The Music and Literacy Connection

Dee Hansen, Elaine Bernstorf, Gayle M. Stuber

The Music and Literacy Connection

Published in partnership with
MENC: The National Association for Music Education
Frances S. Ponick, Executive Editor

Rowman & Littlefield Education
Lanham • New York • Toronto • Plymouth, UK

Published in partnership with
MENC: The National Association for Music Education

Published in the United States of America
by Rowman & Littlefield Education
A Division of Rowman & Littlefield Publishers, Inc.
A wholly owned subsidiary of The Rowman & Littlefield Publishing Group, Inc.
4501 Forbes Boulevard, Suite 200, Lanham, Maryland 20706
www.rowmaneducation.com

Estover Road
Plymouth PL6 7PY
United Kingdom

British Library Cataloguing in Publication Information Available

Library of Congress Control Number: 2006933331

ISBN-13: 978-1-56545-157-5
ISBN-10: 1-56545-157-0

∞™ The paper used in this publication meets the minimum requirements of
American National Standard for Information Sciences—Permanence of
Paper for Printed Library Materials, ANSI/NISO Z39.48-1992.
Manufactured in the United States of America.

TABLE OF CONTENTS

Prelude

> The human mind is the joiner; fitting together the disparate elements of the world to make objects, systems, sceneries. It can bridge distances from the size of an atom's nucleus to the space between galaxies, and leap over time spans of millennia as nimbly as over seconds.
> —Eric Harth, *The Creative Loop: How the Brain Makes a Mind,* p. 9

Johnny has a great sense of rhythm; he can clap on the left side of his body, then the right without missing a beat. His eyes follow the music symbols on the board from left to right. He is great at making up new endings that rhyme or following the previous patterns of a song. He can play the correct durations of the music symbols when the teacher points to them.

If you ask any primary-grade music teacher, he or she can tell you which children might be able to read more proficiently than others by observing their musical behaviors.

What is it that Johnny is doing in music that seems to transfer to reading? How do children learn? What makes a child "literate"? How can we join the best teaching from the reading world and from the music world to enhance the literacy of our children?

The Music and Literacy Connection has practical suggestions for how reading teachers and music teachers can collaborate to move children towards literacy. While much has been written connecting literature and music, we address the specific tasks and skills for decoding, reading comprehension, and writing in the general and music education environments. We also propose parallels between other forms of literacy—listening, speaking, and viewing.

We believe that music learning in a general classroom is not merely playing Mozart in the background or singing turkey songs at Thanksgiving. The instructional activities for classroom and music teachers presented throughout this book use music with intent and integrity. Additionally, the reading strategies we suggest are simply effective instructional practices for teachers of any discipline.

The need for *The Music and Literacy Connection*

For many years, a national effort to increase reading literacy has unfolded through state and federal legislation. Accountability for children's performance on state and national tests has taken away time and resources from many of our music programs. While few would disagree with the intent of the literacy goals, the role of music education in this journey has been questioned by those who have little understanding of the far-reaching value of music study. The purpose of this book is to clearly define the vocabulary and instructional approaches common to both reading and music study to create a productive and positive working environment for teachers of both disciplines. When we look deeply at how young children learn, the fact that music study reinforces reading skills becomes quite apparent. This book will spell out the relationships between music and reading study based on our experience and observations. Well-known brain researcher and educator Patricia Wolfe states,

> Contrary to the popular misconception that music is the property of the right hemsphere, new imaging techniques have shown that music is distributed across specialized regions in both hemispheres. In fact, many musical experiences can activate the cognitive, visual, auditory, affective, and motor systems, depending on whether you are reading music, playing an instrument, composing a song, beating out a rhythm, or just listening to a melody. The mental mechanisms that process music are deeply entwined with the brain's other basic functions, including emotion, memory, and even language. (2001, p. 161)

Research is beginning to confirm the important relationships between music study and language literacy. Among many sources, Armstrong (2003, pp. 57–58) cites several studies that link important aural skills developed in music study to the ability to read words (Bryant, MacLean, Bradley, and Crossland 1990; Shaywitz et al. 1998; Talcott et al. 2000). Susan Strickland summarizes several studies in her article, "Music and the Brain in Childhood Development" (2001). The Arts Education Partnership (http://aep-arts.org) has released excellent studies available to download: *Champions of Change: The Impact of the Arts on Learning* (Fiske 2000) and *Critical Links: Learning in the Arts and Student Academic and Social Development* (Deasy 2002). The reader can also refer to *MuSICA Research Notes* online at www.musica.uci.edu to find articles such as "The Neurobiology of Musical Learning and Memory" by Norman Weinberger (1997). In addition to the MENC Web site (www.menc.org), many advocacy sites include information about current research. Two new sites are www.supportmusic.com and www.musicfriends.org.

We are aware that little empirical research has been done to validate the causal relationships between music and reading literacy. This book is based on our observations and discoveries over many years as we've worked and researched. We strongly encourage researchers to consider examining the auditory and visual processes required for reading and music learning. We believe that parallels exist—we see them as we work. Evidence-based research to support or confirm our observations would be beneficial to music educators and, most important, to children.

Primarily, our intent is to demonstrate the similarities between reading text and music learning so that music and reading teachers can speak a common language with common goals directed toward children's literacy. When children learn to perform, create, or respond to music, they are practicing skills that are also integral to reading. When a question arises about the validity of music study as it relates to national literacy and reading accountability, the music teacher should not feel obligated to stop teaching music in order to prepare children for reading skills. Music study teaches important reading skills as the child learns about and engages in music. The general classroom teacher who uses music as an instructional tool will find children engaged, excited, and motivated.

Targeted audiences

The *Music and Literacy Connection* is written for pre-K to intermediate-elementary music teachers and early childhood and elementary general classroom teachers. It is our hope that general classroom teachers will be able to use music strategies to enrich literacy instruction. Conversely, music educators will be able to use research-based reading strategies in their music instruction. We are also hopeful that teachers of university level education courses such as "Reading in the Content Area" and "Music Methods for Classroom Teachers" will find this book useful.

Organization of *The Music and Literacy Connection*

Four major principles guide the scope, context, and organization of this book:

Guiding Principle 1: Children are active learners.
Guiding Principle 2: Music teachers are literacy teachers and general classroom teachers are music teachers.
Guiding Principle 3: Children construct their own knowledge.
Guiding Principle 4: Literacy is not measured by a single output.

In the Introduction, you will find the theoretical and philosophical basis for our book. Here we provide our definition of literacy; the links between text reading, musical decoding, and comprehension; and a review of federal and state accountability legislation that has, in part, driven the need to provide general and music educators with this book.

The remainder of the book is divided into four sections, one for each of the four guiding principles. Section I, "Children Are Active Learners," provides background for the understanding of how children learn through play, types of play, and the significance of musical play. This section presents an overview of the philosophical underpinnings of the book—that musical environments provide an enriched setting for learning.

Section II, "Music Teachers Are Literacy Teachers and General Classroom Teachers Are Music Teachers," addresses reading strategies for decoding and comprehension both in music and general education. Chapter 7 describes considerations, adaptations, and enrichments for both the general and music classroom. Suggested activities include adaptations for challenged learners.

Our definition of literacy includes speaking, viewing, listening, and writing. Section

III, "Children Construct Their Own Knowledge," includes valuable information for developing the links between music instruction and these important literacy skills.

Section IV suggests ways to assess literacy through music. Based on the principle "Literacy Is Not Measured by a Single Output," we examine various ways to observe and evaluate young children's progress toward literacy in a musical environment. Finally, the appendices contain instructional materials, resources, and assessments.

One of the primary goals of this book is to demonstrate the parallels between text reading and music learning. Figure P.1 provides a visual summary of links between language development and music learning: *learn* musical language, learn *through* musical language, and learn *about* musical language to achieve musical literacy.

Acknowledgements

It is our belief that Eric Harth is correct, "The human mind *is* the joiner" (1993, p. 9). The ultimate beneficiaries of the collaborative power of reading and music are our children. For this belief, we wish to thank the many people who understand our vision and have helped us with our journey into *The Music and Literacy Connection.*

The authors wish to thank MENC for its encouragement and support of our ideas and efforts, our families for their patience and understanding, and our many colleagues who have helped us sort through our ideas over the years. In particular, we would like to thank the following people whose contributions have enriched our book.

Illustrations: Virginia Meserve, Gayle's mother, whose drawings bring our ideas to life.

Music concept map: Aurelia Hartenberger, MENC Southwestern division president, St. Louis, Missouri. Aurelia's ideas helped solidify and validate our thinking.

Instructional resources: Liz Kennedy, program coordinator, Arts Partners of Wichita, Wichita, Kansas. Liz is a treasure chest of resources.

Readers: Anne Miller, elementary music specialist and music therapist, Overland Park, Kansas, and Robin Liston, pre-K music specialist, Lawrence, Kansas. Anne and Robin gave us fresh eyes and great minds.

Researcher: Eric Hansen, who helped us with citation searches.

Contributing educators:

Marcia Daft, master artist with the Wolf Trap Institute for Early Learning through the Arts, Washington, D. C.

Debra Gordon Hedden, associate professor of music education, University of Kansas, Lawrence

Martha Gabel, music specialist, Olathe USD 233, Olathe, Kansas

Greg Gooden, music specialist, Salina, Kansas

Julie Linville, music specialist, Andover, Kansas

Diana Webster, Ell-Saline Middle High School, Brookville, Kansas

Photography: Candice Bell, music major, Baker University, Baldwin, Kansas

Figure P.1
Links to Language Development through Music Learning

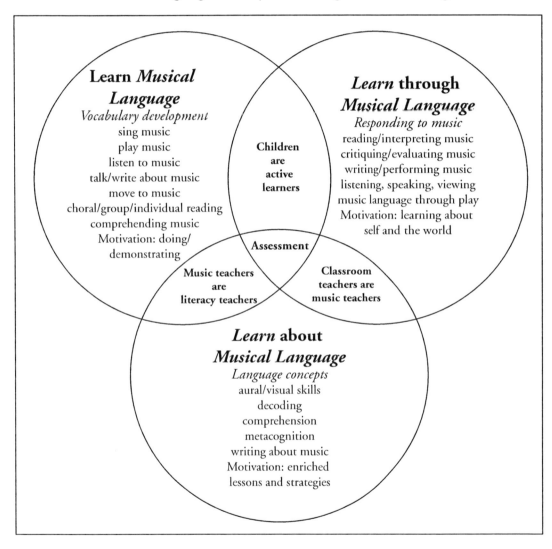

Learn *Musical* Language
Vocabulary development
sing music
play music
listen to music
talk/write about music
move to music
choral/group/individual reading
comprehending music
Motivation: doing/
demonstrating

Children are active learners

***Learn* through Musical Language**
Responding to music
reading/interpreting music
critiquing/evaluating music
writing/performing music
listening, speaking, viewing
music language through play
Motivation: learning about
self and the world

Assessment

Music teachers are literacy teachers

Classroom teachers are music teachers

***Learn* about Musical Language**
Language concepts
aural/visual skills
decoding
comprehension
metacognition
writing about music
Motivation: enriched
lessons and strategies

Threads of the Literacy Fabric: Foundation for *The Music and Literacy Connection*

All the words that come out of our mouths (as well as the lines that emerge from our pens and word processors) ride upon a stream of music. To help individuals achieve literacy, it seems critically important that we acknowledge this important connection between words and music and use it as fully as we can to help our students read and write more effectively.

—Thomas Armstrong, *The Multiple Intelligences of Reading and Writing*, p. 55

In our experiences working with general education and music teachers, we find a gap in understanding each other's vocabulary and educational outcomes. Music educators sometimes feel as though other members of the school faculty consider music time an opportunity for a break or simply time for children to do something else instead of learn the "important, tested" subjects. In reality, as we argue throughout this book, children are learning valuable skills in music class that are an integral part of becoming literate people. It is the definition of "literacy" that is critical here. To that end, most teachers (no matter what their subject) must understand that the knowledge and skills that children learn in every curriculum area contribute in some way to each child's literacy growth.

What is literacy?

Our definition of literacy is broad and comprehensive. While this book primarily targets reading, writing, and music literacy, our belief is that literacy encompasses a wide range of knowledge and skills. Literacy cannot be measured by a single output (Guiding Principle 4). It is a gross oversimplification of the learning process when accountability for a school's success in fostering a child's intellectual growth and progress toward literacy is measured by the results of a single test score in math or reading.

Everyone's definition of literacy is different. Cooper asserts that literacy has often been viewed only as the ability to read and write (1997). He cites the work of researchers and writers such as Vygotsky (1978), Halliday (1975), Clay (1992), and Teale and Sulzby (1986) as contributing to an expansion of that definition of literacy learning. In his text *Literacy, Helping Children Construct Meaning*, Cooper says, "Given what we have learned, we must view literacy as the ability to communicate in real-world situations, which involves the abilities of individuals to read, write, speak, listen, view, and think." Cooper goes on to say,

> In other words, children learn to read, write, speak, listen, view, and think by having real opportunities to read, write, speak, listen, view, and think as opposed to completing contrived exercises that involve marking, circling, and underlining. As they have these real opportunities to develop literacy, children get support along the way from more experienced individuals; these individuals may be parents, peers, or teachers. (1997, pp. 6–7)

The Literacy Dictionary by Theodore Harris and Richard Hodges (1995) is devoted to the many interpretations of the word literacy. Thirty-seven types of literacy are listed, from academic literacy to workplace literacy (p. 141). However, arts literacy and music literacy are not described as separate entities. Soares, in a report prepared for UNESCO, writes, "it is more appropriate to refer to *literacies* than to a single unitary literacy" (1992, p. 11). Soares describes literacies in terms of a broad range of reading and writing practices (figure I.1). "The concept of literacy involves a set of structures ranging from individual skills, abilities, and knowledge to social practices and functional competencies to ideological values and political goals" (pp. 8–10).

The statement at the beginning of this chapter summarizes our position regarding literacy. The study of music and the study of text reading parallel each other in the skills

Figure I.1
What Is Literacy? A Continuum

Ideological values and political goals

Social practices and functional competencies

Individual skills, abilities, and knowledge

and knowledge children must have to become literate citizens. The study of music, however, opens different literacy doors. Through real music experiences, children discover new concepts, new skills, and new ways to express themselves. Music study supports and furthers literacy by its holistic and performance-based instructional approach. Music study provides the real opportunities for learning that Cooper advocates. Developing an understanding of music concepts becomes the highest end of a music literacy continuum if we parallel the ideas of Soares. In Chapters 6 and 10, we discuss in detail the journey to understanding concepts in the music literacy continuum.

Arts educators also argue that arts literacy and music literacy are viable types of literacies. A recent publication by Susan Wright (2003), *The Arts, Young Children, and Learning,* devotes an entire chapter to literacy in the arts. This resource complements the premise of this work.

In this vein, we offer an adaptation of the Soares continuum using vocabulary integral to this book (figure I.2).

Figure I.2
What Is Music Literacy? A Continuum

Ideological values and political goals
High level musical expression: Performance, aesthetics, humanities

Social practices and functional competencies
Functional competencies: Musical performance and application of music elements

Individual skills, abilities, and knowledge
Basic skills, abilities, and knowledge: Facts and organization of music elements and concepts

Creating a common vocabulary

First we need to define specific terms and describe processes associated with both music and language literacy. Clarification of the definitions and descriptions is integral to communication between music teachers and classroom teachers, especially since each group may define many terms and processes differently.

The terms and vocabulary used in *The Music and Literacy Connection* are the result of a synthesis of terminology from many recognized professional organizations. These groups include the International Reading Association (IRA), the American Speech-Language-Hearing Association (ASHA), the National Association for the Education of Young Children (NAEYC), and MENC: The National Association for Music Education. In addition, we have included extensive research and perspectives from scholarly professional journals and texts that are cited throughout this publication.

Auditory and visual processes and skills

In many learning situations, teachers break down the specific learning skills students must master in a process called task analysis. In task analysis, the teacher separates each skill that a child needs to learn into subunits that include specific actions, concepts, vocabulary, and sequences. This process is used both in learning to read text and learning to read music. For both, the task of breaking the codes apart from their explicit symbol systems—alphabet and words or musical symbols—is a task held in common.

> In music classes, teachers frequently break apart the different codes and manipulate the specific aspects of sound that are associated with those codes, such as responses to pitch, dynamics, time/duration, and articulation of individual sounds and groups of sounds in written music. In language reading, teachers work with students to separate the sounds of words into individual phonemes. It may be that one of the aspects we should consider as music educators is the similarity between oral language reading and music reading as the ability to process a sequential presentation of visual code in order to assign meaning through sound. (Bernstorf 2003, p. 10)

Figures I.3 and I.4 describe tasks that are necessary for both reading text and music. These tasks are crucial to children's ability to break the discrete codes of both words and musical symbols. As you read from one column to the next, notice the similarity of tasks. Figure I.3 describes the auditory processes important in language reading and music reading. Figure I.4 describes the visual processes associated with text and language reading and music analysis and reading. The processes are arranged in alphabetical order, not in order of importance.

Figure I.3
Auditory Processes Important in Language, Music Reading, and Music Learning

Term	Language (Reading) Process	Music Reading and Learning
Auditory analysis	Identify phonemes or morphemes embedded in words.	Identify tones/specific sounds embedded in a musical context.
Auditory association	Identify a sound with its source.	Same: (timbre, tone color). Pitched or unpitched.
Auditory attention	Pay attention to auditory signals, especially speech, for an extended time.	Pay attention to auditory signals, especially vocal or instrumental music, for an extended time.
Auditory blending	Synthesize isolated phonemes into words.	Determine contour/pattern, either melodic or rhythmic.
Auditory discrimination	Discriminate among words and sounds that are acoustically similar. Differentiate among frequency, duration, or intensity.	Discriminate among and within specific musical elements: frequency–pitch; intensity–dynamics; duration–beat, meter, rhythm, tempo; sound sources—timbre, tone color.
Auditory figure—ground	Identify a primary speaker from a background of noise.	Listen selectively to a musical line, instrument, pattern, etc.
Auditory memory—sequential memory	Store and recall auditory stimuli of different length or number in exact order.	Store and recall/perform specific musical stimuli. May be demonstrated by rote repetition (short term) or memorization (long term).
Binaural fusion	Fuse into one sounds heard from two separate inputs.	The essence of musical harmony. Also, ensemble and texture in music. Pitch matching and blend in ensembles require this ability.
Binaural separation	Attend to stimuli presented to one ear while ignoring stimuli to the opposite ear.	Essentially the same. In music ensembles, this may also include the monitoring of multiple stimuli in one ear while monitoring one's own musical production in the other ear.
Localization	Ability to localize the source of sound.	Essentially the same.

First two columns from Lucille Nicolosi, Elizabeth Harryman, and Janet Kresheck. *Terminology of Communication Disorders: Speech-Language-Hearing* (Baltimore: Williams and Wilkins, 1989). Third column from Elaine Bernstorf, "Linking Music Learning to Reading Instruction." Workshop presentation handout, Kansas Music Educators Association, Wichita, Kansas, February 2001.

Figure I.4
Visual Processes Important in Language, Music Analysis, and Music Reading

Term	Language (Reading) Process	Music Process
Visual analysis	Identify letters or syllables embedded in words.	Identify specific icons or symbols embedded in a musical or art context.
Visual association	Identify a sound with its visual symbol. Identify object with its picture/icon/word.	Identify musical elements—pitch, rhythm, dynamics, etc.—through graphic representations or symbols.
Visual attention	Pay attention to visual images, especially written language, for an extended time.	Pay attention to visual images (including musical notation) for an extended time.
Visual blending—proximity	Synthesize isolated letters into words.	Determine contour/pattern, either melodic or rhythmic, from icons/notation.
Visual closure—completion/projection	Understand the whole word or message when a part is missing.	Close gaps and complete unfinished forms, see parts as a whole.
Visual discrimination	Discriminate among graphemes that are visually similar. Differentiate among visual stimuli of different types.	Discriminate among and within specific musical elements by sight (pitch intervals; dynamics symbols, meter signatures, rhythm and tempo markings).
Visual figure—ground	Identify a primary image from a background.	Look selectively at a musical line, melodic/rhythmic pattern, or individual notation symbol in music.
Visual memory—sequential memory	Store and recall visual stimuli of different origins.	Store and recall/perform specific musical stimuli. Store and recall visual stimuli of different origins.
Visual continuation	Fuse letters into one word; words into a phrase or sentence. Group visual objects to follow a smooth curve, straight line, or repetitive pattern.	Identify phrases, melodic contour, repetitive patterns.
Visual separation—tracking, focusing	Attend to stimuli presented in one visual field while ignoring stimuli in another visual field.	In music ensembles, this may also include the monitoring of multiple visual stimuli (lines of notation) while monitoring one's own notation line.
Visual—spacial functions	Understand that objects keep their basic shapes regardless of position.	Read musical notation regardless of position within the composition (e.g., multipart, choral lines, piano, stem positions).

From Elaine Bernstorf and Dee Hansen. Linking Music Learning to Reading Instruction (Workshop presentation handout, Kansas Music Educators Association, Wichita, Kansas, February 2001).

As these figures illustrate, the auditory and visual processes associated with language and music analysis and reading involve many individual tasks. When a child is experiencing difficulty with reading or music it is helpful to examine auditory and visual processes as they relate to the task deficiency. In Chapter 10, we suggest possible tasks and assessments in music learning that may help pinpoint the deficiency. Combinations of these tasks are necessary to develop the specific skills needed for students to both read and analyze auditory material for language arts and music education. While music and language and reading analysis have some differences, there are numerous overlaps.

Decoding

The processes described in figures I.3 and I.4 include many of the critical tasks needed to master a set of larger reading skills called "decoding." Wilson and Gambrell define decoding as "the breaking of the visual code of symbols into sounds" (1988, p. 12). Decoding is a critical step toward text reading. Though no child learns in exactly the same way as another, most teachers would agree that the ability to find meaning in text does not come until some decoding skills are mastered.

Decoding terminology varies from source to source. For that reason, the definitions and categorizations in this publication are a synthesis of those sources. There is adequate research, however, to conclude that specific skills must be learned in sequence to read successfully. The publication *Put Reading First* (Armbruster, Lehr, and Osborn 2003), developed by the Center for the Improvement of Early Reading Achievement (CIERA) and funded by the National Institute for Literacy (NIFL), describes in detail effective instructional practices for teaching children to read. *Put Reading First* summarizes the findings of the National Reading Panel Report (2000) in five areas of reading: instruction, phonemic awareness, phonics, fluency, vocabulary, and text comprehension. Armbruster, Lehr, and Osborn state, "While there are no easy answers or quick solutions for optimizing reading achievement, an extensive knowledge base now exists to show us the skills children must learn in order to read well" (p. ii).

Instructional examples as they apply to both an elementary general classroom and a music classroom in these five areas of reading will be discussed in Section II. While these skills are defined in text reading terms, we will discover that they are practiced in parallel during music reading. Figure I.5 describes six major text decoding skills associated with reading that are also in the National Reading Report. Many reading journals and research studies have different, greater, or fewer terms associated with decoding skills. However, in our research and consultations, we find these to be the most commonly addressed and therefore have chosen to target them in our discussion. Teachers must remember that the definitions of these text decoding skills include both the auditory and visual processes and skills described in figures I.3 and I.4.

Figure I.5
Comparative Skills for Reading Text, Music Symbols, and Music Text

Skill	Text Reading	Music-Symbol Reading	Music-Text Reading
Phonological awareness	Sensitivity to all units of sound. Generating and recognizing rhyming words, counting syllables, and separating the beginning sound of a word from its ending sound (Yopp and Yopp 2000).	Sensitivity to all elements of musical sound. Recognizing repeated or imitated sound patterns, sequence, ostinato, matching pitch, etc. Attention to texture, timbre, stylistic nuances.	Learning how to produce the sounds of language in a musical setting. Generating and recognizing how the sound elements of text and the sound elements of music are coordinated within a musical setting (e.g., pairing rhymed text with like phrases, cadences, or repeated rhythmic passages).
Phonemic awareness	A special kind of phonological awareness involving letter-sound correspondences in the smallest units of oral language—phonemes (e.g., "stop" would be expressed in phonemes as s/t/o/p/). Phonemic awareness involves identifying and manipulating the smallest sound units within the written symbol (Young 2000, p. 169).	Instruction that emphasizes how notation is related to the smallest units of musical sounds in systematic ways; music symbol-sound correspondences (e.g., pitches within a phrase, rhythmic subdivisions within a metered measure). Articulation, phrasing, tonguing, performance practice.	In a choral setting, identifying and manipulating sounds as they relate to music symbols, including articulation of pure vowels sounds, diphthongs, elisions, consonants (explosive and affricates). Vocally forming the smallest sound units so that the listener can comprehend the lyrics.
Orthographic or grapho-phonemic awareness	Knowing that letters and diacritics represent the spoken language. Understanding the writing system of a language involves a specific connection between the sequence of letters, characters, or symbols (Bear et al. 2000, p. 402), including spelling patterns that are used to recognize familiar chunks in words (ASLHA 2001). Spelling includes variable and sometime complex, but mostly predictable rules (Moats 1999, p. 19).	Knowing that music symbols represent musical language. Understanding that scales are a series of patterns that are the basis for melody. In Western culture, learning a notational system that has rules about the sequences of pitches and the organization of rhythms that occur in predictable ways. Knowing that pitched and nonpitched instruments are scored differently.	Combining the elements of alphabetic knowledge (as described in the text-skills column) and music-symbol-reading knowledge. Knowing rules for the use and placement of music and text symbols in written music.

Figure I.5 (Continued)

Skill	Text Reading	Music-Symbol Reading	Music-Text Reading
Sight identification	The ability to identify high-utility words that appear most often in print—sight words such as "the," "of," "dog," etc. (Ekwall 1986, p. 25).	The ability to identify and play high-utility notes, types, rests, lines, spaces, rhythm symbols, dynamic markings, fingerings, etc.	Learning the proper vocal enunciation of high-utility words in music lyrics and performing them consistently from song to song.
Cueing systems (context, syntax, graphonic, semantic)	Gathering meaning from words, phrases, or sentences surrounding a word—context. Determining that material sounds "right" based on multiple clues—syntax. Noting that material looks "right"—graphophonic. Noting that material makes sense—semantic (Short et al. 2000).	Gathering meaning from musical phrases and melodic phrases, including placement of accidentals, rhythmic devices, etc. Noting that music looks and sounds "right" based on the rules of a given culture. Noting that music makes sense given the style, period, and composer.	Given a particular style, period, culture, and composer, noting that music and music text sound and look "right" and make sense.
Fluency	Clear, easy written or spoken expression of ideas; freedom from word-identification problems that might hinder comprehension in silent reading or the expression of ideas in oral reading; automaticity (Young 2000, p. 169).	Effortless music performance; freedom from technical problems that might hinder the musical correctness of a performance; automaticity. The ability to execute the musical aspects of a performance smoothly, easily, and readily.	Effortless independent execution of text and music symbols. The ability to perform in a technically flawless manner.

From Dee Hansen and Elaine Bernstorf, *Music Educators Journal*, March, 2002 p. 20. © 2002 by MENC: The National Association for Music Education. Used with permission.

Just as a person continues learning to read text more proficiently, music reading skills also progress. Music decoding skills are refined throughout a person's musical life. With each developmental stage, the skills become more complex and more meaningful. Figure I.6 illustrates the steps to music literacy.

The implications of school reform issues

Through the years, teachers in all curriculum areas have become very involved with school reform efforts. The effects for arts educators have presented an opportunity on one hand and a challenge on the other. Music educators instinctively know that in

Figure I.6
Steps to Music Literacy

Steps to Music Literacy

Through Musical Play:
Performing, Creating, Responding

Comprehension

Knowledge
Comprehension
Application
Analysis
Synthesis
Evaluation

Decoding

Phonological Awareness
Phonemic Awareness
Sight Identification
Orthographic Awareness
Cueing Skills
Fluency

Sensory Processes

Auditory
Visual
Kinesthetic

learning to read music, children practice similar if not identical skills as in learning to read text. We know that children are highly engaged and motivated by singing, playing, listening, and movement. Yet, the challenges of raising test scores in reading and mathematics have directed budgets, personnel, and time resources to those curriculum areas.

No Child Left Behind: Principles and implications for music education

On January 8, 2002, President Bush signed into law the No Child Left Behind Act (NCLB). This new law is the cornerstone of his education reform plan and contains major changes to the Elementary and Secondary Education Act (ESEA), enacted in 1965. It changes the federal government's role in K–12 education by asking America's schools to describe their success in terms of what each student accomplishes. The act contains four basic education reform principles: stronger accountability for results, increased flexibility and local control, expanded options for parents, and an emphasis on teaching methods that have been proven to work.

Building an accountable education system involves several critical steps:

■ States create their own standards for what a child should know and learn for all grades. Standards must be developed in math and reading immediately. Standards must also be developed for science by the 2005–06 school year.

■ With standards in place, states must test every student's progress toward those standards by using tests that are aligned with the standards. Beginning in the 2005–06 school year, tests in math and reading must be administered every year in grades 3 through 8. In the meantime, schools must administer the tests once in each of three grade spans: grades 3–5, grades 6–9, and grades 10–12, as required in The Improving America's Schools Act of 1994. Beginning in the 2007–08 school year, science achievement must also be tested at least once in grades 3–5, 6–9, and 10–12.

■ Each state, school district, and school will be expected to make adequate yearly progress toward meeting state standards. For a school to make progress, each student subgroup must meet or exceed the standard. Subgroups include students who are economically disadvantaged, from racial or ethnic minority groups, have disabilities, or have limited English proficiency.

■ School and district performance will be publicly reported in district and state report cards. Individual school results will be on district report cards.

■ If the district or school continually fails to make adequate progress toward the standards, then they will be held accountable.

(Based on information from the Department of Education's Web site: www.ed.gov/nclb/landing.jhtml.)

What does this mean for music education?

A primary purpose of *The Music and Literacy Connection* is to draw parallels between the process of reading text and the process of reading music. Reflecting on these commonalities, music educators should feel validated in teaching music for its own value. Reading teachers should reflect on the parallels knowing that enlarging their tool chest of instructional approaches is not only valid but enriching for children. We believe that, in time, asking the right questions in active research settings and investigating the physiological workings of the brain will provide evidence that supports the parallels between music and language reading. Common sense says that the parallels exist. We know that children are highly engaged and motivated to learn when in musical environments, and therefore we should strongly support music programs taught by highly qualified teachers in our schools. Reading accountability challenges will not and should not go away. But, neither should providing our children an opportunity to be literate beyond the basic levels of individual skills, abilities, and knowledge as described in Soares' continuum (1992).

We have defined what we believe to be parallels between reading and music learning. Now we look at how children learn. In doing so, we'll examine Principle 1: Children are active learners.

Section I

Children Are Active Learners

Chapter 1

How Children Learn through Musical Play

The years of early childhood are the time to prepare the soil. Once the emotions have been aroused—a sense of the beautiful; the excitement of the new and the unknown; a feeling of sympathy, pity, admiration, or love—then we wish for knowledge about the object of our emotional response. Once found, it has lasting meaning. It is more important to pave the way for the child to want to know than to put him on a diet of facts he is not ready to assimilate.
                    —Rachel Carson, quoted by Peter Haiman in "Developing a Sense
                    of Wonder in Young Children," p. 52.

Imagine a kindergarten classroom that is full of movement, light, color, and young voices. The walls are covered with words, letters, numbers, and pictures drawn by the children. Large paper chains hang from the ceiling and are stretched diagonally across the room. Books of all sizes are in the library. There are exploratory centers for listening, reading, writing, and mathematics. Some children listen to songs they learned earlier in the year, practicing as they follow along in a book. The dramatic play and block centers are full of children reenacting stories or constructing buildings and scenes from the book read by their teacher earlier that morning. Children in the art center are drawing a favorite part of the book; several of them are humming a tune heard during morning group time. Other children sit on the colorful rug, turning pages in the big book of "The Wheels on the Bus" as they sing the song and do the movements. The children in this kindergarten scenario are actively learning in a colorful, engaging, and safe classroom.

In this chapter, we will discuss how children learn by acting on their environment and consider the role that play provides as a context in which children learn best. Theories of play, the importance of play, and the impact of play on learning are frequent subjects in early childhood literature. Any teacher can tell you (with conviction) that play is how children enhance, expand, and just plain enjoy their learning. Play is, or should be, emotionally risk free. Through play, children practice language, cognitive, and motor skills; re-create stories and songs; and develop interpersonal skills in a safe environment. Musical play has been described as a vehicle to improve learning through enhanced emotional connections to information, concepts, and skills. Many researchers (Wolfe 2001; Jensen 2001; Bergen and Coscia 2001; Davies 2000) support the contention that children learn more easily and retain information longer when rhyme, rhythm, and music are used to enhance learning. The Midwest Child Care Research Consortium recommended including musical experiences daily as a way to strengthen the effectiveness of early childhood programs. The researchers indicated that "musical activities and dramatic play are considered to be important experiences for cognitive and social development" (Thornburg, Mauzy, Espinoza, and Mayfield 2003, p. 2). Play provides a meaningful context for learning, and music is a robust avenue to encourage that learning.

Section I examines the role play has in learning. Chapter 1 provides a short overview of some child development and play theories that support the following two premises: (1) children learn through play; and (2) musical play supports literacy learning. It also examines the role of play in developmentally appropriate education. Chapter 2 explores play practices for the regular classroom and the music classroom using music to engage children in learning.

Learning through play

When young children play, they learn to understand the world around them.
—Bernard Spodek and Olivia N. Saracho, "The Challenges of Educational Play," p. 23

The Music and Literacy Connection is based on the premise that children become literate through a broad variety of experiences. What may appear to be play (when children laugh, sing, and move) is in reality an active, engaging, and authentic learning experience. If the purpose of education is to learn, then play, and musical play in particular, supports this purpose. Integrating play into the curriculum and into the classroom is a surefire way not only to encourage, but also to enhance and promote learning. Play allows children to enjoy learning—and enjoyment, as adults and children both know, is the key to continuing engagement. Patricia Wolfe describes the importance of emotion to memory (2001). Emotion is a critical component of learning. In fact, the brain is "biologically programmed to attend first to information that has strong emotional context" (Wolfe 2001, p. 87). Research has provided more and more support for this belief. Emotion, whether positive or negative, helps us remember. Bergen and Coscia sum it up for teachers, "Educators can use this knowledge by being aware of the emotional aspects of learning and trying to enhance the learning of important content by providing experiences that are embedded in positive emotional contexts" (2001, p. 56).

Play is a highly motivating way to support learning in both children and adults. The strong connection between emotion and learning makes it clear that the high interest provoked by play will enhance cognitive, motor, and social-emotional skills (Bergen and Coscia 2001, p. 61). There has been a recent upsurge of research on the workings of the brain that supports the belief that young children are active learners and that active learning occurs during the self-expressive fun time called play. In summary, play provides the means by which children practice skills, attitudes, and knowledge in a safe environment.

Musical play, in particular, enhances memory and therefore learning (Wolfe 2001; Bergen and Coscia 2001; Jensen 2001). The connections among emotion, learning, and music are too strong for teachers to ignore. Jensen summarizes it well: "music making enhances the systems that allow us to perceive and respond appropriately to a world rich with emotions and complex social structures" (2001, p. 32).

Children learn through play

A major premise of developmentally appropriate practice is that young children learn best through play. "Play is an important vehicle for children's social, emotional, and cognitive development as well as a reflection of their development" (Copple, Bredekamp, and Neuman 1997, p. 14). Children construct their own learning based on interactions with others and with the environment. Play is a "highly supportive context" (p. 14) for this construction of knowledge and gives children many opportunities to explore and understand their world.

Belief in the value of play for knowledge construction is based on work by major theorists in child development, such as Jean Piaget and Lev Vygotsky. In addition, Mildred Parten's social levels of play provide us with a way to observe and describe children's play (1930). The work of these theorists, as it relates to play and learning, will be described in detail.

David Elkind studied under Jean Piaget and has written many articles and books promoting play as the context for learning—and for enjoying that learning. He notes (and teachers agree) that children play because they enjoy it! "Children play because they are predisposed to play, not because they are trying to learn or achieve something" (Elkind 2003, p. 46). Adults, however, have spent a lot of effort proposing theories that explain and describe the meaning and the value of children's play. Language learning is a part of play and is included in the theories described in the next section (Elkind 2003). First, it is important to provide a context in which to consider their work as it relates to the music and literacy connection.

Theories of child development that support play
Jean Piaget

Piaget is arguably the best known child development theorist. Born in 1896, he began to develop his observational skills at a very young age. He tried to explain children's play within the context of his theory of cognitive development. Piaget believed that children actively construct their own knowledge and that this construction occurs during play. Piaget distinguished three types of play: practice play, symbolic play, and games with rules. A fourth type of play, constructive play, was not considered by Piaget to be a separate type of play, but a "midway point between play and work" (Chaille and Silvern 1996, p. 74). Piaget believed that play changes with, and therefore reflects, children's development (Rogers and Sawyers 1988, p. 12). Piaget's descriptions of play types help us understand the stages of children's development.

The first type is *practice play* which occurs during infancy. It is defined as the "exercise [of] structures for no other purpose than the pleasure of functioning" (Chaille and Silvern 1996, p. 73). Practice play can be seen whenever a baby or older child keeps repeating a skill or movement. The child is merely repeating a movement or skill that is already mastered and is fun to do. Riding a bike, dropping a spoon or bowl, or hitting a mobile to watch it spin—all are examples of practice play. It can be seen whenever a child acquires a new skill. According to Piaget, learning does not necessarily take place in practice play; however, personal understanding can be, and often is, constructed by the child during this play. For example, when children are jumping rope or riding a bike, they gain more control as they practice their skills. The skills used in practice play become more complex as we grow older (Rogers and Sawyers 1988). Singing the alphabet song is a type of practice play as long as it is under the child's control rather than being performed at the direction of an adult (Rogers and Sawyer 1988, p. 14).

Babies transition from the sensorimotor stage of cognitive development to the pre-operational stage around the age of two. They have developed object permanence and gradually become capable of representing their learning by a variety of methods: verbal signs, symbols, and expressions of feelings. Toddlers start using pretend play, which allows them to practice or reproduce their sensorimotor experiences in a play experience. Pretending that dolls are alive and empty cups have tea in them for a tea party is what Piaget called *symbolic play.* At this stage, children are using symbols to represent or act out their experiences. For example, a child pretends that a block is a car or his hand is an ax in the story of Hansel and Gretel. This type of play is the beginning of *representation,* in which young children use one object to represent another. Another example is children putting blocks on a plate to be "food" or pretending to be someone else (mom, dad, sister) while playing in the housekeeping area.

During this stage, children incorporate more and more social interaction in their play. Such play helps children to begin to organize their understanding of their own world. In this type of group activity, children must negotiate and solve problems so that they can continue to play. Such interaction is an important aspect of social discourse and of learning to understand another's perspective. They also become more adept in language which, in turn, enhances their pretend play. Hirsch-Pasek and Golinkoff (2003) note that current research supports the connection between play and learning.

Pretend play or make-believe play provides children a mechanism to separate themselves from their present reality. Such play promotes the ability to manipulate symbols such as using a block for an apple or a word for a person.

The third stage of play involves playing *games that have rules* (Spodek and Saracho 1998, p. 18). This play is typical of older children and begins to be seen during the early years of elementary school. Games with rules require social interaction, negotiation, and an understanding of how the child's social group works. According to Piaget, children at this stage of play are learning to use symbols that are collectively understood.

Lev Vygotsky and Daniel Elkonin

In one of their many articles and books on Lev Vygotsky's work, Bodrova and Leong describe the Vygotskian approach to play (2003b). Vygotsky was born in Russia in 1896. His work focused on the social and cultural aspect of learning. Along with Piaget, Vygotsky believed that play has a strong link to cognitive development. According to Vygotskian theory, play is the preeminent educational activity of early childhood. Vygotsky believed that "the influence of play on a child's development is enormous" (Vygotsky 1978, p. 96). Through play, young children achieve a true understanding of concepts. Through representative play, they understand that a stick can be a horse. Children become able to separate one specific meaning from an object (the stick) and apply their conceptual understanding of the outside world (the horse) to that object. In other words, children understand that you can hold a stick and ride it like a horse to enhance your play experience.

Daniel Elkonin was a student of Vygotsky. In the United States, he is known as the inventor of the Elkonin blocks used in Reading Recovery and other remedial reading programs (Bodrova and Leong 2003a, p. 12). Although he has contributed much to the understanding of phonemic awareness, his study of play has also contributed significantly to the field of early childhood education. Elkonin identified four basic ways that play influences the development of children (figure 1.1). These outcomes of play activity provide an important foundation for future learning in the primary grades (Bodrova and Leong 2003a, p. 13).

Figure 1.1
Elkonin's Four Expected Outcomes of Play Activities

Influence	Description
Play affects the child's motivation.	During play activities, young children become better able to delay gratification. As they sing a song about putting their toys away or use rhythmic instruments to extend their pretend "jungle" play they are expanding the time spent on an activity.
Play facilitates cognitive "decentering."	Pretend play allows children to take others' perspectives. A young boy tells a story using a different instrument for each of the main characters. This ability will later support the development of reflective thinking and metacognition.
Play advances the development of mental representations.	When young children use blocks to represent food or clap hands to demonstrate the syllables in their names, they are learning to separate the meaning of an object from the object's physical form. Eventually, they will be able to use words rather than objects, promoting the development of abstract thinking and imagination.
Play fosters the development of deliberate behaviors—physical and mental voluntary actions.	Children use rules when they play. Rules can be demonstrated through physical actions such as moving on all fours when pretending to be a cat or changing speech patterns when saying nursery rhymes or singing silly songs. This "deliberateness" in play provides a foundation for developing memory and attention skills.

Based on Elena Bodrova and Deborah J. Leong. 2003. Chopsticks and Counting Chips: Do Play and Foundational Skills Need to Compete for the Teacher's Attention in an Early Childhood Classroom? *Young Children* 58 (3), p.13.

Mildred Parten: Social development and play

In a classic study of social participation, Parten identified several levels of peer play that range from simple to complex (Rogers and Sawyers 1988, pp. 20–21). Her levels of play (figure 1.2) are still frequently used when researching play in the classroom, although other theorists and educators have disagreed with her hierarchy of play behaviors. Factors such as setting, culture, and ability may change the level of maturity assigned to a level of play. For example, solitary play may not mean that the child is socially immature. Some children need to work quietly or want to explore the materials first. According to Owocki, children are expected to move back and forth among the play levels throughout their early years (1999). Teachers see children at all levels of play (and in the arts we often see creative adults at all levels of play). However, Parten's descriptions are useful in discussing play and musical play in the context of the child's social, emotional, and cognitive development.

Figure 1.2
Parten's Levels of Social Play

Type of play	Example
Unoccupied	Susan looks at others playing musical instruments, but does not participate. She just stands or moves around to other areas of the room. If there is nothing to watch, Susan may play with her own body, stand passively, or follow the teacher around the room.
Onlooker	Nathan watches other children play in the block center. Some children are using small blocks to tap out a beat for the marching toy animals used by other children. Nathan is definitely involved in the watching, but does not become an active participant. Nathan may ask a question or talk about the animals with the other children. *Note*: This is typical of two-year-olds.
Solitary, independent play	Sara is playing by herself, turning pages in the big book, "The Wheels on the Bus." Other children are close by, but she does not interact with the others or alter what she is doing. She is engaged with her book.
Parallel play	Michael picks up a wooden drumstick from the instrument tub. Three or four other children also select instruments. The presence of the other children has some meaning for him, but Michael does not try to influence or interact with them. *Note*: This type of play seems to be a safe way to set the stage for more intense group interaction and is the most common type of social play observed in all age-groups.
Associative play	Fred and Lucy are sitting near each other, each holding a book of nursery rhymes. They are reading the rhymes aloud and occasionally show the other pictures in their book. Their focus, however, is on their own book and their own reading. For this play level, specific roles are not defined and there is no organized goal such as building a block structure or playing a game.
Cooperative play	Six children are marching around the carpet, each playing an instrument as they sing the song "The Wheels on the Bus." This type of play has a common goal, one that can be realized only if all of the participants carry out their individual assigned roles. In this case, the children are a marching band.

Based on Cosby S. Rogers and Janet K. Sawyers. 1988. *Play in the Lives of Children.*
Washington DC: National Association for the Education of Young Children, pp. 20–21.

The examples in figure 1.2 are only an introduction to the Parten play stages. We encourage you to investigate the work of other early childhood music educators about specific characteristics of musical play and development. In particular, Barbara Andress has described examples of how children move through the play stages with various types of music activities (1998). Her recommendations and the extensive research on early childhood music by Wendy Sims provide two important resources for teachers who want to develop music programs specifically for early childhood settings (Sims 1993, 1995; Andress 1985, 1989; Andress and Walker 1992).

Contributions of play to learning

Piaget observed how children learn by watching them as they made mistakes and corrected them during play. According to Jensen, "we don't become smart by always making the right choices—we become smart by eliminating bad choices" (2001, p. 90). Play is the vehicle for learning in the early childhood years, because play has intent and purpose for young children. Play actively engages students in the examination and understanding of big ideas. Through play, children can reflect on their previous learning and practice new skills in a stress-free environment. Such reflection allows children to think about previous choices, adjust dispositions, and practice skills. Playful activity is a means of enhancing the skills, abilities, and dispositions children already have in place.

Play as a context for learning clearly supports cognitive development as Piaget suggested. Research is beginning to support musical play as a specific type of play that enhances cognitive development. Figure 1.3 lists a number of ways play contributes to learning.

Play builds autonomy in a child. During play, children are in control of their time, their choices of materials, playmates, and setting. Play encourages the development of social skills through interaction with friends and teachers. In general, play allows for risks to be taken within a safe environment; as a result, learning increases. Indeed, play demands that we risk. In play, there is no fear of failure because, in *true* play, there is no failure!

Brain research in the context of play and music

The creation of new ideas does not come from minds trained to follow doggedly what is already created. Creation comes from tinkering and playing around, from which new forms emerge.
—Selma Wassermann, "Serious Play in the Classroom:
How Messing around Can Win You the Nobel Prize," p. 12

Current brain research has increased our knowledge of how children learn, and has provided us with more and more information about how we can help all children to learn and grow to their potential. Neuroscientists now believe that it is the interaction between our heredity and our environment that makes us who we are. The first few

Figure 1.3
Play and Its Contributions to Learning and Cognitive Maturity

1. Play provides children with the opportunity to practice new skills and functions. As children master skills, they can integrate the new skills or reorganize them.

2. Play offers numerous opportunities for children to act on objects and experience events. Piaget's belief was that children learn through acting on the environment; play gives children a wide range of experiences where they "act" on their environment.

3. Play is an active form of learning that unites the mind, body, and spirit. Until about the age of nine, children's cognitive structures function best when they are playing. Emotional and social maturity are enhanced through play.

4. Play enables children to transform reality into symbolic representations of the world. Children often "practice" what they see at home.

5. Through play, children can consolidate previous learning. Children can construct and reconstruct what they have learned. Eventually they will be able to say, "Ah-ha!"

6. The play environment is "psychologically safe." As they play, children can retain their playful attitude—a learning "set" that contributes to flexibility in problem-solving. Creativity and inventiveness are enhanced in play.

7. Creativity and aesthetic appreciation are developed through play. As children play with objects, art mediums, sounds, words, and language, they learn about the properties of each and are able to practice the skills necessary to use each item—for example, practicing rhythmic language enhances knowledge and appreciation of the uses of words.

8. Play enables children to learn about learning—through curiosity, invention, persistence, and a host of other factors. Attention spans are longer in play and interest is high.

9. Play encourages children to become self-motivated learners. Have you ever seen a child who wanted to stop playing?

Based on Cosby S. Rogers and Janet K. Sawyers. 1988. *Play in the Lives of Children.*
Washington DC: National Association for the Education of Young Children, pp. 57–59.

years of life account for much of the brain's growth. It is certainly clear that early experiences are very important and that the developing brain is actually molded by those experiences as well as by genetic input (Wolfe 2001; Jensen 2001; Diamond and Hopson 1998). Such experiences, particularly during the early years, physically shape the brain and actually influence the child's responses (and, eventually, the adult's) to the variety of experiences life offers.

Research also demonstrates the importance of social interaction and emotional connection. Children need to be talked to, read to, and loved to create connections between the brain cells, thus shaping the brain so individuals respond appropriately to their environment. Children need to interact with others, both adults and other children, in order to learn language, social, and cognitive skills. Adult-child interactions such as reading, talking, and singing songs are excellent ways to build brains by encouraging language and synaptic growth.

A strong component of learning is emotion. Young children need to be held, cuddled, and comforted in order to be able to handle stress and control their own emotions as they grow older. Davies notes that "the hemispheres of the brain work together when emotions are stimulated, attention focused, and motivation heightened." Davies continues, "Rhythm acts as a hook for capturing attention and stimulating interest. Once a person is motivated and actively involved, learning is optimized" (2000, p. 148). Music clearly enhances learning.

Research suggests that socio-emotional safety is essential for healthy brain growth in the first years of life and, in fact, "contributes to sustained optimum brain development throughout childhood" (Bergen and Coscia 2001, p. 64). As Jensen reminds us, learning in play is "low threat, high feedback, and high fun" (2001, p. 90). In fact, all the components needed for learning to occur can be found in play. Children have time to learn, time to practice learning, and time to correct mistakes in a low-risk environment.

Since learning is dependent on experience, it is important that the experiences are appropriate for the age of the child so that they do not create a stressful environment. Children, like adults, cannot learn when they are stressed, fearful, or overstimulated. A safe environment with a moderate level of challenging material and an adult who encourages a child to try will enhance brain development, thus increasing a child's ability to think at a higher level. Musical play is one excellent means of getting young children to listen and play with language—a great preliteracy and literacy experience (Wolfe 2001; Jensen 2001).

Bergen and Coscia express the belief of most early childhood educators that "play does serve a number of important functions that can be hypothetically related to brain research" (2001, p. 61). They suggest that the repetition which is inherent in the enjoyable activity called play may strengthen synaptic connections and create "levels of mastery" which support brain development and growth. Bergen and Coscia suggest that "educators who give opportunities for play are likely to be supporting brain functioning" (2001, p. 61). Since 2001, however, new brain research and new understanding of the implications of that research have given us a clearer understanding of the importance of play in children's learning and development. In their book *Einstein Never Used Flash Cards: How Our Children Really Learn—And Why They Need to Play More and Memorize Less*, Kathy Hirsh-Pasek and Roberta Michnick Golinkoff state that "researchers have discovered that play is related to greater creativity and imagination and even to higher reading levels and IQ scores" (2003, p. 208). In fact, the authors state that "based on the research evidence, a new equation is in order: PLAY = LEARNING" (p. 208). "Researchers are in universal agreement that play provides a strong foundation for intellectual growth, creativity, and problem solving. And it also serves as a vehicle for emotional development, and for the development of essential social skills" (p. 214).

Play promotes creativity and problem solving. Musical play is a highly creative activity that supports learning. Stevenson noted this in her article "Creative Experiences in Free Play" (2003). When she allowed her students time to play, they expanded and enhanced their own learning and skill levels. Teachers can foster learning by providing quality time for play because play supports and enhances cognitive growth and development. We know that one size of teaching does not fit all children. Teachers need to support play by providing time and a variety of opportunities, space, and appropriate materials in an enriched environment. Through play, teachers can have it all: active engagement, high interest, and long-term learning.

Chapter 2

The Role of Music in Play and Literacy Learning

Music creates inspirational moments and opportunities to make sense out of chaos.
—Marcia Earl Humpal and Jan Wolf, "Music in the Inclusive Environment," p. 107

Setting up the playful learning environment

We believe play can, and should, provide the environmental and curricular structure for teaching and learning for young children. Musical play is a specific form of play that can be used to enhance general learning or it can be a specific subject area to be taught and learned. Music therapy and music education are two fields that recognize these important roles for music in a child's development. Most early childhood specialists also recognize the important roles that music can play in a child's learning. A study by Thornburg and colleagues reinforces this belief by recommending that music be part of all early-childhood programs that want to be considered high quality (2003). According to the American Music Therapy Association (AMTA),

Music should be used to promote learning for the following reasons:
1. Music reaches children at different levels, thus it can promote a range of skills such as social and communicative interactions, motor skills, and self-expression;
2. Music may make play more joyful and thereby naturally increase play; and,
3. Music can be included in many activities and its enjoyable qualities may motivate children to participate in those activities. (Kern and Wolery 2003)

Music as an educational strategy

In early-childhood programs, and many primary grade classrooms, music engages children and provides important opportunities for incidental learning. Finger plays, traditional nursery rhymes, and songs like "B-I-N-G-O" reinforce concepts such as one-to-one correspondence, phonemic awareness, and the understanding of the systematic relationship between the letters of the alphabet and the sounds connected to each letter. Pat Wolfe endorses the use of music—in particular rhythm and rhyme—to enhance memory. In fact, she suggests that "information embedded in music or rhyme is much easier to recall than the same information in prose" (2001, p. 165). Isn't it easier for most young children to sing the "ABC Song" than to say the alphabet? Although teachers of young children know that being able to sing the song does not necessarily correlate with letter recognition, singing provides the emotional hook and the playful place for starting to understand the alphabet.

The use of rhythm and rhyme as an educational strategy provides young children with an easily remembered and nicely structured format for literacy learning. When used in conjunction with movement such as finger plays, this educational strategy provides an "extra sensory input to the brain and probably enhances the learning" (Wolfe 2001, p. 166).

David Lazear provides several examples of using kinesthetic intelligence to support learning in his book *The Seven Ways of Teaching* (1991, p. 62). Sara Stevenson, in her article "Creative Experiences in Free Play," suggests that providing children with time to play not only increases their capacity for learning, but also allows them to make the music and the skills they have learned meaningful to them (2003). In essence, she supports our premise that play allows children to construct their own knowledge in a way that is enjoyable to them (Guiding Principle 3: Children construct their own knowledge). She also points out that children make their own music which is "highly meaningful to them and must not be cast aside" (p. 45).

Children often hum, sing, or chant words, rhymes, and songs that they have created either to help them replay previously learned information or simply enjoy musical language play. It is clear—from both current research on brain development and past theories about learning through play—that music enhances learning in all areas and in particular, in the areas of language and literacy. Teachers must understand and believe in the value of play and of music in order to support learning and language in young children. The reading activities in *The Music and Literacy Connection,* including decoding, comprehension, listening, speaking, viewing, and writing, represent our ideas for activities that promote literacy. When observing children participating in these activities, some may think that they represent child's play. They do! And, that is exactly why they are vital to the music and literacy connection.

Adults who work with children must know how to support children's learning through appropriate language and age-appropriate materials—challenging as well as familiar—that are made available in a supportive environment. Adults know how to support literacy as well as other types of cognitive learning. Talking with and to children is a critical part of language learning as well as preliteracy and literacy development.

We also know that music enhances learning. Bergen and Coscia say it clearly, "Anyone who has been around young children knows that they have high motivation to attend to and explore visual arts media and the rhythms, melodies, and tempos of music" (2001, p. 53). Educators know that literacy learning, as all learning, happens most easily when students have high interest levels and strong emotional connections to the material. Musical play and musical activities clearly provide an emotional environment in which learning can occur.

We realize that teachers must be comfortable and competent to support literacy learning through multiple and integrated teaching processes. Musical play is one way this can be done. Teachers must believe that children really do learn through musical play. The following are some suggestions for classroom procedures that support literacy through play:

- Select and use instructional strategies that accept and support playful and engaged learning. Use phonological awareness strategies, including musical activities such as listening to and singing songs that include rhyme and alliteration.
- Design and orchestrate a curriculum that incorporates play into activities and strategies, including songs that can be taught alongside appropriate children's literature.
- Create an environment that supports play through carefully arranged spaces, thoughtfully selected materials, and appropriate teacher expectations for behavior and learning. Include instruments, recordings, and open spaces for movement, listening, and activity centers. Include a book center with books that illustrate songs the children are learning during music activities.
- Use assessments that allow the trained teacher to gather specific information about each child's level of understanding through careful observation of the child's behavior, whether the activities are related to reading music or text. Document the child's cognitive development, including divergent thinking, creativity, problem-solving ability, and concept development.
- Remember that play supports language development, particularly through comunication with peers and adults. Vocabulary will grow easily through enjoyable activities such as talking, reading, and singing together.
- Incorporate musical play as a "primary mode for children's social development" (Stone 1995–96, p. 49). During music play activities, encourage children to interact with others, learn to get along, take turns, cooperate, and negotiate.
- Provide a safe environment in which children can express feelings through pretend play. Children can easily replay over and over again an unsettling event in a safe environment. Many songs provide scenarios with demonstrated emotions. For example, "The Wheels on the Bus" allows children to be assertive and directive (move on back), sad (wah, wah, wah), and comforting (sh, sh, sh). Other favorite children's songs also have references to emotions ("Santa Claus Is Coming to Town"—pout, cry, shout).

■ Allow different types of movement in play and music activities to assist children's development of physical skills, including both fine and gross motor skills.

Remember that "play provides the natural and experiential learning that supports the child's construction of his [or her] own knowledge of the world and his or her place in it" (Stone 1995–96, p. 104).

Children's musical development

An excellent source for determining age-appropriate musical activities for children can be found in *Music in Childhood: From Preschool through the Elementary Grades* by Patricia Shehan Campbell and Carol Scott-Kassner (2002). The next three figures (2.1–2.3) represent a few of the many valuable tables and charts found in this text. To assure a successful musical play environment, the activities must be structured so that they are appropriate for the abilities and skills of the children.

The teacher's role in play and literacy development
Play environments

Teachers must understand and then recognize the variety of knowledge, skills, and dispositions that can be observed during play. Children have a wide range of opportunities to use both written and oral language during play (Chaille and Silvern 1996). Sociodramatic play is a particularly wonderful way to observe children using and expanding their language skills. For example, children frequently experiment with language and even accents as they become a storybook character or family member. Musical language in the form of songs, rhythmic sounds, and finger plays can be heard in any preschool and kindergarten classroom as well as in early primary grades. According to Spodek and Saracho, "children experiment with words and manipulate their use, meaning, and grammar. They do not necessarily emphasize the meaning or value of words; rather they experiment with rhythm, sounds, and form" (1998, p. 21). Providing children a time and place to experiment with language and language prosody, particularly through musical expression, can be an excellent way to reinforce literacy learning in a supportive, yet fun way.

We have already described how play allows children to master new knowledge at their own pace and in their own way, and how it reduces anxiety and tension that can inhibit learning. For adults, particularly teachers, structured play is often a means to an end. From a child's point of view, play is something you don't *have* to do—it is just fun! Children don't anticipate the desired end; they simply enjoy the process of learning. Figure 2.4 describes how play and learning are related. In school settings, the play environment is generally viewed from two perspectives, the child's and the teacher's. In this figure, play is a continuum, from "free play" to "work." Learning moves along a continuum from "discovery learning" to "drill and practice."

Figure 2.1
Children's Rhythmic Development

Age	Developmental Skill
Less than one	Demonstrates rhythmic swaying, rocking, bouncing
One to two	Demonstrates babbling in irregular rhythmic patterns Performs dance-like rhythmic movements
Two	Sings spontaneous songs framed around regular rhythmic pulses and patterns
Three	Sings spontaneous songs with some feeling for meter and with regularly recurring rhythmic patterns Imitates short rhythmic patterns
Four to five (kindergarten)	Taps in time to a regular set pulse Begins to develop rhythmic clapping and patting Replicates short rhythmic patterns on instruments
Six to seven (grades one and two)	Distinguishes fast and slow, long and short Can perform songs faster and slower Can PRW* quarter-, eighth-, and half-note rhythms
Eight to nine (grade three)	Can PRW dotted-quarter and eighth notes (♩.♪), and syncopated quarter- and eighth-note rhythms (♪♩♪) Can recognize and conduct music in $\frac{2}{4}, \frac{3}{4}, \frac{4}{4}$, and $\frac{3}{8}$ meter
Nine to ten (grade four)	Can PRW sixteenth-note patterns (♬♬ ♬♩ ♩♬) Can recognize and conduct music in cut time and compound meters ($\frac{6}{8}, \frac{9}{8}$)
Ten to twelve (grades five and six)	Can PRW dotted eighth- and sixteenth-note patterns (♬ ♬.) Can recognize and conduct music in asymmetric meters ($\frac{5}{8}, \frac{7}{8}$)

*Note: PRW = perform, read, and write

From Patricia Shehan Campbell and Carol Scott-Kassner. *Music in Childhood: From Preschool through the Elementary Grades* (with CD), 2nd ed., p. 97. © 2002. Reprinted with permission of Wadsworth, a division of Thomson Learning; www.thomsonrights.com, fax 800-730-2215.

In the early elementary classroom, play is used to "foster problem solving, thinking skills, and academic skill learning" (Bergen 1998, p. 83). Consciously planning to use a variety of types of play may provide the best opportunity for learning for the largest number of children. An understanding of play and its enhancement of learning can

Figure 2.2
Children's Melodic Development and Teacher's Guidance

Age	Percept and Concept	Teacher Actions
Less than six months	Responds to differences in pitch. Can match vocally sustained pitches and begins to imitate sounds.	Sing with words or neutral syllables such as "loo." Sustain pitches in middle register. Imitate sounds. Generate new ideas.
Six to eighteen months	Differentiates between pitch contours. Sensitive to phrase endings and intervals.	Continue vocal play. Sing nursery songs and other simple songs from child's culture. Play recorded music.
Eighteen months to four years	Able to recognize familiar phrases and songs based on contour and rhythm. Increased ability to replicate familiar material. More attention to absolute value of pitches than to relative value. Sensitivity to phrase, shown through movement.	Sing many songs with children. Engage in vocal play, extending the range upward and downward. Add words to vocal play upward and downward and high and low to match pitch patterns. Experiment with keyboards and computer programs that reinforce contour and pattern discrimination skills. Show contour and phrase with bodies.
Four to eight years (kindergarten to grade three)	Beginning to conceptualize aspects of pitch and melody such as high and low, upward and downward. Able to demonstrate this knowledge first (age four to five) through showing and later (age five to six) through telling. Sensitivity to intervals and to tonality emerges. Continued development of phrase as unit.	Provide many opportunities through singing, movement, use of bells, and use of computer programs to demonstrate pitch concepts and contours. Have children vocally supply endings to familiar songs. Help them add musical vocabulary to describe melodic events. Respond to phrase endings.
Eight to twelve years (grades three to six)	Can identify discrete aspects of pitch motion such as steps, leaps, and repeated tones. Perceives patterns moving downward most easily—later moving upward. Recognition of melodic sequence. Can build concepts of scale and mode around age ten to eleven.	Continue to build experience with melodies through singing, shaping through movement, and playing instruments. Add reading of contours and patterns using precise notation.

From Patricia Shehan Campbell and Carol Scott-Kassner. *Music in Childhood: From Preschool through the Elementary Grades* (with CD), 2nd ed., p.132. © 2002. Reprinted with permission of Wadsworth, a division of Thomson Learning; www.thomsonrights.com, fax 800-730-2215.

Figure 2.3
Children's Harmonic Development and Teacher's Guidance

Age	Percept and Concept	Teacher Actions
Five to seven (kindergarten to grade one)	Developing sensitivity to relation between melody and harmony—harmonic fit. Small number of children beginning to notice separate vertical events. May perceptually combine two pitches into one.	Help children distinguish between accompanied and nonaccompanied music. Ask children to indicate when chords need to change as accompaniment to a melody.
Eight to ten (grades two to four)	Stronger ability to notice numbers of vertical events. Beginning to sense closed or strong and open or weak cadences.	Build triads and add to songs. Sing songs with combined lines such as ostinatos and rounds. Add Autoharp accompaniments to songs.
Eleven to twelve (grades five to six)	Able to correctly identify number of simultaneous events. Clear sense of strong and weak cadence. Can harmonize accurately by ear.	Keep refining perception of simultaneous sounds through listening. Have them use simultaneous sounds and cadences creatively. Give students melodies to harmonize with basic chords.

From Patricia Shehan Campbell and Carol Scott-Kassner. *Music in Childhood: From Preschool through the Elementary Grades* (with CD), 2nd ed., p. 141. © 2002. Reprinted with permission of Wadsworth, a division of Thomson Learning; www.thomsonrights.com, fax 800-730-2215.

direct a teacher's curricular and environmental decisions. Stone advocates for play as an important part of the early elementary classroom. "We must not succumb to the narrow definition of learning that undervalues or eliminates play as a curricular tool in the classroom" (1995–96, p. 45).

Teachers' behavior

Teachers make hundreds of decisions daily and many of these decisions revolve around "how": How to most effectively and most appropriately interact with individual children. Teachers of young children must understand that there is no one way to teach young children and that there must be a balance between directive teaching (demonstrate, direct) and nondirective (acknowledge, model) with emphasis on less directive methods. Figure 2.5 is a continuum of teaching behaviors that can be used along with the descriptions of the play behaviors of children and the learning process (or play in the classroom) in figure 2.4.

Figure 2.4
The Play Environment: Child and Teacher Perspectives

Play— Child's Perspective	Environment	Learning Process— Teacher's Use of Play
Free play The child chooses whether to play, what to play, how to play, and when to play.	The room has several centers (blocks, art, dramatic play, book and listening, musical instruments). Children are given adequate time to interact with the materials and each other as well as with adults in the room.	*Discovery learning* The teacher has set up the classroom with materials that will support children as they generate their own concepts.
Guided play There is a loose framework of social rules (such as in dramatic play scenarios that reenact a story) that children must understand and follow. The teacher may monitor and, if necessary, redirect the play or provide more materials.	The musical instrument center includes several rhythm patterns written on cards that the children can use to practice playing. The rhythm patterns are from repeated words and patterns of songs that the teacher has been modeling and students have been practicing over the last few months.	*Guided discovery learning* The teacher has carefully constructed certain experiences so that certain types of learning or discoveries are more likely to occur. For example, the teacher "leads" the child by modeling and scaffolding until the child experiences and identifies the modeled concept.
Directed play Children may not have a choice as to whether they can participate in this form of play. This can be enjoyable and should use playful activities.	The "games" center has places for only two children (a teacher-imposed rule). Children can use dramatic play with fire hats and hoses or use blocks to build a house or barn. Social rules, of the classroom and the children, are important in this type of play.	*Reception learning* This is meaningful verbal learning based on language and prior knowledge. Teachers therefore need to know their students well so they can select activities that will promote this type of learning. For example, setting up a field trip to a fire station would support later dramatic play around the concept of fire fighters.
Work disguised as play Children are "almost playing," performing tasks that are not necessarily inherently playful, but that the teacher can make enjoyable and fun.	Children are asked to play the rhythm pattern from a card on a drum or block by imitating the teacher. The children have had prior experience using instruments, manipulatives, and blocks to play patterns.	*Rote learning* This is "verbal learning," but may not be inherently meaningful to the children. *Note*: Young children are less able to make this type of information meaningful unless they have help in developing understanding and skill practice.

Figure 2.4 (continued)

Play— Child's Perspective	Environment	Learning Process— Teacher's Use of Play
Work Children must follow the teacher's directions and do not typically have the option of being playful and diverging from the original activity.	The teacher gives the children a task such as saying a sight word seen on a card, identifying a musical symbol at sight, or completing a worksheet.	**Drill-repetitive practice** Children are asked to repeat over and over a certain piece of information that may not necessarily be in a meaningful context.

Another interesting theory about the importance of play is the brainchild of James Catterall, director of the Center for Imagination, Graduate School of Education, UCLA. He described an experience with scientists who were attending a UCLA seminar. Each of the scientists talked about their science and their "art." One spoke of the aesthetics of color in relationship to chemistry, one displayed four computer-generated works of art, a psychologist talked about creativity, and mathematician Paul Winter talked about music. Catterall pointed out that "the scientists in that room had

Figure 2.5
Teaching Continuum Related to Play Behaviors

Description/Label	Teacher Behavior
Acknowledge	Give attention and positive encouragement.
Model	Display the desirable behavior (implicit) or provide a minimal description of process (explicit).
Facilitate	Temporarily assist a "ready" child get to the next step.
Support	Similar to facilitating, but with more adult involvement.
Scaffold	Set up challenges and assist children to work on the edge of their current competence (to do this well, teachers must know the continuum, their children, and where their children are in the learning process).
Co-construct	Actively do a project or an activity with a child.
Demonstrate	Actively participate in the activity with the children as observers.
Direct	Give specific directions to children to complete a task or activity.

made time to play with their ideas. ... A scientists plays with ideas, creates theories, rearranges things, ... goes back to the playroom ... " (2003, p.116).

Later in the discussion Catterall criticized the way we typically teach science in school—the teaching of "final form science":

> We've taken play out of the curriculum, but it needs to go back. I think that applies tremendously to the arts. The arts, in many senses, are about playing with ideas to the point where you want to express them, perhaps even to audiences. Maybe you want to express them in your backyard for your neighbors or express them on your office wall for yourself. But if you haven't played with the ideas, your product probably isn't finished. (2003, p. 116)

To conclude this chapter, we encourage teachers to embrace our first guiding principle: Children are active learners and leave you with this thought:

> There are two kinds of teachers: cookbook teachers and checkerboard teachers. A cookbook teacher sits down in the evening and measures out so much arithmetic, so much spelling, and so much music according to a pedagogical recipe. The next day, he spoonfeeds it into his pupils. Suppose instead, the teacher was getting ready for a game of chess or checkers. When she sits down with her "opponents," the vital factor is the reaction of the other mind to the moves she is making. Of course, cookbook teaching is easier. But from the child's point of view, checkerboard teaching offers possibilities for real adventure, and for the teacher, it is a lot more fun! (Foulkes 1991, p. 15)

As we move to our ideas for teaching reading, we hope to foster checkerboard teachers—those who arouse the emotions, generate excitement for the new and unknown, and help children find lasting meaning. We believe that children do know how to produce or construct their own knowledge—they play.

Section II

Music Teachers Are Literacy Teachers and General Classroom Teachers Are Music Teachers

Chapter **3**

Music in the Reading Environment: Decoding

> Learning to read and write is a complex and multifaceted process that requires a wide variety of instructional practices.
> —Carol Copple, Sue Bredekamp, and Susan Neuman, *Learning to Read and Write: Developmentally Appropriate Practices for Young Children,* p. 14

Mrs. C., the first grade teacher, is sitting with seven students in a reading circle. Each child has an erasable board with a marker and a copy of the book *Goat in a Boat.* Mrs. C. asks the children to listen to the word she says and write the beginning sound of the word on their boards. "The first word is 'boat,'" she says. The children write a letter and show her the results. She congratulates the ones with a correct response ("b") and asks the two students who wrote "g" and "d" to erase their letter, write a "b," and say the sound with her. This continues until a list of ten words has been said and written. The children then exchange their boards and markers for the books at their feet. They open their books and prepare to take turns reading a page or two aloud as Mrs. C. listens, corrects mistakes, and says "good job" to those who complete their task correctly. The reading begins with one student and continues around the circle until all seven students have had a chance to read.

Teachers devise many activities to help students gain important decoding skills. As the teacher in the scenario worked with her students to read *Goat in a Boat,* she emphasized two significant decoding skills: phonemic awareness and orthographic (graphophonemic) awareness. (See Introduction, figure I.5.) In teaching the children phonemic awareness, she used flashcards that contained letters and blends of letters that represented the sounds of the words in the story. The children practiced verbalizing these sounds so that when they encounter them when reading, they will be able to transfer the sounds on the flashcards to those in the text. "Effective phonemic awareness instruction teaches children to notice, think about, and work with (manipulate) sounds in spoken language" (Armbruster, Lehr, and Osborn 2001, p. 5). The teacher also helped her students reinforce the letter-sound relationship (orthographic or grapho-phonemic relationship) by writing the symbol for the beginning sound (the onset) of key words such as "boat." "Alphabet and letter-sounds must be learned as discrete units. Their [children's] first understanding develops through exploring the beginning sounds of words. Once they understand how the alphabet represents sounds, children begin to view the writing system—the orthography—as a series of patterns that are organized at the level of syllable" (Bear et al. 2000, p. 93).

Enhancing reading strategies using music

How could a general classroom teacher enrich and motivate her students in a traditional instructional setting by using music activities? In truth, many teachers "use music" by having children sing or chant during breaks in their work. Some teachers use songs as a way to learn the content of reading or mathematics such as memorizing grammatical structure or multiplication tables. However, when the goal is to improve literacy, those uses of music will probably not help children learn specific reading skills. When teaching reading, it is important for all teachers to understand that children benefit from a variety of approaches. The scenario in this chapter demonstrated rote instruction. Encouraging children to engage in singing or chanting in a directed or guided setting allows them to construct meaning from the learning activity. The National Association for the Education of Young Children (NAEYC) encourages teachers to allow children to play with words. "Songs and chants offer endless opportunities for children to enjoy and explore language" (Burns, Griffin, and Snow 1999, p. 55). For instance, if the teacher, in addition to the traditional instruction, invites the children to suggest other words that begin with "b" or "g" and create a rap with the words, their understanding of sound and symbol relationships will be reinforced. Play invites children to construct their own meaning in a safe and motivating environment.

Why don't classroom teachers use music activities?

While some classroom teachers comfortably use music activities, others feel intimidated or unqualified to use music in their classrooms. And classroom teachers using music activities may not feel as though they can teach music concepts, given pressures to improve test scores in reading. Children whose schools have music specialists benefit from their expertise in teaching the fundamental concepts and performance skills of music. Ideally then, classroom teachers and music teachers collaborate to assure that all children receive qualified instruction in the content and skills of both curriculum areas.

The first step in the collaborative process is to understand the similarities and differences in each other's vocabulary and concepts. Therefore, we will return to our list of decoding terminology (Introduction, figure I.5) and describe some commonly used music activities that can easily be used in a general classroom to reinforce children's reading skills.

Phonological awareness

Phonological awareness involves the ability to identify and discriminate the characteristics of sounds. "Phonological awareness refers to the whole spectrum, from primitive awareness of speech sounds and rhythms to rhyme awareness and sound similarities, and at the highest level, awareness of syllables of phonemes" (Copple, Bredekamp, and Neuman 2000, p. 84). A child who is phonologically aware can perceive and produce rhymes, divide words up into their syllables, and notice that groups of words have the same sounds at their beginning, middle, or end. "Recent research has confirmed that children who have a greater degree of phonological awareness when they enter school are better equipped to learn to read" (Burns, Griffin, and Snow 1999, p. 46).

Musical activities are a natural way to foster phonological awareness. Using songs, chants, or movement, children can manipulate sounds in many ways. "The same parameters of pitch, dynamics, duration, and articulation that make sounds musical can transcend linguistics. Music can exist with or without words" (Bernstorf 2003, p. 10). Children can listen to recordings in a general music class and identify repeated or imitated sound patterns. The song "Skip to My Lou" (figure 3.1) offers classroom teachers many opportunities for children to experiment with sound.

Figure 3.1
Skip to My Lou

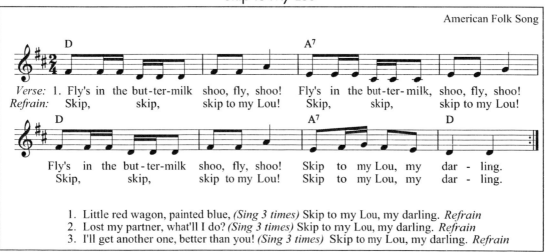

American Folk Song

Verse: 1. Fly's in the but-ter-milk shoo, fly, shoo! Fly's in the but-ter-milk, shoo, fly, shoo!
Refrain: Skip,   skip,   skip to my Lou! Skip,   skip,   skip to my Lou!

Fly's in the but-ter-milk shoo, fly, shoo! Skip to my Lou, my dar - ling.
Skip,   skip,   skip to my Lou! Skip to my Lou, my dar - ling.

1. Little red wagon, painted blue, *(Sing 3 times)* Skip to my Lou, my darling. *Refrain*
2. Lost my partner, what'll I do? *(Sing 3 times)* Skip to my Lou, my darling. *Refrain*
3. I'll get another one, better than you! *(Sing 3 times)* Skip to my Lou, my darling. *Refrain*

From Patricia Hackett and Carolynn A. Lindeman. *The Musical Classroom: Backgrounds, Models, and Skills for Elementary Teaching,* 5th ed. © 2001, p. 366. Reprinted by permission of Pearson Education, Inc., Upper Saddle River, NJ.

Children could
- Move to the song, singing the lyrics and walking or skipping in a circle to the beat
- Clap or tap the syllabic divisions of the words as they sing
- Identify the repeated parts of the song (Shoo, fly, shoo!)
- Make up new verses with words that fit the musical rhythm
- Experiment with variations in dynamics (intensity of sound) or tempo (speed)

Song lyrics are full of rhyme, rhythm, and alliteration. Classroom teachers can enhance their students' reading skills by planning music activities that draw attention to the qualities of the language. "Children should play with sound and rhymes through a variety of games and songs" (Burns, Griffin, and Snow 1999, p. 47). A simple way is to use a hand drum, set of bells, or tambourine to tap the beat or highlight rhymed words or a repeated melodic pattern. These activities are fun and contain important opportunities to develop skills that are critical for successful readers. Many prereading skills develop at the preschool level, though continuing these activities in kindergarten and into later primary grades may be necessary. Take, for instance, the song "Who's That Yonder" (figure 3.2).

Figure 3.2
Who's That Yonder

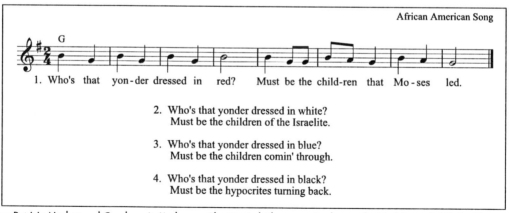

African American Song

1. Who's that yon-der dressed in red?   Must be the child-ren that Mo-ses led.

2. Who's that yonder dressed in white?
   Must be the children of the Israelite.

3. Who's that yonder dressed in blue?
   Must be the children comin' through.

4. Who's that yonder dressed in black?
   Must be the hypocrites turning back.

From Patricia Hackett and Carolynn A. Lindeman. *The Musical Classroom: Backgrounds, Models, and Skills for Elementary Teaching*, 5th ed. © 2001, p. 389. Reprinted by permission of Pearson Education, Inc., Upper Saddle River, NJ.

Teachers might ask children to change the colors at the end of the first phrase, then make up words that rhyme. Classmate names could replace "the children." This song could be very easily accompanied by an Autoharp or bells.

Learning to listen to and participate in the production of sound is critical to aural discrimination and phonological awareness. The Orff approach to music instruction often uses rhythmic chants that can easily be used in a general classroom.

Words of one, two, and three syllables form the building blocks of music, because they provide the substance for the recitation of longer and shorter durations equivalent to quarter, eighth, half, whole, and sixteenth notes, as well as triplets. Because language is so fundamental to children's daily lives, they comfortably and easily express rhythmically its phonemes and phrases. (Campbell and Kassner 2002, p. 99)

Using children's names, types of foods, animals, and so forth, teachers can create chants to help children experience word sounds through music. Also, traditional chants such as "One, Two, Buckle My Shoe" may not be familiar to this generation of children, though they are excellent ways of encouraging children to play with words and numbers. (See Appendix I for examples of activities and chants.)

Phonemic awareness

Phonemic awareness is a type or subset of phonological awareness. *Put Reading First* defines phonemic awareness as "the ability to hear, identify, and manipulate individual sounds—phonemes—in spoken words" (Armbruster, Lehr, and Osborn 2003, p. 10). Phonemes are "the smallest part of *spoken* language that makes a difference in the meaning of words. English has about forty-one phonemes" (p. 4). Phonemes are visually represented by using a slash mark in between each phoneme in a word, such as "hat": h/a/t, a word with three sounds or phonemes.

Note that phonemic awareness and the teaching strategies inherent in "phonics" instruction are different. "Phonemic awareness is the understanding that the sounds of spoken language work together to make words. Phonics is the understanding that there is a predictable relationship between phonemes and graphemes, the letters that represent those sounds in *written* language" (Armbruster, Lehr, and Osborn 2003, p. 3). Children must have a variety of experiences with words and language to develop phonemic awareness.

When considering the effect of reinforcement on learning, it is easy to understand why a child's experience with music supports reading. Remember that the acquisition of language and reading skills and the acquisition of music learning skills require virtually the same auditory and visual processes. Figure 3.3 has specific exercises that develop phonemic awareness. In parentheses we have linked the auditory and visual processing skills to phonemic awareness skills. (See figures I.3 and I.4.) You will also find music exercises built around the song "Che Che Koolay" (figure 3.4). Notice how the phonemic awareness processes are the same, but taught through music.

How reading teachers can use music and how music teachers can facilitate reading

There are many traditional uses of music to facilitate phonemic awareness. Songs in which we manipulate individual phonemes are the most obvious examples. "Apples and

Figure 3.3
Exercises to Develop Phonemic Awareness

Phoneme isolation (auditory analysis)
Children recognize individual sounds in a word.
Teacher: What is the first sound in "koolay"?
Children: The first sound in "koolay" is /k/.

Phoneme identity (auditory memory)
Children recognize the same sounds in different words.
Teacher: What other words in the song start with /k/?
Children: "kof," "kah," and "coom."

Phoneme categorization (auditory discrimination)
Children recognize the word in a set of three or four words that has the "odd" sound.
Teacher: Which word doesn't belong? "Koo," "kof," "tah"?
Children: "Tah."

Phoneme blending (auditory blending, visual continuation, visual discrimination, visual blending—proximity, visual association)
Music exercise: Children listen to the sounds of "kool" and then its separate phonemes. They take turns writing and singing it.

Phoneme segmentation (auditory analysis, auditory blending, auditory discrimination, visual continuation, visual discrimination, visual blending—proximity, visual association)
Children break a word into its separate sounds, saying each sound as they tap out or count it. Then they write and read the word.
Teacher: How many sounds in "kool"? (k/oo/l)
Children: Three sounds.

Phoneme deletion (auditory analysis, auditory attention, auditory discrimination)
Children recognize the word that remains when a phoneme is removed from another word.
Teacher: What is "kah" without the "k"?
Children: "Ah."

Phoneme addition (auditory analysis, auditory attention, auditory discrimination)
Children make a new word by adding a phoneme to an existing word.
Teacher: What word do you have if you add /s/ to the sound "kool"?

Based on Bonnie B. Armbruster, Fran Lehr, and Jean Osborn. 2003. *Put Reading First: The Research Building Blocks for Teaching Children to Read.* Jessup, MD: The Partnership for Reading, pp. 5–6.

Figure 3.4
Che Che Koolay

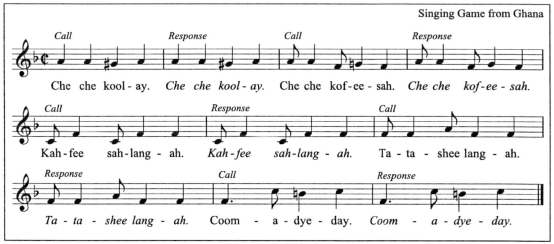

From Patricia Hackett and Carolynn A. Lindeman. *The Musical Classroom: Backgrounds, Models, and Skills for Elementary Teaching*, 5th ed. © 2001, p. 286. Reprinted by permission of Pearson Education, Inc., Upper Saddle River, NJ.

Bananas" is a typical use of phoneme manipulation. ("I like to eat, eat, eat, apples and bananas. I like to āt, āt, āt āpples and bānānās.") Both classroom teachers and music teachers feel comfortable using these types of songs and activities, especially since the songs themselves present phonemic isolation examples.

Another traditional manipulation of phonemes may occur in activities where students create sound stories. As children make sound effects, they use individual phonemes and combinations of phonemes that may or may not be words. One of the first activities that develops phonemic awareness is the production of animal sounds. Some animal sounds are individual phonemes like /s/, the "ssss" for a snake sound, but many animal sounds are combinations of two phonemes, a consonant and vowel sound like /mu/—moo, /ba/—bah, /ne/—neigh. These are developmentally appropriate for young children in the auditory realm, but they can be difficult when it comes to their written form. Virtually every culture has some animal song where children make the animal sounds. Songs like the American favorite "Old MacDonald Had a Farm" and the Spanish song "Come to My Farm" are sung in homes and schools around the world.

In addition, children may manipulate phonemes to make other types of sound effects. The typical "sh" sound used for the wind or for "be quiet" is actually a diagraph that is produced as a single phoneme. The /r/ sound that children use to make car sounds or sirens is another example. These sounds are heard when children are playing alone or with others. They occur in every language. What is interesting is that we seldom show children how to read or write individual phonemes or nonsense syllables. "Old MacDonald" is a song learned by almost every child. One reason this song has become a standard for all children is because it highlights several levels in language development. There are two primary parts that children will initially sing, "ee-i-ee-i-oh" and the animal sounds (notice this is not the name of the animal but the sound it makes).

The repeated phrase "ee-i-ee-i-oh" is one children will sing long before they can sing the entire song. There are several reasons why this may be so. First, the phrase has no consonants, only vowels. Second, the children generally produce a single phoneme on each pitch that is sung (not an entire syllable, but a single phoneme). They will sing "ee," the diphthong "i" as a single phoneme "ah," and then a single "o." Young children will tend to blend these sounds into a single extended sound that is manipulated rather than totally separated vowels. As they develop linguistically, the children will separate the vowels with more clarity—frequently they will also nod their heads or do some kind of movement to show the separations. Their movements demonstrate awareness of the "rhythm" of the "words."

"Moo," "bah," and "neigh" are among the most stable and earliest sung animal sounds because they focus on a vowel sound paired with one of the early developing consonants, /m/, /b/, or /n/, added to the front. If observed closely, young children may not actually produce the "chick-chick" sound but rather an approximation (often with a hint of the earlier developing consonant "t" instead of a clear "ch"). Linguistically, these early productions mesh with language development as the animal sound "moo," "bah," "neigh," and "chick" tend to function as stand alone expressions. The children will reach for a toy cow and say "moo-moo" as if that is the noun that names the object. Likewise they may call a dog a "bow-wow" and a cat a "meow." These "words" use vowels and consonants that are produced earlier in language development and are very much like the sounds the animals make, so children associate the animal with the sound. Why shouldn't a dog be called a "bow-wow"? After all, that is the name the animal appears to call out as its own. Seldom will children label a dog as a "grrr" or a cat as a "purrr." Why is this? Because the /r/ sound is one that comes later in the developmental sequence. Children who have developmental disorders in phonological awareness will tend to produce fewer sounds (phonemes) and will actually substitute phonemes that are easier for them to make for the "real" phonemes. They may make all of their sounds in the front of their mouth, for example singing "tat" instead of "cat"; or they may move the placement of all their sounds to the back (for example, /kæk/ instead of /kæt/, to use the International Phonetic Alphabet). This example shows how children sometimes will adjust what they understand about sound to what they can produce or what they have experienced.

Given the slower production and greater separation of phonemes that are sung compared to those that are spoken, children may have better phoneme production and awareness when music is present. We all know of instances where an individual's phoneme production is much better when singing than speaking. We also know of children who can imitate adult singers both in vocal quality and diction, yet when they speak, they use diction and vocal quality more characteristic of their developmental ages. As educators, both classroom and music, we need to recognize that children sometimes are able to produce sounds by rote that they do not truly understand in a meta-cognitive way. As children begin to manipulate sounds and match them to specific objects, locations, or people, we realize that they are creating their own mental lexicon. One aspect of this is when children begin to see something visual that triggers their language production, such as the logo for McDonald's or their name on a chart in the classroom. Even very young children may ask for a hamburger when they see the McDonald's golden arches logo. Or they might say some form of the word "McDonald's." Such associations between two-dimensional graphics and sounds are early signs that children are making associations between visual and aural perceptions. These are the behaviors associated with children who "read" flash cards of words at extremely young ages. Seldom are these children able to "read" words that have not been practiced or rehearsed. As musicians, one purpose of rehearsal is to make the aural/oral response associated with specific patterns—reading musical phrases—automatic. These "reading" responses are somewhat different than the decoding required for reading unfamiliar words or unfamiliar musical patterns (sight-reading).

Phonemic awareness and phonics instruction

Developing phonemic awareness requires teachers to focus on single phonemes. Music activities deal almost exclusively in syllables. What is important about syllables in music is that the syllables we sing are blended phonemes at the single *sound* level instead of the single *meaning* level.

Many songs have nonsense syllables. Nonsense syllables are simple blended phonemes that are used as sound markers. They function as timing and pitch elements without any meaning. That is why we sing "la, la, la" when we want to present pitch and rhythm without additional meaning loads or because we can't remember the words. It keeps the process moving. Wouldn't it be interesting if children were allowed to say "la, la" when they couldn't read a word in order to keep moving in the sentence? That practice might address some of the fluency issues with beginning readers.

Sight identification

Children who are gaining proficiency in reading are able to instantly recognize commonly used words, letters, and numbers. Sight-identification skills are often acquired through activities that allow students to practice high-frequency words in multiple contexts. For instance, teachers can use flash cards, or ask students to identify the words in a text before reading. Musical activities can help engage students in these activities.

Animal songs again may reinforce reading in music activities. Having children hold up cards with the animal names when they hear their animal in a song can be quite useful. We seldom do it, but having students hold up or point to cards with high-frequency words such as "in," "out," or "around" with songs like "The Hokey Pokey" is an excellent way to reinforce prepositions. These are easy for classroom teachers. Music teachers can reinforce words such as "up," "down," "step," "skip," "high," "low," "fast," "slow," "loud," and "soft" by providing a laminated pointing sheet or a set of answer cards with common words. This would allow children to be actively involved, answer questions in class, and learn to read simultaneously. Because we use many of the same terms over and over in our classes, we can reinforce reading through our classroom activities. Reading teachers teach children to instantly recognize high-frequency words, words that appear many more times than most other words in spoken or written language (Harris and Hodges 1995, p. 107). Music teachers also introduce "high-frequency notes," symbols for individual sounds. Again, the task is matching a "visual" to a "sound." In music, however, visual symbols match specific sounds one-to-one. We almost always have a single syllable matching a single sound. Even if music is melismatic (more than one pitch to a single syllable), there is a new note for each new sound or sound combination. This allows the child to "see" and "touch" individual sounds as they are heard.

Graphophonemic awareness

Also referred to as orthographic awareness, graphophonemic awareness is identifying and manipulating a grapheme, the smallest part of written language that represents a phoneme in the spelling of a word. A grapheme may be just one letter, such as "b," "d," "f," "p," or "s," or several letters, such as "ch," "sh," or "th." When children acquire orthographic awareness, they are able to use letters or approximations of letters to represent sound.

When teachers begin to introduce graphophonemic awareness, they generally use words that are associated with things—nouns—like "ball," "cat," and "car." In this way, symbols (graphemes or letters) are matched with visual objects or drawings of objects. We match the visual thing to the visual "sound." Songs such as "The Alphabet Song" ("Twinkle, Twinkle, Little Star" tune) and "B-I-N-G-O" are frequently used by classroom teachers to introduce graphemes.

The song "B-I-N-G-O" works so well because each individual letter matches an individual sound. However, we are all familiar with the fact that young children who sing "The Alphabet Song" tend to sing or say "l, m, n, o" all mashed together as a single syllable instead of separate sounds. This is because children recognize the sound pattern set up by short (s) and long (l) sounds in the first phrase "a, b, c, d, e, f, g" (short, short, short, short, short, short, long) and try to repeat or imitate it in the second phrase. Children have already learned the rule that in musical settings there are repetitions of phrases. If we sing the original song, "Twinkle, Twinkle, Little Star," we realize that the "s, s, s, s, s, s, l" pattern is repeated exactly throughout the song and that there is a single syllable for each pitch. Children who have heard the original have processed this pattern. A gentle reminder—sound precedes (and overrides) symbol. The music teacher has a distinct advantage in helping children associate sounds and symbols because of the consistent structure of sound in music. Remember that children can often produce sounds by rote that they do not truly understand in a metacognitive way. That is why direct instruction in orthographic or graphophonemic systems is critical to helping students truly understand and be able to decode the symbols in both language and music.

The English language has twenty-six symbols called the alphabet. These symbols are designed to represent the "sounds" of the language. This can be confusing for children and speakers of other languages as the symbols may stand for more than one sound and sounds may have more than one symbol. This is especially true for English vowels. The use of icons, graphics, or manipulatives can bring another dimension to learning. One example is the additional symbols we draw over vowels to show whether they should be pronounced as "long" or "short" vowels. Adults who study language production as linguists, speech pathologists, and diction teachers actually learn an additional alphabet to help them with the confusion of multiple symbols for the same sounds, the International Phonetic Alphabet (IPA). Many choral directors and voice teachers use the IPA to help their students produce specific phonemes to get better diction or blend. Suggestions for how alphabetic symbols can be manipulated in music classrooms are discussed in the following chapter and in Chapter 7.

Music symbols are even more complex than alphabetic symbols. There are multiple systems to represent the same sound, for example, traditional music notation on the staff, alphabetic letters, Curwen hand signs, and a set of monosyllables (solfège). As our students advance, we use both arabic and roman numerals to describe relationships between the sounds that are being studied. Creative teachers also allow their students to use "scribbles" and invented notation to help them learn. Such methods are described more fully in the section "Considerations, Adaptations, and Enhancements" in Chapter 7, as well as in the writing section (Chapter 9).

Cueing system awareness

Musical activities are particularly engaging when developing cueing system awareness. (See figure I.5.) Children delight in songs and chants that develop their ability to tell whether the words "sound right," "look right," or "make sense."

Children who are developing cueing system awareness are attracted to song parodies and jump rope chants. Parodies seem to spontaneously erupt from children (especially boys) in second grade. Some children are heard to tease each other by inventing new "verses" to jump rope chants while others make up funny parodies of their favorite songs to entertain each other. Such activities demonstrate language skills. Children who are not able to manipulate language in these ways may feel somewhat outcast from their peers. Classroom and music teachers who help children work together as a class to make up song parodies, create new chants, and to perform appropriate language manipulation feats may assist poorer readers or students who do not naturally have strong language skills.

Fluency

Fluency provides a bridge between word recognition and comprehension. Fluent readers are able to successfully execute all of the decoding skills described thus far. Because fluent readers do not have to concentrate on decoding the words, they can focus their attention on what the text means. Therefore, fluency is important in being able to understand what is read. Fluency is necessary for reading comprehension—the ability to construct or assign meaning by using clues in the text and prior knowledge (Cooper 1997, p. 11).

Classroom teachers can use choral reading to encourage fluent reading with young or hesitant readers. The feeling of movement with fluent readers is important. The effect of inertia on poorer readers can sometimes be alleviated when they join a group of fluent readers. At other times, poor readers may become frustrated when they lose their place. In a very obvious way, the inherent structure of music—with a feeling of pulse or beat—allows learners to experience fluency. The nature of music encourages students to maintain fluency over accuracy when producing rhythms and pitches during music sight-reading. When singing, even more than when playing an instrument—and especially more than with choral reading—the reader tends to maintain fluent production even if it means singing a wrong note or putting in "la, la, la" when the words are too difficult to read. The experience of fluency is inherent in virtually every music event. Movement and dance are similar. The movement provided by the music will encourage individuals to continue the task (singing, playing, dancing) even when they are not accurate. Rather than stopping—an interruption to fluency—the participants will finish the task and then do it again to get it right. Having students in a music setting sight-read without stopping and without using rote imitation is one of the best ways to facilitate reading *and* fluency.

Ideas for classroom teachers

- Build word walls as children encounter new vocabulary. Emphasize the sounds of the words by creating chants or rhymes. Set these to a rhythmic pattern or a melody to help reinforce their pronunciation and meaning.
- Write the lyrics to a familiar song on an erasable board, then try these exercises:
  1. Have the children change the words, experimenting with beginning and ending sounds, phonemes, or syllables.
  2. Erase key phrases of the song and have children replace them by verbally chanting either the original or new lyrics.
  3. Highlight, or write in a different color, repeating or rhyming phrases. Have children tell you why those phrases are in different colors.

- Sing a familiar song. Have children identify all the words in the song that begin with a letter or sound they are studying.
- Have children move in rhythm to a poem or song. Have them create a movement that they will do when they hear a repeated section or word(s).
- Look for resources for language and music activities. One good resource is "Linking Lyrics through Song Picture Books" (Barclay and Walwer 1992).

We have explored how music can be used to heighten children's engagement with basic decoding skills and tasks. Chapter 4 will investigate how music teachers can teach music reading with processes that parallel those in text reading.

Chapter **4**

Reading in the Music Environment: Decoding

Awareness of having better things to do with their lives is the secret to immunizing our children against false values. ... The child who finds fulfillment in music or reading or cooking or swimming or writing or drawing is not as easily convinced that he needs recognition or power or some "high" to feel worthwhile.

—Polly Berrien Berends, *Whole Child/Whole Parent*

Mrs. B., an elementary-school music teacher, is standing at the front of her room with twenty-six students sitting in folding chairs, their legs dangling over the edges. Each child is given a card that has a drawing of one animal (bear, cat, sheep, or goat). Mrs. B. asks the children to listen to "Have You Seen My Honey Bears," an Israeli folksong, and point to the picture of the animal as she sings the animal names. She sings again and holds up larger versions of the pictures that match the animal drawings. She asks the children to check to see if they are correct. Then, she asks the students to hand in the cards as she calls out each animal name. First, she picks up the bears, then the cats, then the sheep, and then the goats. After she picks up the animal cards she gives each child another card with three lines drawn on it (— — ——). She asks, "Do you think these cards have the animal names, too?" The children answer yes or no. Mrs. B. asks the children to listen to the song again and watch her while she shows them how they can use their new card to "read" the animal names. As she sings the song, she points to the lines when she sings the words (honey bears; silly cats; wooly sheep; billy goats). Many of the children begin pointing in imitation, even as the teacher is pointing. Mrs. B. asks the children to point along with her while she sings the song again and points to the lines while the children point to their own pictures.

This continues as she assists students so that they are all able to point to the lines while she sings the animal names. When the children are able to easily point to the lines with the animal names being sung, Mrs. B goes to the chalkboard. She draws the short, short, long (— — ——) lines on the board. She writes the names of the animals with syllabic separations under each set of lines.

She says, "We are going to sing our song one more time and I'll show you how we read the animal names in music." She erases the lines and draws in the music notation for — — —— (two eighth notes and a quarter note) while she leaves the words written in syllables. Mrs. B. points to the picture as the children sing. She says, "That's how musicians read words and music at the same time."

Music teachers develop many activities to help students understand the important decoding skills needed for reading music. As they demonstrate music decoding skills, they frequently demonstrate language reading skills—word or syllable—at the same time. As our teacher in the scenario worked with her students to read the short-short-long rhythm pattern for the song "Honey Bears," she emphasized two important decoding skills: syllabic separation and orthographic (graphophonemic) awareness (see figure I.5).

In teaching children syllabic awareness, Mrs. B. used cards with line drawings (icons) representing the lengths of the sounds being sung in the song. The children practiced saying the sounds and touching the cards when they encountered them in the four verses of the song. Because of these experiences, the children should be able to associate the pattern of the sounds on their picture cards with the words divided into syllables and rhythmic notation encountered in a piece of music. "Effective phonemic-awareness instruction teaches children to notice, think about, and work with (manipulate) sounds in spoken language" (Armbruster, Lehr, and Osborn 2003, p. 5). In this case, the teacher helped her students reinforce the syllable-to-sound relationships (orthographic or graphophonemic relationships) that are common in reading music.

The first-grade reading circle scenario in Chapter 3 was concerned with single phonemes. In "The Honey Bear Song" example, it can be seen that music educators work with children at the syllable level from the very beginning. This may be the reason that some children enjoy music and singing from music texts even when they struggle with traditional reading activities that require decoding to the individual phoneme. The nature of vocal music demonstrates the syllable and sound segmentation that is the major building block of the writing system.

Enhancing music and reading strategies: Completing the connection

In Chapter 3, we discussed ways that a general classroom teacher could enrich lessons and motivate students by using musical activities. In this chapter, we discuss how music teachers can help students improve their language and music literacy. By extending traditional music activities one step further, we can demonstrate the literacy link between music and language. The reading scenario in Chapter 3 demonstrated rote instruction. The music scenario in this chapter demonstrated use of iconic representation and direct instruction. By adding one additional activity, music teachers can help complete the learning loop that connects music with language reading and symbol interpretation. Such an activity is suggested below. This extension should add only one or two minutes to the initial lesson. The regular use of such extensions helps students experience and understand the music and literacy connection.

Scenario extension

When the children are able to easily point to the — — —— lines with the animal names being sung, Mrs. B. goes to the chalkboard. She draws the short, short, long lines on the board. She writes the names of the animals with syllabic separations as she sounds out each syllable. Then she passes out papers with the words written under the short-short-long lines like her example on the chalkboard. She asks the children to sing the song again while she shows them how to point to the animal names and "read" them. She then asks the children to point to the animal names with her while they all sing together. As the children continue to enjoy this song and sing it regularly, the teacher can simply write the names of the animals on the board (without the syllabic divisions) as a reminder of the order of the verses. This is an additional step along the road to reading.

On another day, the children may be encouraged to think of other animals whose names will work within the song structure. This activity reinforces the syllabic structure and the short-short-long rhythm pattern simultaneously. It becomes evident that children understand by the suggestions they make. A child who makes up the verse "Have you seen my puppy dog?" or even "Have you seen my elephant?" will be demonstrating the short-short-long pattern better than a child who suggests "Have you seen my cat?" or "Have you seen my tarantula?" The ability of some children to follow the short-short-long pattern demonstrates that they are moving along the reading continuum.

For children who are not able to easily follow the pattern, it is necessary to break down the task. The teacher may want to make up cards with suggested animal names, some that fit the pattern and some that do not. Then, the children can be guided to find the cards that work. By writing the words chosen in syllable separation form on the chalkboard and pairing them with the correct notation pattern, the teacher is able to help the children check to see if the words they chose do fit the pattern.

Developing specific decoding skills in the music classroom

Some reading activities can easily be used in the music classroom to help children reinforce their skills.

Phonological awareness

Phonological awareness is the ability to identify and discriminate the characteristics of sounds. Music education activities are designed to help students refine their discrimination skills. Students learn to discriminate within the four primary characteristics of sound: frequency, time, intensity, and source. In music education activities, children go beyond these gross parameters to specific musical qualities within the parameters: frequency (pitch), time (duration—beat, meter, rhythm, and tempo), intensity (dynamics), and source (timbre, tone color). Combinations of these qualities determine musical form. In music education, teachers use specialized terminology, distinct examples, and repeated experiences to isolate specific aspects of each parameter.

Timbre. When children participate in music activities (especially when they produce their own sounds by singing or playing instruments), they learn to manipulate the individual characteristics of sound. When playing barred instruments, children learn that the sound is clearer when the mallet hits directly in the middle of a bar. With recorders, they learn that they must control their breath to produce the best tone or to play longer and shorter sounds. Music class provides time for exploring sound in isolation, in patterns, and ultimately in meaningful offerings with or without language. Children from different linguistic backgrounds easily choose pictures of the instruments they hear played on a recording, even if they cannot say the names of those instruments.

Pitch. Pitch is a primary parameter for music and one that is the center of many lessons in music class. Children may listen to the song "Love Somebody" and be asked to choose the correct visual representations of steps or skips for the different pitch patterns on the words "Yes, I do!" at the end of each phrase. They may then be given melody bells and allowed to play those same pitches by "reading" the answers that they chose. In music, pitch can be written in more than one way. Music teachers may use icons, the musical alphabet, a number system, solfège syllables, or standard music notation.

Figure 4.1 shows the diatonic scale represented four ways. It could be argued that Curwen hand signs may also be read. At times, teachers may use more than one of these forms of pitch representation in the same lesson as a way of breaking down a more challenging task or adapting to the needs of individual students who may be at different reading levels.

Time. Time is another major component of music. We frequently use the term "rhythm" as a description for the quality of time in music. In reality, we should differen-

Figure 4.1
Diatonic Scale

tiate between the different time elements by using specific terms to describe music duration: beat, meter (groups of beats), tempo (the speed of the beat), and rhythm (the relative length of individual sounds). Our impulse to use the term rhythm to describe all elements of time in music may be because we are subconsciously aware of the importance that rhythm has in language. The phonological building blocks of rhythm are syllables, especially in English, which is syllabic. In order to become literate, children must be able to sound out these units of language. Syllables provide the rhythm of language. They also provide the basis of many rhythmic patterns in music.

Phonemic awareness

Through singing, children have wonderful opportunities to manipulate sound. Specific phonemes can be manipulated, vowels can be held for shorter or longer durations, and consonants can be articulated in various ways. One of the most important skills we teach in singing is how to adjust consonants and vowels to make music more musical. We even move consonant sounds from the end of one syllable to the beginning of another to preserve the vowel line. This is a sign of excellent choral music instruction, the step beyond mastery of pitches and rhythms. Control of phonemic production is a goal in choral technique—control the shape of the air column and you control the resulting diction, blend, rhythmic precision, and even intonation.

With young children, we don't describe the manipulation of phonemes in technical detail the way we do with older students in advanced choral singing or voice lessons, but we model them extensively. We all have witnessed young children who mimic opera singers or their favorite pop singers. They are able to sing words they don't understand and produce musical renditions that are quite accurate to the model they have heard.

Imagine a young child learning to sing the French song "Allouette," but having no idea what the words mean. The child is aware of the sounds and enjoys singing them, but doesn't understand what letters represent those sounds in written language.

The child likes the sounds as musical sounds. They are not meaningful words because she has not had experience with them in the context of language. For her they are delicious phonemes that are fun to articulate and music to her ears, but primarily they are music, a song. In fact, because the child never studied the relationship between the phonemes and graphemes of French, she is still unable to decode the sounds of that language from a written sample. Many years later, when that child became a music teacher (author Elaine Bernstorf), she encountered those words again and was then able to match the sounds to the written syllables that were in the textbook. Only then did she realize that she had never seen the written words before. She had learned the song by rote, probably from a record played at home or maybe from echo singing it at school. Perhaps if that child had been exposed to the graphemes when she first learned the music, she might have been eager to read and write that wonderful language that sounded so lovely.

It is important for children to have textbooks or "big books" in music just as in other subject areas so they can see the sounds they are singing. Even in a time of budget constraints, it is important that written language and written music be available for students so they develop phoneme-grapheme awareness. Using cue cards, chalkboards, or overheads (electronic or traditional) is worth the extra effort they require. However, the textbook has no meaning without good instruction. It is important that we bring both music notation and written language to life with specific and focused activities involving sight identification, orthographic and graphophonic awareness, and cueing if we intend to have fluent readers of language or music.

Sight identification

Sight identification can be enhanced through a variety of music activities. In the music room, many teachers post music vocabulary words on bulletin boards and special posters. Students become familiar with these words because the same music terms are used daily. Many young children begin to recognize the words "piano" and "forte" even when they don't really understand their meaning. A musical sight vocabulary is important. Most music teachers refer to the glossaries of their music series texts or their district curriculum for suggested terms to include. (It can be a problem when children transfer from one school to another and the teacher uses a different music vocabulary, especially for pitch or rhythm. As radical as it may be, perhaps it is time for music educators to consider a standard list of high-frequency words for children in music education classes.) What music teachers may not consider is adding additional sight words. Music teachers (as well as physical education teachers) can make verbs and prepositions come alive for young children. In kindergarten and primary regular classrooms, nouns are the predominant sight words: chair, table, window, desk. In a music classroom, teachers have a great opportunity to use verbs (sing, play, move, dance, step, skip, hop, jump), prepositions (in, out, up, down, before, after), adjectives (loud, soft, higher, lower), and adverbs (quickly, softly).

By putting key words on cards for movement activities, music teachers may save their voices and enhance sight-word identification simultaneously. It could be argued that the only sight words in a music room should be music vocabulary, but perhaps we are limiting ourselves with this practice. By creating sight cues for any important vocabulary associated with music, we support reading. However, as music teachers, it is critical that we be certain that musical vocabulary is always visible and that we use the displayed terms correctly. (See the word wall section in Chapter 6.)

Another important aspect of sight identification is the use of music-phrase cards and rhythm-pattern cards or pitch-pattern cards. Figure 4.2 has a list of typical words, phrases, and patterns.

Music teachers use textbooks, prepared overheads, and different types of listening maps to assist children in representing musical qualities graphically. In a manner of speaking, we have our own set of sight words. Examples may include the typical Orff rhythm patterns; Curwen hand-signs for pitch; step, skip, same; crescendo and decrescendo signs; and alphabet labels for form (ABA, rondo, D.C. al fine). We use these sight words regularly in our classes. They are seldom reinforced anywhere outside of the music room. It may not be reasonable for other teachers to incorporate music-vocabulary sight words into their teaching, but it makes perfect sense for music educators to find simple ways to incorporate standard frequent-use vocabulary words into music. (Consult local curriculum guidelines and peer teachers for appropriate vocabulary words to include.)

Orthographic or graphophonemic awareness

Text awareness. Favorite action songs and dances are repeated over and over. A familiar song with actions is "If You're Happy and You Know It, Clap Your Hands." Many teachers use graphics of hands (clap), feet (stomp), and head (nod) when they teach this song. These pictures are helpful in fostering independence as children begin to "read" which verse to sing from the picture cards. But what if we take the activity one step further? By using sight-word or sight-phrase cue cards paired with the picture cards, we gradually introduce written language that is predictable because of the repetitive process of the song. In this case, we actually introduce sight phrases. As a result, students may build a repertoire of sight nouns and verbs. However, this type of activity cannot be carried out from behind a piano, guitar, or Autoharp. The activities will need a recorded accompaniment or to be presented a cappella. It is important that the words are visible during the action. Over time, children may take on the role of the reading assistant, but initially the teacher must present the word cards or have an assistant (parent volunteers or older students who come in during their recess). A positive experience with written language in music class may provide a special boost for a student who struggles with reading in other settings.

Figure 4.2
Words, Phrases, and Patterns for Word Walls

The following are potential vocabulary words that may be appropriate for word cards or a reference poster. Please consult glossaries in the textbook series you may be using for additional words and for suggested vocabulary for specific grade levels. Pattern cards can include common rhythmic (♫ ♩ | ♪♩ ♪♩ ♩ | ♩) or melodic patterns in solfège or notation (*sol-mi, sol-mi-la-sol mi, do-re-mi-re-do-do-do*, etc.), common chord progressions shown by letter or roman numeral, and common forms (AB, ABA, rondo). Allowing suggestions for phrases from favorite songs will help the students develop their own "theme charts."

Frequency-Pitch
Melody
up, down, same
step, skip, same
repeat, contrast
scale, major, minor, pentatonic

Harmony
chord, triad, interval
consonance, dissonance
monophonic, homophonic, polyphonic

Intensity-Amplitude
Dynamics
loud, soft
piano, forte
crescendo, decrescendo

Articulation
staccato, legato, marcato

Form
part, phrase, section
AB, ABA
rondo
verse-chorus, verse-refrain
theme, variation

Time-Duration
Beat

Meter
duple, triple, mixed

Rhythm
long, short, same
even, uneven
whole, half, quarter, eighth, sixteenth, rest
syncopation
fermata

Tempo
fast, slow; faster, slower
accelerando, ritardando
andante, allegro, moderato, presto, vivace

Timbre
Tone color
strings, winds, brass, percussion
soprano, alto, tenor, bass
dark, light, bright, mute

Notation awareness. Music is generally based on the syllables of language. When teaching young children, we frequently group syllables and notes into patterns and phrases to help the children read notation.

In many children's songs, there is a one-to-one match of written-language syllable to musical note. This one-to-one syllable and note lineup actually helps children visualize the individual sounds they are singing and saying. The visual-aural match aids notation awareness, which is vital to learning to read music. Single syllable words usually go with a single note. Words that have more than one syllable are written with dashes separating each syllable. Good alignment between the syllables and the notes gives children even more visual cueing to encourage reading skills. This is an important point that will be discussed more thoroughly in the descriptions of adaptations and enhancements in Chapter 7.

Some music education methods are designed to enhance the syllable-note relationship even more directly. Kodály rhythm syllables (such as *ta, ti-ti, ta-ah*) are nonsense syllables that help children internalize time patterns. Solfège syllables (*do, re, mi, fa, sol, la, ti, do*) are used to help children internalize pitch relationships. These syllables assist children in understanding sight-sound relationships. Interestingly, Kodály primarily chose syllables that comprise a single consonant-vowel combination. Such syllables are easily sung and sounded out by young readers. Given the closed sets of syllables in Kodály and solfège and the repetition of certain patterns such as *ti-ti tah* and *sol-mi* that occur frequently in children's songs, children who engage in syllable-based music reading may have a better chance of becoming effective and efficient readers of both music and language.

Older students may participate in more sophisticated singing situations. The choral music they encounter may still have one text syllable to one music syllable, but the syllable may not be as simple as Kodály's with a single consonant and single vowel. At this stage there is a different strategy for reading and music production. Choral teachers move to working with smaller grapheme and phoneme units. They systematically work at the grapheme-phoneme level to improve diction. They help students sound out individual phonemes to maintain a strong vocal line. They teach singers to "get to the vowel," usually by shortening consonant sounds and enhancing the more vocally resonant vowel sounds. They teach choirs to alter the written notation, especially rhythm, to enhance both vocal quality and diction. Students may even write in altered rhythmic notation to help them perform better. For example, students may be asked to sing a whole note as a dotted quarter note with a quarter rest. Such adjustments actually alter rhythms and help students move away from just producing syllables to producing syllables that emphasize beginning or ending consonants.

Cueing systems. During music activities, children may be asked to fill in words, make up parts, or participate in question-and-answer musical games. Making up songs or parts of songs requires a series of interrelated adjustments. Consider the song "If You're Happy and You Know It." This song is frequently used to allow children to make up new verses. Peers eagerly wait to hear whether the made-up section sounds right. What does that mean? Sounding right, in the language context, is based on multiple cues including syntax, graphophonic, and semantic. (See figure I.5.) In this case, there are also music cueing systems. This does not mean that the child must match the pitches exactly and use exactly the same rhythm pattern. Frequently the child doesn't sing exactly the same pitches or rhythm but stays within the same pitch contour and maintains the same rhythmic meter and phrase length (number of beats). For example, a child may sing "if you're happy and you know it jump up and down" using very short sounds in a triplet pattern to make the "jump up and down" fit into the meter. In this case, music cueing systems were used because the child maintained the meter (number of beats for the phrase) and followed the pitch contour line, but adjusted the rhythm pattern to include shorter sounds for "jump up and down."

It is important that we help students put their own meanings into new contexts. Young children are not able to do this easily. Some older children also experience difficulty. They tend to be the poor readers. These children may need extra help to participate. One suggestion is to have prepared samples of verses and let them decide if the verses sound right. Having a variety of examples (some following the pattern and some not) will help them experience cueing systems in language and in music.

The National Standards for Music Education (Consortium of National Arts Education Associations 1994) provide a sound basis for lesson planning. National Standards 3 and 4, for improvisation and composition respectively, are particularly important building blocks for developing comprehensive musicians. The Standards are also important in guiding students to read and write music (Standard 5). Review all nine standards on the MENC Web site (www.menc.org/publication/books/standards.htm). By giving students opportunities to improvise using the four major characteristics of sound (pitch, time, intensity, timbre), we are helping them understand the sound components that govern verbal language as well as the language of music. Such experiences also allow students to gain control over the cueing systems of music and of language. It is important to encourage students to use these cueing systems in their written form even though it takes extra time and effort. Use paper or magnetic rhythm strips, a laminated staff with note heads such as poker chips or metal washers with craft sticks for stems. Using individual chalkboards may provide additional opportunities for refining students' reading skills.

Fluency. After children have some mastery over skills that are learned earlier (phonological awareness, phonemic awareness, sight identification, orthographic or graphophonemic awareness, and cueing systems) they will push for opportunities to test their fluency. Children in a music class who think they have finally mastered a song will ask, "Can we do it faster?" This is their way of expressing a desire to demonstrate fluency. Children who are not advancing as quickly along the skill pathway may withdraw in such settings. It is important to help all children develop fluency.

Children who may not be able to sing or read at faster tempos can be successful playing an ostinato or the steady beat. While they may not be able to master the intricacies of the language patterns, they will still be developing in other ways. Sometimes these children sing louder or change the timbre of their voices or instruments. They are trying to demonstrate what they *are* able to do fluently. We usually provide opportunities for fluency activities, but we may not realize how important they are for promoting both music and language growth. When we describe mastery in language we use the term fluency. When describing this same type of mastery in music settings we use the term musical or musicianship. The more we assist students in developing musicianship, the more we may be assisting them in language fluency as well.

Summary

Music educators should be aware of the similarities between oral language reading and music reading (Bernstorf 2003, p. 10). In this chapter we have suggested activities for reinforcing language skills in the music classroom. These suggestions include the following:

- Label nouns in the music classroom.
- Provide verb, preposition, adjective, and adverb cue cards for action songs and as playing guides for instruments.
- Help students make up verses to action songs.
- Let students fill in short patterns or phrases from a set of suggested written answers.
- Have students fill in short patterns independently or produce phrases from their own ideas.
- Take a little extra time to write student answers so they can be seen as well as heard again by all students.
- Help students fix answers that do not fit the pitch or time pattern rather than rejecting those answers or just applying a teacher fix.
- Help students fix answers that do not fit the linguistic pattern (for example, the part of speech) for the song.

These actions cannot occur in music programs where music instruction is rote and there are no opportunities for improvisation or composition. By going one step further and regularly introducing written language, icons, and music notation, music educators provide fertile opportunities for developing not only visual and auditory processes and skills, but decoding skills that are critical for strong literacy.

Our purpose is not to become reading teachers. We should not compromise good music instruction to do silent reading or reading tutorials. We need to use the parallel

metacognitive and metalinguistic skills that students experience through good music instruction. Well-trained music educators have a unique role as they teach multiple systems of reading through the medium of music. Music teachers complement the reading curriculum. This may be why virtually all cultures have music teachers, whether they are called professional music educators or storytellers. Music education provides critical opportunities in the learning process for children to truly experience the music and literacy connection.

Chapter 5

Music in the Reading Environment: Comprehension

It is not enough to be content with motivating students to learn to read a book; they must learn to read the world.

—Carolyn Piazza, *Multiple Forms of Literacy: Teaching Literacy and the Arts,* p. iii

Mr. Henry's third-grade class is studying Mexico. Today they are visited by musicians and dancers who live in their community but were born and raised in Guadalajara. The children listen and watch as the dancers swirl rhythmically to the strong melodic sounds of the guitarists, singers, and brass players. The spokesperson for the group invites the children to dance with them. Mr. Henry and the music teacher have both received a study guide from the group in advance, so the children have been prepared for this moment. The children also sing the comedy ballad "Don Gato" with the group. They learned the song in music class, first in Spanish, then in English. In Mr. Henry's class, the children read the English version of the story, *Puss in Boots,* and the Spanish version, *El Gato con Botas,* both by Charles Perrault (1990 and 1991). They wrote and illustrated story maps of "Don Gato" and created graphic organizers to show how the song and the story were similar and different.

Mr. Henry's use of a variety of instructional strategies improved the children's reading comprehension and helped them gain an appreciation of Mexican culture. It is important that students experience a concept or topic in multiple ways so that their emotional response will help them learn. Using musical experiences in the regular classroom creates colorful, engaging, and inviting environments—important elements in establishing literacy.

In this chapter, we will review common instructional strategies for developing reading comprehension and describe musical activities that can be woven into reading lessons. David Cooper defines reading comprehension as "a strategic process by which readers construct or assign meaning to a text by using the clues in the text and their own prior knowledge" (1997, p. 11). Comprehending text is different from decoding. At a high level of decoding ability, children can read and pronounce the words of the text fluently. But when they comprehend the text, they also assign meaning to it. Later, we'll discuss the implications of Bloom's Taxonomy (1984) as it relates to activities that promote reading comprehension.

In reviewing the scenario, we find that the children have not only studied literature from Mexico, they have learned to dance, sing, and create visual representations of the text and music literature. Because the performing group provided the teacher with a study guide, students were better prepared to experience the presentation and understand the stories. This preparation is part of a process called "schema theory" (Rumelhart 1980).

> Schemata are structures that represent the generic concepts stored in our memory. Schema theory explains how these structures are formed and related to one another as we develop knowledge. ... The process of comprehension depends on the reader's schemata. The more closely those schemata match the schemata intended by the author, the easier it is to comprehend the text. (Cooper 1997, p. 10)

Jackie Wiggins emphasizes the importance of teaching for conceptual understanding. She says, "It is important to take the time to be sure that all students have accessed an appropriate context for understanding what you are about to teach. Throughout a lesson, teachers must constantly assess student perspective, bearing in mind that contextual understanding is crucial to conceptual understanding" (2001, p. 9). Cooper describes a scenario of children about to read a story concerning birds in winter. Rather than asking children if they have ever seen birds in the winter and what kinds of birds they see, he suggests that teachers dig deeper into the real meaning of the story. The main concept is really about the survival of birds during blizzards (1997, p. 104). Too often we trivialize the underlying concepts of a story or song in our efforts to activate prior knowledge.

Imagine if Mr. Henry assigned *Puss in Boots* to his students with no other linked activities. No doubt they would have enjoyed reading it. The children would have brought to the reading their own schemata or prior knowledge and would have understood the text in their own way. But, the integrated activities enriched the entire class. Together they grew in their understanding of the sounds, sights, language, and movement of the stories.

Notice that the activities in the scenario emphasized the literature and culture of Mexico. The songs and dance could have been taught in music class and the reading skills could have been taught in reading class. However, the objective was for the children to experience the culture and literature of Mexico. This unit would most likely be classified as integrated or cross-curricular. There are several different approaches to integration. (Appendix IV describes several models of interdisciplinary or cross-curricular integration.) In the scenario, two teachers taught units on Mexico at the same time. They coordinated their instruction so that the concepts were not redundant, but built upon each other. Robin Fogarty referred to this type of integration as sequenced (Fogarty 1991, p. 34). This is a commonly found model of integration in schools. Another model Fogarty refers to as threaded (pp. 63–65). In the threaded model, "thinking skills, social skills, study skills, graphic organizers, technology, and a multiple intelligences approach to learning thread through all disciplines" (p. 64).

During school improvement or accreditation, schools will often ask teachers in all disciplines to support reading and mathematics by integrating shared, research-based teaching strategies. In this way, various successful approaches to teaching reading and mathematics are used in a building, with positive results for all programs. With that in mind, this chapter highlights several commonly used instructional strategies for reading and demonstrates how to use music as the text. In Chapter 6, we demonstrate how the same reading strategies can successfully be used as tools in a music class. One could also think of this as a type of parallel integration, where teachers are increasing children's learning skills by using shared instructional strategies.

When we react to music or literature, we are responding as a "natural process of constructing meaning" (Cooper 1997, p. 299). Cooper describes two basic categories of responses: personal and creative. In a personal response, children describe how the literature has affected them personally—how it relates to their life experiences. In a creative response, children create "art, music, drama, and so forth" (p. 299). Naturally, common sense dictates that a balance of responses be sought to teach skills pertinent to reading comprehension. Responses to literature, however, do not always have to be responses to a book. Lyrics can be used to reinforce children's reading skills. Let's look at how children might respond to the song "Follow the Drinking Gourd" (figure 5.1) using common reading comprehension strategies, in three settings: before, during, and after learning the song. These activities would precede reading the children's book *Follow the Drinking Gourd*, by Jeanette Winter (1988).

Figure 5.1
Follow the Drinking Gourd

From Jane Beethoven et al. *The Music Connection, Grade 3*, pp. 186–7.
Copyright © 1995 by Silver Burdett Ginn, Inc. Reprinted by permission of Addison-Wesley Educational.

Strategies used before reading

Prereading instructional techniques help children acquire prior knowledge or schemata before reading a new book or singing a new song. "When there is a gap between children's background knowledge and ideas in the text, there is a temptation to fill it by supplying the information through teacher explanation" (Maria 1990, p. 94). On occasion, a teacher's brief explanation may suffice to prepare students for new ideas in a text. But, having students actively involved in the prereading exercise is usually more effective.

Graphic organizers are a way to visually organize thoughts and can be used to promote complex thinking and build vocabulary in classroom activities as well as assessments. Many Web sites are available that provide ideas for constructing and using graphic organizers (see resources at the end of the chapter). All graphic organizers, of course, can be modified to fit the lesson, so teachers are encouraged to create them on an overhead transparency, blackboard, or computer as the lesson emerges.

Mind maps are used to help students in the middle grades and higher understand the types of information that make up a definition. Each map has three types of information: Class 1—What is it? Class 2—What is like it? Class 3—What are some examples? (Cooper 1997, p. 247). Figure 5.2 is a mind map that supports "Follow the Drinking Gourd." This map could be generated by the teacher and children during class. To build a mind map, generally the teacher places the title in the center of the map and gives at least one example of a term or concept that relates to that title. The teacher then encourages students to brainstorm further terms.

Figure 5.2
Mind Map for "Follow the Drinking Gourd"

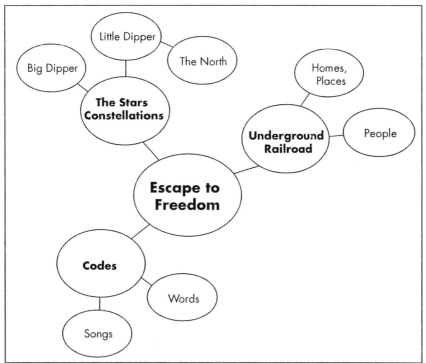

Semantic mapping, developed by Pearson and Johnson (1978), is also an effective tool. Semantic maps are used to help children understand the relationships within a given topic. The ovals represent the concepts and lines with arrows and words next to them represent the relationships (Cooper 1997, p. 126). The semantic map in figure 5.3 helps children understand the concepts behind "Follow the Drinking Gourd."

Figure 5.3
Semantic Map for "Follow the Drinking Gourd"

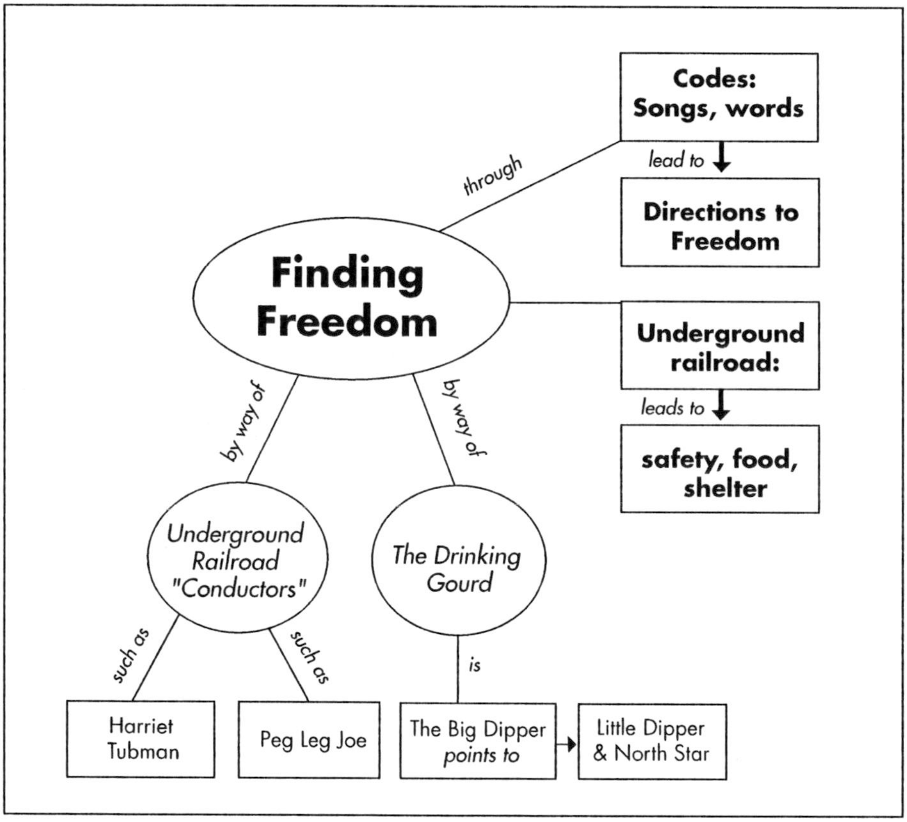

Another graphic organizer is a Know-Want to Know-Learn (K-W-L) chart developed by Ogle (1986). This prereading activity is best used for expository text. While "Follow the Drinking Gourd" is a song, some aspects of it can be considered expository because of the historical background. Katherine Maria encourages teachers to use a semantic map first so that children become aware of the vocabulary they will encounter and then use a K-W-L chart to activate prior knowledge based on the vocabulary (1990). The K-W-L chart would, obviously, be used prior to, during, and after learning

Figure 5.4
K-W-L Chart for "Follow the Drinking Gourd"

What I know	What I want to know	What I have learned
■ I've heard of slavery. ■ I know where to find the Big Dipper. ■ I think escaping to freedom would be hard. ■ We fought a war to get rid of slavery.	■ What are code songs? ■ What is the Underground Railroad? ■ What is the "drinking gourd"? ■ Where was the war fought? ■ When did all of this happen?	■ I learned that a lot of the Civil War was fought right here where we live. ■ I learned how people helped the slaves so they could escape to the North. ■ I learned that the "drinking gourd" is really the Little Dipper.

the song. Figure 5.4 is an example of a K-W-L chart third-grade children might create for "Follow the Drinking Gourd."

Another prereading strategy, developed by Hansen (Hansen and Pearson 1983), is "inferential strategy." This strategy uses prediction to prepare readers. "Designed for narrative text, this strategy encourages children to compare something from their own lives to something that might happen in the story" (Maria 1990, p. 105). With "Follow the Drinking Gourd" this strategy has two parts: (1) Explain the strategy to the children. Let them know that the class will try to identify some things that are familiar to them before singing the song. (2) Construct at least two questions for each concept in the song. Here is a sample of how the dialogue might unfold:

T: We are going to sing a new book today! But before that, I will be asking you some questions to help you understand what this song is about, based on your own experiences. Why do you think slaves might try to escape from their homes?

S 1: I learned about slaves when we visited a plantation in the South. Sometimes they weren't treated very well.

S 2: They couldn't do what they wanted to—they had to work for their masters.

T: What do you think being a slave would be like?

S 3: You'd have to do what you were told or be punished.

S 2: If I were a slave, I would want to escape, too.

T: If you were going to escape, how would you find where you were going?

S 3: I'd get a map or I'd ask other people that I trusted.

S 4: I'd follow a road, but in the woods next to it so no one could see me.

T: What if you discovered that there is a formation of stars called the Little Dipper whose handle has the North Star in it. Let's say you didn't have a map, could you follow the stars north to freedom?

S 1: Sure—except if it's cloudy!

Strategies used during reading

The teacher then introduces "Follow the Drinking Gourd." As the children listen to and learn the song, the teacher uses several additional reading comprehension strategies. One of the most powerful ways to foster reading comprehension is with questioning strategies.

A popular and effective questioning strategy is called "Question-Answer-Responses" (QARs) developed by Raphael (1986, pp. 516–522). QARs is an inquiry technique that improves a student's comprehension by asking questions of increasing degrees of difficulty. There are four levels of questioning in QARs:

Level 1 (Q 1)—Right there: Literal questions with answers found easily in the text.

Level 2 (Q 2)—Think and search: The answer is in the story, but the reader needs to put together different parts of the story to find the information.

Level 3 (Q 3)—Author and me: The answer is not in the story. Readers need to think about what they already know and what they read in the text and fit the two together.

Level 4 (Q 4)—On my own: The answer to the question is not in the text. A reader could answer the question without reading the story. The reader's own experiences are the basis for the answer.

QARs begins with literal questions and moves to questions that ask students to infer, evaluate, or synthesize using prior knowledge. Likewise, Bloom's Taxonomy (1984) remains a foundation for understanding questioning and thinking processes and also moves from simple to complex. From knowledge level to evaluation level questions, the taxonomy leads us through graduated levels of thinking. Many people have constructed sets of verbs that they think capture the essence of the taxonomy. Figure 5.5 attempts to capture the nuances of the different levels.

Another excellent process for understanding types of questions has been created by Larry Lowery (1998), science educator at the University of California in Berkeley. Figure 5.6 shows his levels and definitions of questions.

Below are examples of starter questions for the four levels of QARs using "Follow the Drinking Gourd." The categories of questions from Bloom's Taxonomy and Lowery are also shown. Note how the questions all move toward higher-order thinking.

Level 1–Right there
Now that we've learned the lyrics to the song, what does the song ask us to follow?
Bloom—knowledge level; Lowery—narrow instructional, confirming

What is the old man doing in the song?
Bloom—knowledge level; Lowery—narrow instructional, confirming

When should we follow the drinking gourd?
Bloom—knowledge level; Lowery—narrow instructional, confirming

Figure 5.5
Taxonomy of Educational Objectives

Knowledge	Comprehension	Application	Analysis	Synthesis	Evaluation
Recalling specific and isolable bits of information. Refers primarily to what might be called the hard core of actions or information in a field of knowledge.	Knowing what is being communicated and being able to make some use of the material or ideas in it in oral, written, verbal, or symbolic form.	Being able to use a theory, principle, idea, or method (an abstraction) correctly to solve a problem that contains elements new to the student.	Emphasizing the breakdown of material into its constituent parts and detecting the relationship of the parts and the way they are organized.	Putting together elements and parts to form a whole. This process involves re-combining parts with new material, reconstructed into a new and more or less well-integrated whole.	Making judgments about the value, for some purpose, of ideas, works, solutions, methods, material, etc. using criterion as well as standards for appraising accuracy, etc.
Knowledge of Dates, events, persons, places, sources of information, specific facts, ways of organizing, studying, judging, and criticizing ideas and phenomena, theories and structures, principles and generalizations, major ideas, methodologies, techniques.	**The ability to** Translate—put a communication into another form of communication. Interpret—reorder ideas into a new configuration; see interrelationships, generalize, summarize. Extrapolate—make inferences based on a given—not on abstraction.	**The ability to** Apply the appropriate abstraction without having to be prompted as to which abstraction is correct or be shown how to use it in that situation, given a problem new to the student or containing elements new to the student.	**The ability to** Identify or classify the elements of a situation. Make explicit the relationships among elements to determine their connections and interactions. Recognize the organizational principles, arrangement, and structure.	**Involves** Drawing on elements from many sources and putting these together in a structure or pattern not clearly there before. Efforts should yield a product able to be observed through one or more of the senses and clearly more than the materials the student began with.	**Involves** Drawing on some combination of all other taxonomy levels. Includes distinct criteria, highly conscious and carefully considered. Based on internal or external standards. Not an opinion.
Action statements/verbs How do you; What is; Explain how to; Recall; When; List; Define; Name.	**Action statements/verbs** Reword; Why; Describe in your own words; Restate; Report; Discuss; Translate, Interpret; Distinguish; Differentiate.	**Action statements/verbs** Predict; Employ appropriate procedures leading to solutions; Apply laws, generalizations, and principles to create practical situations.	**Action statements/verbs** Detect fallacies in arguments; Check consistency of a hypothesis; Recognize particulars; Recognize causal effects.	**Action statements/verbs** Integrate the results of an investigation into an effective plan; Design (given specifications); Create a phrase of music in the style of; Write a.	**Action statements/verbs** Appraise; Make judgments and values; Apply self-developed standards to a choice or decision.

Adapted from Benjamin Bloom et al. *Taxonomy of Educational Objectives, Handbook 1: Cognitive Domain.* Published by Allyn and Bacon, Boston, MA. Copyright © 1984 by Pearson Education. Reprinted/adapted by permission of the publisher.

Figure 5.6
Types of Instructional Statements or Questions

Narrow Instructional

Statements or questions for which a teacher expects a certain, predictable response or set of convergent responses.

Q1, Q2 (Raphael); Knowledge, Comprehension (Bloom)

Broad Instructional

A broad statement or question for which a teacher seeks a variety of acceptable, although generally unpredictable responses. Use thinking processes which synthesize information or ideas in ways unique to the individual.

Q3, Q4 (Raphael); Application, Analysis, Synthesis, Evaluation (Bloom)

Confirming

Require students to remember information: recall a fact, define a term, identify. Teacher has particular response in mind.

Examples
- What instrument plays the melody?
- How many types of voices sing this song?
- How many flats and sharps?
- Looking at the title, what is this song about?
- What note should you be prepared to play at measure one?

Integrating

Require students to compare or synthesize information in a direction planned by the teacher. Compare, contrast, associate, explain, state relationships, arrive at conclusions.

Examples
- Explain what you mean by thick texture.
- Why do you think he composed it that way?
- How can this be performed more effectively?
- What makes this music sound marchlike?

Open-Ended

Allow the student to explore ideas freely in student's own terms. Encourage synthesis of ideas, hypothesize and develop a meaningful resolution, deduce and predict.

Examples
- What can be done to resolve this problem?
- Predict what will happen if …
- What would happen if we changed the tempo?
- What if we try it this way?

Valuing

Require the student to synthesize information in order to come to a judgment concerning the answer. Justifying a choice, defending a position, or presenting evidence for a judgment.

Examples
- Why do you prefer the first one to the second?
- Explain why you think this is the best way to do this.
- Why do you think it was written/performed/created this way?

Feeling

Expect the student to express feelings and emotions from a purely affective perspective. Share feelings, become aware of own feelings or those of others.

Examples
- What kind of music makes you happy?
- How does the combination of colors make you feel?
- What types of feelings did you have after hearing/performing this music?

Adapted from Larry F. Lowery. 1998. "Asking Effective Questions." Workshop handout at the Lawrence Hall of Science, Graduate School of Education, University of California, Berkeley.

Level 2–Think and search

What clues in the song help you find your way when you escape?
Bloom—analysis level; Lowery—narrow instructional, integrating

What do you think the drinking gourd is?
Bloom—analysis level; Lowery—narrow instructional, integrating

Level 3–Author and me

Do you think slaves had an easy time escaping?
Bloom—synthesis level; Lowery—broad instructional, valuing

Were there people who helped them?
Bloom—synthesis level; Lowery—broad instructional, open-ended

Do you think there are places that still have slavery?
Bloom—analysis level; Lowery—broad instructional, open-ended

Level 4–On my own

Make a sculpture that describes your idea of freedom.
Bloom—synthesis level; Lowery—broad instructional, feeling

Read the book *Follow the Drinking Gourd.* How does this story relate to freedom?
Bloom—synthesis level; Lowery—broad instructional, open-ended

While moving to higher order thinking, the children are constructing meaning—comprehending the text. Too often our questions to children stop at the knowledge and comprehension levels. We don't ask them to think. The questions used with "Follow the Drinking Gourd" are an example of how lyrics can foster reading comprehension and at the same time add interest, because the text is set to music.

Strategies used after reading

Vocabulary building strategies are one way to reinforce the words and concepts students have learned when reading. In building vocabulary, children either recognize a word or they understand the meaning of a word. Children need broad exposure to vocabulary in order to recognize or understand words. All the arts, and especially music, introduce children to new words and concepts for their vocabulary treasure chest. When a child learns a song like "Follow the Drinking Gourd," the reading teacher can introduce new vocabulary words such as "quail," "gourd," "riverbank," "pegfoot," "Big Dipper," "Little Dipper," "Polaris," and "North Star." The music teacher, on the other hand, might include completely different vocabulary: "eighth notes," "quarter notes," "key of G," "verse-refrain," and "D.C. al fine." "Increasing the volume of students' reading is the single most important thing a teacher can do to promote large-scale vocabulary growth" (Nagy 1988, p. 236).

Techniques for building vocabulary abound. Here are a few examples:

- Journals. Have students make a personal list of words that interest them or that they would like to discuss with a group, a peer, or you. Students should choose words that interest them or puzzle them rather than having them simply identify all the words they don't know.
- Use a broad variety of words when speaking. Use music vocabulary when you teach about music. See Chapter 4 for common music sight words. The language should always be used in the context of music.
- Discussion circles. After students have finished a project or performance, encourage them to respond to and talk about points of interest, using the correct vocabulary. For example, if the students sing on a program, have them tell you what music vocabulary they learned. Make those words new spelling words for the week.
- Word banks, word files, and word books. At the primary level, the word bank is motivational because words and sentences can be written on cards shaped like coins and dropped into banks made of plastic bottles, boxes, or other containers. Students can "withdraw" words from the bank and review them frequently. Students should be encouraged to use the banked words in their writing and class work. Imagine children using words such as timbre, texture, vivace, ensemble, or marcato in their writings!
- Writing. Reading comprehension and writing go hand in hand in the learning process. Chapter 9 encourages classroom teachers to use music as a prompt for writing.
- Word expansion activities. Mind maps, semantic maps, webbing, Venn diagrams, and so forth can be used to expand vocabulary.
- Bulletin boards or word walls. It is fun for students to develop bulletin boards to display words of interest or words on a particular topic. Word walls promote awareness of vocabulary and can be built over a lesson, unit, or year. Word walls offer a sort of subliminal visual for children. They see the words when they come to class, though they may not be referred to daily. When the word does appear in text or conversation, children should have at least an image of it in their heads.

What music teachers can teach reading teachers

So far in this chapter we have dwelt on reading comprehension strategies in a reading setting, using music as the literature. But music teachers use instructional strategies in their classrooms that can be of enormous benefit to a reading teacher.

Modeling

Because learning to perform music often involves mentoring or guidance from a peer or teacher, music teachers naturally demonstrate how to play, sing, and move. For example, a teacher helping students sing a song so that all the vowel sounds are the same will form the vowel with her mouth, using her hand to help emphasize the shape of the sound. She will encourage her students to mirror her and use highly descriptive visual metaphors or imagery to spark their imaginations. Music teachers frequently find themselves "performing" for their students in an effort to model accepted performance techniques. Reading teachers working with students on oral reading lessons would benefit from watching music teachers use these strategies. Music teachers do not simply sing a song in the manner that they "read" a story orally. They break down the song into its repeated patterns, themes, and discover its overall structure. Reading teachers do this with poetry, but often not until children are older and may have already "tuned out" on reading.

Teaching conceptually

Music teachers naturally ask children to sing, play, move, or compose in ways that demonstrate their understanding of music elements and concepts. Wiggins states:

> To teach musical elements with no music present is not teaching music at all. Studying tempo or dynamics or direction in a nonmusical setting is not studying music. Most important, when extracting a particular musical element for study, it is essential that the students understand the relationship between that element and the musical work from which it is drawn. It is not enough for the teacher to have that knowledge: the students need to have knowledge of the musical context from which the particular musical elements are drawn and of their function within that context. (2001, p. 36)

Certainly, the same holds true for reading text. We celebrate, even promote contests and award prizes based how many books children can read. The question is: how do we know that the children understood the ideas behind the books they read? How did they demonstrate their understanding? Did they answer some "right there" questions that were simply regurgitating what was written in the text, or did they actually have to think and respond at a higher level? It takes years of practice for people to become musicians, mathematicians, or scientists, years to be able to put knowledge into skillful practice. Students must be able to demonstrate understanding of the conceptual basis of their learning. Good music teachers can teach other teachers how to help children do this.

Teaching language fluency

Reading or speaking fluently is not simply recitation with no technical mistakes. Expression and diction are critical components of oral reading. What better source of how to teach these skills than a music teacher? Children would benefit very much from adding rhythm, pitch, dynamics, and phrasing to their reading—music elements that are taught as a matter of course in a music class. Reading teachers should consider having hand drums, bells, Autoharps, and other instruments in their classrooms to turn dry text into lyrics.

Syllabic divisions are fun to learn with a rhythm pattern. In music class, teachers frequently separate vowels and consonants to communicate lyrics more effectively. Even in instrumental music, players articulate the beginning and ending sounds of notes using tonguing, bowing, and breath. Good musicians are masters of articulation—forming the precise sounds needed to communicate the meaning or effect. Reading teachers need only ask the music teacher for help in teaching these skills.

When we think back to our interpretation of literacy as part of a continuum, we see that the reading process can move beyond simple decoding skills by using music and the arts as part of the learning process. Using the arts as part of the instructional process enlarges the child's connections with a theme or concept, engages and excites the learning environment, and expands vocabulary. Music and the arts encourage and support reading comprehension. For music teachers, the act of learning about music can also be encouraged and supported by using common reading strategies in the music classroom. In Chapter 6, we will see how these strategies can make music learning more meaningful and promote music literacy.

Resources for graphic organizers

- http://www.graphic.org. How graphic organizers can help you and your students.
- http://www.fromnowon.org/oct97/picture.html. Using graphic organizers as a thinking tool.
- http://www.inspiration.com. Ideas for using Inspiration's copyrighted software.
- http://w3.ag.uiuc.edu/AIM/Discovery/Mind/c-m2.html. Types of concept maps.
- Bromley, Karen, Linda Irwin Devitis, and Marcia Modlo. 1999. *50 Graphic Organizers for Reading, Writing and More.* New York: Scholastic Professional Books.

Chapter 6

Reading in the Music Environment: Comprehension

Our efforts to help students understand the connnections among the disciplines consist of providing opportunities for them to understand concepts deeply and see commonalities in other world views.   —Jackie Wiggins, *Teaching for Musical Understanding*, p. 291

Miss Anderson's jazz unit had expanded over the years. At first, she just played some music by famous jazz musicians, had her students sing some songs from her basal classroom series, and told them a bit about the history of jazz. She discovered that her students didn't remember much about jazz when she mentioned it in class the following year, so she created a unit that allowed her students to take a deeper journey into jazz. She got some videotapes, invited jazz musicians to her school, taught her students how to write a twelve-bar blues, charted the history of jazz by using graphic organizers, and assigned student research projects and presentations. The unit itself lasted nearly a semester, but her students learned how the elements and concepts of music were interwoven by studying jazz.

For any type of learning experience to be meaningful, there must be opportunities to look and relook at the learning through multiple lenses. The students in this scenario will take away positive memories of jazz music and, we hope, love it for the rest of their lives.

How we learn is no longer a mystery to researchers, but it is complex. We take in information through our senses: sight, sound, smell, taste, and touch. Our brains filter the information and send it to the appropriate processing place. Wolfe describes the brain as a sieve: "By some estimates, 99 percent of all sensory information is discarded almost immediately upon entering the brain" (2001, p. 79). So, for us to keep information, it must be reinforced by further experience or retained because of interest spurred by emotion or meaning. Then how do we make music learning meaningful? How do we move from the simple process of decoding symbols in music reading to making and understanding the music we experience and perform?

When we introduce students to new music or musical sounds, they may not have had previous experience of them or formed prior knowledge—schemata. The classroom or rehearsal experience may be enjoyable and emotionally satisfying. The band may learn the notes and play them accurately, but a deeper understanding of music will not magically unfold unless the teacher provides those learning opportunities. This is the transition from fluency to comprehension; from playing notes flawlessly to performing with deep understanding. In a classroom situation, we certainly don't expect children to perform jazz music with the deftness of a professional. However, we do want them to understand the nuances: what makes it sound and feel the way it does, where it origi- nated, and notable performers. University of Chicago learning theorist Mihalyi Csikszentmihalyi writes, "If nobody paid attention to music, the language of musical notation would probably not be sufficient to get children interested enough to develop their music skills" (1978, p. 211). Educational psychologists who have researched the effect of intrinsically motivating instruction on learners have found that information must be presented in such a way that the learners can "hook" into the concepts or skills through sequential and engaging instruction. We have the natural emotion stimulator— music—but our intrinsic motivation to learn, perform, listen to, and experience music grows with understanding and with comprehension. Csikszentmihalyi's research suggests that the central requirement for creating an intrinsically motivating experience is the acquisition of skills that lead to more competence. "A person who has not learned how to mix pigments cannot enjoy painting for long; he or she will not be able to match goals with actions" (p. 211).

To foster an understanding and love of music, perhaps we can borrow instructional strategies from those who teach reading comprehension. Let's review some basic reading comprehension strategies that translate easily into music teaching. Figure 6.1 defines various reading comprehension strategies, then suggests ways that music teachers can use them in their classrooms or rehearsals (Hansen 2002, pp. 12–14). See Appendix IV for common activities in all arts forms: music, dance, drama, and visual art.

Music teachers already use most of these activities in the classroom or rehearsal. Also, the music activities suggested do not deal with the text, but with the music itself. "In order for musical understanding to grow, an individual must interact directly with music through performing, listening, creating, or some combination of the three processes" (Wiggins 2001, pp. 26–27). What music educators do not clearly articulate to administrators and peers is that music educators *do* use reading comprehension strategies—both for understanding the meaning of the music through concepts and ele- ments as well as understanding the lyrics of songs. With current reading accountability concerns, music educators can help others understand, by bridging the gap between

Figure 6.1
Reaching Comprehension: Common Reading Strategies, Activities, and Parallel Music Activities

Reading Strategy	Reading Class Activity	Music Class Activity
Finding the main idea	Find critical facts and details in narrative (stories) or expository (informational) literature.	Identify themes, melodies, or motifs through repeated rhythmic and melodic patterns, tonal centers, etc.
Sequencing	Identify the beginning, middle, and the end of a story.	Determine the form through repetition of cadential patterns, melodic and rhythmic structure, phrase structure, climatic points (golden mean), etc.
Summarizing	Pull together information in a meaningful way through written or oral presentations.	Analyze compositional elements, discuss historical context, create an original piece in the style of a given composer or style period.
Making predictions	Reach conclusions and predict outcomes based on prior knowledge combined with new knowledge.	Explore the effects of key changes or changes of modality, meter, style, and tempo on existing music. Write a new ending, or change the affective elements in the music.
Using imagery	Use imagination to create pictures in the mind about what students have read or studied and then communicate what they "see."	As children rehearse music, imagine elements of nature (birds soaring, a thunderstorm, etc.) to transform note playing into music making.
Retelling	Respond to stories by retelling, role-playing, drawing pictures, and storyboards.	Listen to and describe musical performance. Move to music, sight read and reread for precision, improvise on an existing melodic or rhythmic motif.
Writing	Construct meaning through written expression. Reread and write about a story, or create a new story based on given story elements.	Compose and arrange music. Reflect on evaluations of performances or write about music in journals for persuasive writing assignments (see Chapter 9).

From Kansas State Department of Education. 2000. *Literacy Instruction Now: Knowledge for Teachers Implementing State Standards (LINKS)*. http://www.ksde.org/outcomes/links.pdf.

"their" vocabulary and ours, that we support reading comprehension through music learning activities. We reinforce reading strategies in our classrooms, furthering children's experiences with those strategies.

In our observations, we find that music teachers may overemphasize the literature aspects of a piece of music. They teach games and activities that explore the meaning of the lyrics rather than teach about the musical elements and compositional principles. Certainly a song like "Follow the Drinking Gourd" (Chapter 5) warrants concentration on its cultural and historic elements that support National Standard 9. However, we should strive for a balance between literature study and music learning.

Let's break down the music elements of the familiar song "Brother John" (figure 6.2) using the reading comprehension strategies from figure 6.1. Then we'll investigate how other reading comprehension strategies, such as inquiry and graphic organizers, can be used to further our students' understanding of music elements and concepts. Remember, the tasks should be presented in the context of the song, after the children listen to or sing the entire piece.

Figure 6.2
Brother John

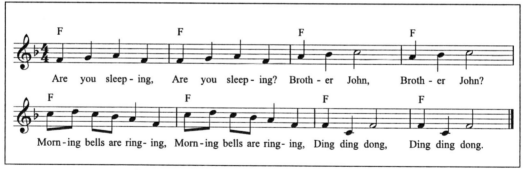

From Jane Beethoven et al. *The Music Connection, Grade 3*, p. 41. Copyright © 1995 by Silver Burdett Ginn, Inc. Reprinted by permission of Addison-Wesley Educational.

Finding the main idea. Have students identify the repeated rhythmic and melodic patterns visually and aurally. Have them sing, choose patterns, or write the important patterns as a group or individual activity.

Sequencing. Introduce or reinforce the terms "phrase," "bars," and "period." Notice how the second phrase seems to answer the first. Have students devise movements that reflect the patterns in the two phrases. Challenge activity: Have students move to the melody and rhythms as a round. Have them sit on the floor when they have reached their group's final cadence.

Summarizing. Graphic organizers are tools to help our students more clearly understand the organizational principles of music. At times, we present music in graphic form so that it can be seen as well as heard. (Of course, the most used graphic organizer in the world, in our opinion, is the musical staff.) Patricia Wolfe asserts,

> Not only are visuals powerful retention aids, but they also serve to increase understanding. The ability to transform thoughts into images is often viewed as a test of true understanding. But some people appear to process information the other way around, literally seeming to comprehend information by visualizing it. (Wolfe 2001, p. 153)

A common practice in teaching early music-writing and symbol-recognition skills in music is for children to create iconic charts before writing on a staff. These visual or graphic organizers further children's understanding of duration and pitch. Have children outline the melodic contours of "Brother John" with colored pencils on plain paper. Use a different color for the first phrase than the second and place the lines of the first phrase above the second (see figures 6.3 and 6.4—without color). This exercise (a graphic organizer) allows students to practice aural and visual discrimination skills important for reading both text and music. Children may need to first identify the rhythmic and melodic elements separately, depending on their prior knowledge and experience. When they are ready, combine the two. Working in cooperative groups would be helpful in this exercise, so that students could participate in group discussion and peer evaluation.

Figure 6.3
Melodic Contour Drawing for "Brother John"

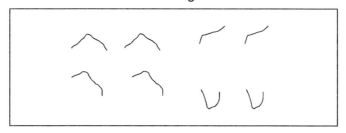

Figure 6.4
Rhythm and Melody Drawing for "Brother John"

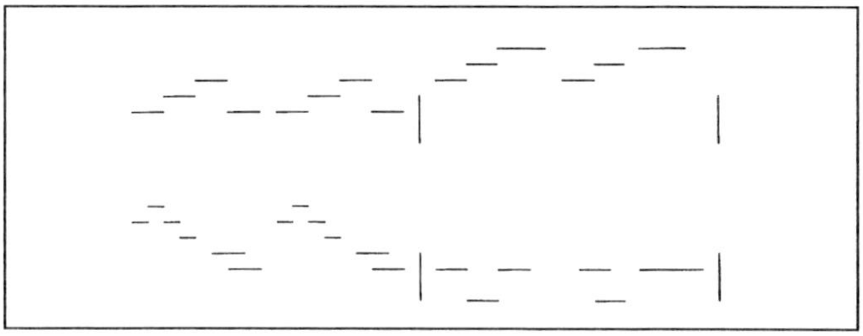

The following are some simple suggestions to improve children's conceptual understanding and comprehension of the music elements in "Brother John":

Making predictions. Experiment with a change of mode. Play "Brother John" in a minor key with a slower tempo. Discuss how this changes the feeling of the music. What did you do to the scale pattern on which "Brother John" is based to make it sound differently? Introduce or reinforce the concept of minor. Discuss what impact this mode change might have on the lyrics of the song.

Using imagery. When children sing the phrase "Morning bells are ringing," have them imagine their voices are bells—light and lilting—to help them stay in tune and together.

Retelling. Have children work in pairs to devise an improvisation on "Brother John." They could add eighth notes or dotted patterns to the second and fourth lines. Children could create movement to illustrate their drawings of the melodic contour. Add instrumental or vocal ostinatos or descants. Sing the song as a round.

Writing. Children could write the ostinato pattern, first creating it on bells, then writing it graphically, then finally placing the notes on a staff. Children could rewrite the song, turning it into a blues.

This is not to suggest that all of these activities would be used for every song taught in a music class. Just as in a reading class, occasionally books should be read just for fun, and some music should be performed simply for the joy of making music. In planning a curriculum, give careful consideration to what children should be able to know and do at their specific developmental level. Long-range planning at the district level as well as by individual teachers is essential in assuring that curricular objectives are met. The National Standards for Music Education (Consortium of National Arts Education Associations 1994) have content and achievement standards that many school districts have adopted. These standards provide a high bar at which our goals for music education should be aimed, though thoughtful preparation and planning are integral to successful implementation. (Appendix V includes an example of such a district curriculum, aligned with the National Standards, that suggests instructional activities and assessments by elementary grade level. The examples of teaching units and student work in Appendix III were created and classroom tested by Kansas Music PROPEL trainers.)

Comprehending music elements: conceptual understanding

Music is an aural art. The music concepts and elements that we study are expressed through sounds that generally appear as symbols or words on paper. Many people without music training seem to have a difficult time working with music elements and concepts in cross-disciplinary activities because of their lack of musical background. The fundamentals of music seem very abstract to them, as they may for our students. For this reason, attempts at integration center on lyrics or the emotional impact of the music because they are easily recognizable. Attempting to find cross-curricular parallels with the music itself—the nuts and bolts of why a given piece of music sounds like it does and what that has to do with the conceptual basis of another curriculum area—requires some prior knowledge about how music is constructed. Part of a music specialist's job is to help classroom teachers make those links. Fostering understanding of music in cross-curricular activities means that students learn about historical, mathematical, or social studies connections to music elements and concepts—not just the lyrics, but the music itself. We can't really consider singing the song "Dry Bones" a legitimate connection with science study of human skeletons. We could, however, connect the "skeleton" of music—music elements, the structure that holds it together and makes it what it is—to the bones in the human body. For example, we can draw parallels—that some bones provide the frame of the body and move the body along (e.g., percussion or low strings), while other bones allow smaller articulated responses that must be performed with intricate timing and precision (e.g., violins). If we go beyond making connections at the lyrics level, and get into the music by thinking more deeply about what makes music what it is, we have then taught our subject area with integrity.

Aurelia Hartenberger (2003) offers a conceptual framework that organizes musical-content understanding using music concepts that spiral through the critical thinking process of Bloom's Taxonomy of the Cognitive Domain: knowledge, comprehension, application, analysis, synthesis, and evaluation (see figure 5.5).

Hartenberger's framework starts with the scientific properties of sound, including frequency, time, intensity, and timbre. Frequency is the vibrations per second known as pitch. Time is the temporal organization of sound known as duration. Intensity is the degree of loudness known as volume, and timbre is the quality of sound known as tone color. Frequency, time, intensity, and timbre are real, measurable properties of sound, representing the cognitive domain level of "knowledge." They can be identified and defined with precise parameters. The musical organization of sound—pitch, duration, volume, and tone color—represents the basic macroconcepts underlying the general structure of all music.

In music classrooms, these basic concepts are not necessarily learned sequentially, but rather during the interplay of the various cognitive levels, while performing, responding, and creating music. Hartenberger describes the types of activities associated with each of Bloom's levels as follows (also see figure 6.5 and Appendix III):

Knowledge level. Students memorize facts and recall basic terms in the science of sound.

Comprehension level. Students begin to organize the scientific properties of sound into macroconcepts specific to music. The scientific terminology of frequency, time, intensity, and timbre is replaced by the more subjective terms pitch, duration, volume, and tone quality.

Application level. Students construct, generalize, and experience microconcepts such as melody, harmony, dynamics, articulation, beat, and rhythm.

Figure 6.5
Levels of Conceptual Understanding In Music

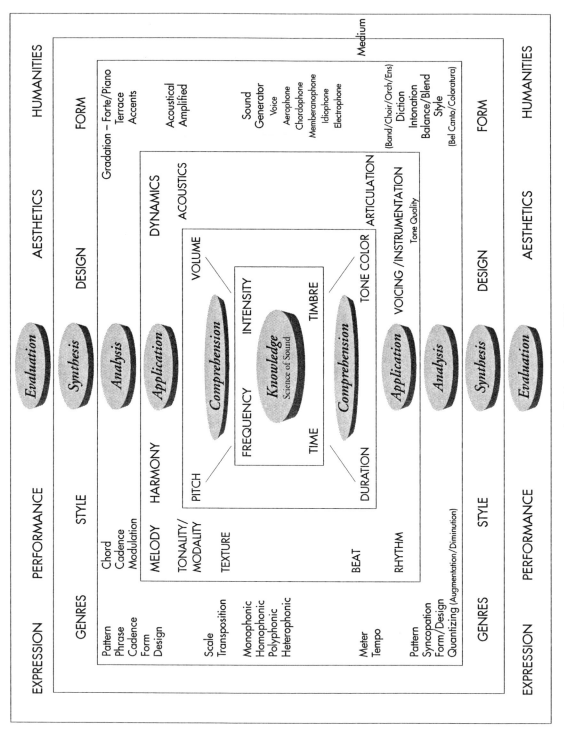

Aurelia Hartenberger. 2003.

Analysis level. Students discover, compare, and examine the structural qualities of music in miniconcepts such as patterns, phrases, chords, gradations in dynamics, sound generators, styles, and how composers manipulate rhythmic duration (e.g., augmentation, diminution, and hemiola), balance, blend, and so forth.

Synthesis level. Students explore and formulate relationships between macro-, micro-, and miniconcepts to create and distinguish genre, style, and form in music. The processes of creativity are emphasized at this level. Synthesis involves putting together or recombining various parts with new material so as to develop something new. Music classrooms that encourage improvising and creating and composing are rich with synthesis level activities.

Evaluation level. Students are asked to make judgments based on either internal or external standards. Guided self-reflection and peer evaluation are valuable activities that reflect this level.

According to Hartenberger,

> A concept-based curriculum must teach thinking beyond the facts to achieve integration. By definition, concepts are timeless, universal, broad, and abstract. They may be thought of as groups or clusters of related phenomena. To achieve a conceptually driven integrated curriculum, lessons must be designed to include metacognitive activities that focus on conceptual lenses that go beyond the content in each area. For the understanding of how music integrates and enhances learning across content areas, the elements of contextual knowledge, artistic processing of musical concepts, and developmental structure of musical concepts are essential. (2003, p. 1)

Appendix III has extensions of this work, including charts that offer specific descriptions of activities for each of Bloom's levels. Also, Hartenberger reviews the sequential levels of the artistic process and their relationships with the affective and psychomotor domains and Bloom's Taxonomy.

Robert Marzano has studied instructional strategies that have a significant positive impact on learning (Marzano 2003). In figure 6.6, from his book *What Works in Schools: Translating Research into Action,* Marzano summarizes the most effective instructional strategies.

At first glance, a music teacher may not see music education parallels in these general-classroom-based teaching strategies. Yet each of these strategies is as relevant in a music classroom as in a reading classroom. When we help children learn the construction of music and how to perform it, we are enriching their mental abilities in dealing with "nonlinguistic representations—using pictures or symbols such as graphic representations, physical models, mental images, or dramatic enactments" (Marzano 2003, p. 86) to communicate understanding of content. Marzano goes on to suggest specific behaviors that are associated with each of the instructional strategies (figure 6.7). Consider how these behaviors translate in the musical learning environment.

Figure 6.6
Categories of Instructional Strategies that Affect Student Achievement

Category	Average Effect Size	Percentile Gain	Number of Effect Sizes	Standard Deviation
Identifying similarities and differences	1.61	45	31	0.31
Summarizing and note taking	1.00	34	179	0.50
Reinforcing effort and providing recognition	0.80	29	21	0.35
Homework and practice	0.77	28	134	0.36
Nonlinguistic representations	0.75	27	246	0.40
Cooperative learning	0.73	27	122	0.40
Setting objectives and providing feedback	0.61	23	408	0.28
Generating and testing hypotheses	0.61	23	63	0.79
Questions, cues, and advance organizers	0.59	22	1,251	0.26

Sources

Marzano, R. J. 1998. A theory-based meta-analysis of research on instruction. Aurora, CO: Mid-Continent Research for Education and Learning (ERIC Document Reproduction No. ED 427 087).

Marzano, R. J., B. B. Gaddy, and C. Dean. 2000. *What works in classroom instruction?* Aurora, CO: Mid-Continent Research for Education and Learning.

Marzano, R J., D. J. Pickering, and J. E. Pollock. 2001. *Classroom instruction that works: Research-based strategies for increasing student achievement.* Alexandra, VA: Association for Supervision and Curriculum Development.

In addition to organizing and classifying levels of conceptual understanding in music, teachers need to use a variety of instructional strategies to aid children's learning. The instructional strategies that follow parallel those found in reading literacy. Though these are not specifically Orff, Dalcroze, and Kodály activities, they can easily be adapted to those strategies.

Figure 6.7
Instructional Categories Divided into Specific Behaviors

General Instructional Category	Specific Behaviors
Identifying similarities and differences	▪ assigning in-class and homework tasks that involve comparison and classification ▪ assigning in-class and homework tasks that involve metaphors and analogies
Summarizing and note taking	▪ asking students to generate verbal summaries ▪ asking students to generate written summaries ▪ asking students to take notes ▪ asking students to revise their notes, correcting errors and adding information
Reinforcing effort and providing recognition	▪ recognizing and celebrating progress toward learning goals throughout a unit ▪ recognizing and reinforcing the importance of effort ▪ recognizing and celebrating progress toward learning goals at the end of a unit
Homework and practice	▪ providing specific feedback on all assigned homework ▪ assigning homework for the purpose of students practicing skills and procedures that have been the focus of instruction
Nonlinguistic representations	▪ asking students to generate mental images representing content ▪ asking students to draw pictures or pictographs representing content ▪ asking students to construct graphic organizers representing content ▪ asking students to act out content ▪ asking students to make physical models of content ▪ asking students to make revisions in their mental images, pictures, pictographs, graphic organizers, and physical models
Cooperative learning	▪ organizing students in cooperative groups when appropriate ▪ organizing students in ability groups when appropriate
Setting objectives and providing feedback	▪ setting specific learning goals at the beginning of a unit ▪ asking students to set their own learning goals at the beginning of a unit ▪ providing feedback on learning goals throughout the unit ▪ asking students to keep track of their progress on learning goals ▪ providing summative feedback at the end of a unit ▪ asking students to assess themselves at the end of a unit
Generating and testing hypotheses	▪ engaging students in projects that involve generating and testing hypotheses through problem solving tasks ▪ engaging students in projects that involve generating and testing hypotheses through decision making tasks

Inquiry

We learned about inferential strategy, QARs (Raphael 1986), types of questions (Lowery 1998), and how scaffolded questions relate to Bloom's Taxonomy in Chapter 5. The questions used there related directly to the text of "Follow the Drinking Gourd." They could be used by either a reading teacher or a music teacher. In contrast, the following sets of questions relate directly to the music elements of "Brother John."

Inferential strategy questions

Part 1. Explain that first you will be asking children questions about "Brother John" to familiarize them with the music elements of the song before singing it. You will be asking questions about the melody and rhythms in the song.

Part 2. After the students have sight-read the song with the accompaniment, guide the students through a visual analysis of the music:

T: Do you notice any places where the notes of this song repeat?

S: The notes in the first measure are played again.

T: Do you see any other places where the notes repeat?

S: They repeat all over the place! The words are always done two times.

S: The notes do the same thing.

T: What about the rhythms? Do they repeat?

S: Yes, they repeat just like the notes and words.

T: If you were to draw the melody of this song, what would it look like?

S: We would draw the first measure and then do it exactly the same.

S: Then the third, fifth, and seventh measures.

T: Let's do it!

The children then draw rhythmic and melodic contour maps.

Question-Answer-Responses questions

Using the Question-Answer-Responses (QARs) technique, a teacher might ask the following questions. Bloom's Taxonomy levels and the Lowery question types have been included.

Level 1 (Q 1) Right there

The notes in the first measure, F-G-A-F, are repeated. Who can tell me in which measure you find them again?

What note is flat in the key signature?

Bloom—application; Lowery—narrow instructional, confirming

Level 2 (Q 2) Think and search

Are there other groups of notes in the song that are repeated? Which measures?

Describe what measures of the music have the same melody and rhythm.

As we look at the key signature and the notes of this song, in what key is it written?

Bloom—comprehension, analysis; Lowery—narrow instructional, integrating

Level 3 (Q 3) Author and me

Let's sing the song using the melody of the third and fourth measures as an accompaniment and repeat it over and over while we sing the song. Does anyone remember what kind of musical harmony we would be playing?

Given the key of the song, what do you think the best notes to harmonize this song would be?

Bloom—analysis; Lowery—narrow instructional, integrating

Level 4 (Q 4) On my own

Let's take turns playing an ostinato accompaniment with the song. You may play one measure or two, using any of the notes in the chord, but you must repeat it over and over while we sing.

Bloom—application, synthesis; Lowery—broad instructional, open-ended

In this example, the teacher leads the children to a study of ostinato harmonization. Similar questioning and instruction can lead the children to an understanding of phrase structure, repeated patterns, or scale patterns. By carefully constructing questions and activities in a music classroom, music educators can engage children's higher-order thinking skills. As a result, musical play—responding, performing, and creating—becomes the conduit for conceptual understanding. The learning environment in a music class should be the model for other curriculum areas that usually emphasize memorization without understanding.

Building a vocabulary

Within the scope and sequence of local curriculum, developing a comprehensive music vocabulary is critical to music learning. Children need to know what the music symbol looks like, what it is called, how it sounds, and most important, they must experience it. Just because children can identify a quarter note as a symbol does not mean that they can perform it correctly in a measure of music. Children need to have multiple exposures to the symbol or word that represents the music concept or element itself—they must see the word; hear the word; and play, sing, or move to the word. A rich music vocabulary provides the wealth of descriptive terms needed to communicate what is happening in music and to be an expressive writer or speaker. Classroom teachers probably won't teach such words as timbre, texture, phrase, staccato, legato, or diminuendo. How much more articulate our children are when they can incorporate those words into their everyday vocabulary.

Below are photos of music word walls in an elementary classroom. This teacher has built the wall during the school year. Because all grade levels come to the music classroom, not all words will be studied by every class. The teacher points to the words appropriate for the particular class in which the word is learned. Other children see the words—a visual representation of a term they will or have studied.

Cooperative learning

Cooperative learning is an instructional strategy that has been widely used in general classrooms for many years. In cooperative learning, "teachers can structure lessons cooperatively so that students work together to accomplish shared goals" (Johnson et al. 1984, p. 2). The following elements must be present to assure a positive experience with this process (Felder and Brent 1994):

1. **Positive interdependence.** Team members are obliged to rely on one another to achieve the goal. If any team member fails to do his or her part, everyone suffers the consequences.
2. **Individual accountability.** All students in a group are held accountable for doing their share of the work and for mastery of all of the material to be learned.
3. **Face-to-face promotive interaction.** Although some of the group work may be parceled out and done individually, some must be done interactively, with group members providing one another with feedback, challenging one another's conclusions and reasoning, and perhaps most important, teaching and encouraging one another.

4. **Appropriate use of collaborative skills.** Students are encouraged and helped to develop and practice trust-building, leadership, decision-making, communication, and conflict-management skills.

5. **Group processing.** Team members set group goals, periodically assess what they are doing well as a team, and identify changes they will make to function more effectively in the future.

Here are some cooperative learning exercises based on an instrument families unit.

Teacher: Please divide into your music teams. Decide who will be the recorder today and make sure that person has paper and pencil.

Exercise 1: Recalling prior material

We've been learning about instruments of the orchestra. In your groups, list the instrument families and as many instruments as you can for each family. You have two minutes—GO!

Exercise 2: Stage-setting

Here are some questions that we'll be considering today. Work together to begin formulating your answers. (Notice that questions 2, 3, and 4 require some higher order thinking.)

1. Name instruments made of these materials: wood, metal, skin, and gourds.
2. Why does the material from which an instrument is made make a difference in its sound?
3. Think of a song we sing and choose two instruments from two different families that could accompany that song. Defend your choice.
4. What would happen if we chose instruments from a different family? How would the sound change?

Exercise 3: Problem solving

Choose one person from your group to come to the instrument shelves and retrieve the instruments you chose for question 3. In your group, quietly begin to describe how your accompaniment might sound. Have your recorder write down your ideas. I'll come to each group and help you. When your ideas are finished, return your instruments to the shelf.

Exercise 4: Explaining the solution

Each group will have two minutes to share their ideas. Once everyone has shared, we'll try out a few of your ideas with some instruments.

Exercise 5: Analytical, evaluative, and creative thinking

With the information we have learned about instrumental families, we will begin some activities to help us understand them even better. In the next few weeks we will do the following:

- Listen to music and write about it by telling stories and describing how the combination of instruments makes the music sound as it does.
- Create our own compositions with guidelines that we will generate together.
- Play melodies and accompaniments using instruments in all families.

Exercise 6: Generating questions and summarizing

After selected lessons and assignments and at the end of the unit, the teams generate summarizing questions. Children can also generate their own questions for the rest of the class to ask. Here are some examples of summarizing questions:

- Describe how different types of materials affect the sound of music.
- Explain why composers choose some instruments over others when they write a piece of music.
- Describe the difference between the sound of electronically generated music and music that is performed by a "real" instrument.

Techniques for cooperative learning groups

Think-pair-share. Children think and formulate their own ideas first, compare their answers with their teammates, then share with the whole class.

Thinking-aloud pair problem solving (TAPPS). In this problem-solving strategy, students work in pairs, with one person as the problem-solver and the other as the listener-encourager. Then they reverse roles with the same or a different problem (Lochhead and Whimbey 1987).

Jigsaw. Students begin in home groups, with each member of the team responsible for one aspect of a problem or question. Then the home teams redivide into "expert" teams, each team responsible for one aspect or component of the problem or question. Each expert team is given the information or resources necessary to formulate a response. After adequate time and discussion, everyone returns to their home team and shares what they have learned in order to contribute to the whole (Aronson et al. 1978).

Recommendations for cooperative learning groups

1. Keep groups to no more than three or four students.
2. Try to select groups that include different genders, races, and ability levels.
3. Try to select the groups based on your perceptions of how they might work together. Teacher selected groups have been shown to perform better than self-formed groups (Feichtner and Davis 1991).

4. Make sure the roles that you assign for individual team members rotate from assignment to assignment.

5. Make sure the criteria and assessments for the assignments are clear.

6. Assess the work quality of the group, not individuals. However, adjustments in individual grades might need to be made if there are noncontributors. Using a rubric that is designed to reflect the work of the entire group but given individually to each team member is useful.

Reflecting on musical understanding

We have discussed several instructional strategies that can be used effectively to further the understanding of music. The overall goal is to promote literacy, in a broad and overarching sense. Elliot Eisner, professor of art at Stanford University, eloquently sums up this goal:

> Children who have not learned how to see and mentally explore the various forms of arts and science will not be able to write, not because they cannot spell, but because they have nothing to say, nothing to reconstruct from sensory exploration of the environment. (1981, p. 470)

Music educators enlarge students' worlds. The vast array of colorful and enlightening experiences we give our students changes lives and attitudes. Music educators *are* in the business of literacy learning.

Chapter 7

Considerations, Adaptations, and Enhancements

The outcome of education must not be a foregone conclusion; rather it must be an unending quest for enlightenment. An enlightened Education is, by its very nature, neither rigid nor unde-fined, but flexible, as it must serve as the given context of our society, while accommodating the ever-expanding universe of our children. One grows by helping others. One helps others by growing.
—William Thomas Sly, founding director Creative Educational Systems,
printed on the title page of all Creative Educational Systems books

Music in the reading environment
Decoding considerations

Using music in the reading environment provides students with enjoyable experi-ences that target decoding skills. In the scenario from Chapter 3, Mrs. C., the first grade teacher, used music in a reading circle. Singing during circle time is common. Most reading teachers use songs with lyrics related to the themes of the material students are reading. Teachers who are comfortable with music will sing the songs themselves. Teachers who are not comfortable may use recordings. But what songs should be used? There are literally thousands of children's songs available to enhance the reading environment. However, obtaining such materials may come at a cost for the teacher both in time and money. In school districts where there are designated vocal music teachers, the music teacher frequently provides a valuable resource for song material. In fact, the music teacher may be the primary "librarian" for songs and music materials in a school or school district. Coordination and collaboration between reading and music teachers provides children with a rich environment for both reading and music. The purpose of this chapter is not to provide or explicitly describe these materials, but rather to consider principals to use when evaluating and choosing such materials.

Frequently, a music teacher is not readily available to help the reading teacher find materials. In such situations, teachers often use traditional song melodies. Many teachers will use a few familiar melodies with new words (usually related to the themes being used in the reading program) thus providing "piggyback" song material. Teachers may create their own piggyback songs using familiar melodies such as "London Bridge." Other teachers use the songs (again, usually piggyback songs) provided by commercially produced reading and literacy programs.

Over the years, some piggyback songs have actually become traditional songs. For example, "Twinkle, Twinkle, Little Star" is a tune traditionally used for "The ABC Song." "Hot Cross Buns" and "Three Blind Mice" share the same melody. "On Top of Spaghetti" is a parody sung to the tune of "On Top of Old Smokey." Many hymn tunes have multiple sets of words as seen in church hymnals around the world.

Traditional melodies have stood the test of time. They are singable and memorable and have usually been learned in one of two ways. Many traditional songs are learned by rote. Children eventually learn to sing them by sheer exposure, as the songs are repeated over time. At the other extreme are examples such as traditional hymn tunes with multiple verses. In this situation, only the texts are read by the congregation. The familiar melody is named and the singers read the specific text to the melody indicated. Another variant is when familiar words (such as those from "Amazing Grace") are sung to a nontraditional melody. In either case, the decoding is one dimensional. Either the music is familiar so that text decoding is the primary task or the text is familiar but set to a different melody to help the singer focus on the words instead of performing automatically. Seldom do such songs allow for simultaneous decoding of music and text. In fact, that is precisely the point.

Piggyback songs and parodies are found in most regular classroom settings. Such materials have a place and allow classroom teachers to include music when they are not strong musicians themselves. However, if the children are not already strong readers, there is a tendency to revert to rote learning, which does not reinforce decoding skills for either reading or music.

Comprehension considerations

Seldom is the text of a song the primary vehicle for learning factual material in a reading classroom. When students are tested for comprehension we hardly ever see a song as the reading example. Poetry is used at times, but rarely is music the primary vehicle for assessing comprehension. Yet how much information do we learn from music?

Throughout our history, ballads, spirituals, and folk songs have played a special role in conveying important information or truths in their texts. Our students may sing patriotic songs or songs naming all the states and come away with a better understanding of our nation. Hymns and works such as *Messiah* are used to aid the comprehension of scriptures and truth. While not a primary vehicle for assessing comprehension, vocal music has a valuable role in promoting comprehension of a variety of ideas, fact, and themes.

Reading comprehension can be a valuable by-product of music instruction and music experiences. Classroom teachers should and will continue to use music, especially songs, to help children comprehend their world. This aid to comprehension should be recognized and music teachers should use the highest quality music and text. Materials that have stood the test of time and are endorsed by music specialists will be among the best for both decoding and comprehension in the reading classroom. Both music and reading classes will benefit from recordings that are well performed, have a reasonable tempo, and model good vocal quality.

Reading in the music environment
Decoding considerations

One of the most important tasks in the music classroom is learning to read musical notation. Instrumental music centers on the decoding of symbols to produce musical sounds through some type of body response: fingering, blowing, bowing, striking, pressing, and so forth. There is generally a one-to-one match between the symbol on the page and the action of the body. For this reason, many students often feel successful reading music even when they find text reading extremely difficult. When learning vocal music, the brain must decode both the musical symbols and the alphabetic symbols. This is a dual process requiring both orthographic and graphophonemic awareness.

Music teachers frequently divide sight-reading tasks so that students are working on one type of decoding at a time. The music symbols may be decoded while the students sing on "la." Or the choral director may have the choir speak the words aloud to become familiar with the text before attempting to sing those words with the appropriate pitches. Including sight reading in festivals and contests shows the importance of musicians demonstrating their decoding abilities as a group. Again, the group needs an additional level of decoding awareness to perform these tasks as a unit.

Alignment

For music teachers, there is a dimension of coding that classroom reading teachers do not encounter. This dimension is the visual alignment of text and music notation. While such alignment is important, it is sometimes overlooked. We notice when children have difficulty decoding music, but we may not be aware that the decoding difficulties are caused by visual misalignment of the notes and syllables. For the best learning, children should use music that is clearly aligned spatially for both pitch and duration. Pitch alignment is usually quite uniform as the lines of the staff are generally equal in distance. However, in an effort to reduce costs, publishers frequently change the length of measures based on the number of notes to be printed rather than using measures of uniform size to demonstrate a steady movement of the music over time.

Children can become quite confused if they see a single half note in a measure less than half the length of a measure with four eighth notes.

Inconsistency of spacing is one problem that students may encounter when reading music, another is how the notation aligns with individual syllables. When music is properly aligned, the visual match between each syllable and its musical pitch supports reading. However, when there is not a clear match, students' reading will generally get worse and they will make either text or pitch errors. Students will tend to default toward the most logical response. For example, if a descending scale is being sung, they will sing the correct pitch but may sing the incorrect syllable or word. If the rhyme structure is clear, the students may sing a reasonable rhyming word and will frequently guess the correct word if they are following the meaning of the text. These factors may be important to music teachers when they are assisting students with sight-reading. To make reading easier, you may wish to point out how text and notation align throughout a piece of music. Showing students how to look for horizontal and vertical alignments, rhymes, and repeated patterns may help them in reading both text and music.

Size

When children have problems with decoding music, one of the first things to consider should be the size of the notation and the size of the text. In the regular classroom, reading materials for young readers are in large print, using at least a fourteen-point font. Most music textbooks have text and notation of a reasonable size, even when the alignment is not consistent. However, music teachers often rely on commercial materials. In many cases, there are song sheets that go along with recorded music. Teachers may be allowed to copy the song sheets to use in the classroom, but they frequently have small text and notation. This may be fine for the teacher, but may not be helpful for the children. As a result, the teacher will usually adapt materials in one of two ways. Either the teacher will not use the printed materials at all, and the children will learn the song strictly by rote; or the teacher may retype the text and enlarge it or print the text on a chart. Again, the music may be learned by rote even if the text is read.

Given the copyright issues associated with music reproduction, teachers are often reluctant to make adaptations of commercially available materials. In addition, there are significant costs of time and paper for teachers to develop their own music materials. Some teachers will use an enlarged copy on an overhead projector, but teachers may fear this is a possible copyright infringement. Also, for some students, the visual discrimination required to process a projected image may cause additional decoding issues.

Comprehension considerations

Teachers need music materials that reinforce classroom themes to help children with comprehension in music and reading. Reading teachers frequently use music materials for teaching both decoding and comprehension skills; but what does comprehension mean in music? For music educators, comprehension encompasses both text and notation; but it may actually extend beyond simple text or notation, to a combination that transcends both forms of literacy.

In its simplest form, music text is a story such as a ballad or a chorus-verse form. The text may include nonsense syllables. Music texts often have rhymes, but almost always have repeated rhythms and pitch patterns. Such organization in music is important for comprehension.

Musicians also look for ways to "comprehend" the composer's aesthetic message. A common technique that composers use is word painting. In word painting, a composer illustrates the lyrics by using specific musical patterns or expressions to enhance the meaning of the words, for example, using ascending melodies to describe birds flying off into the sky or melismas (moving note patterns) for words describing a babbling brook. To demonstrate their understanding of music texts, singers and players might emphasize a passage where the message becomes more intense with a crescendo (getting louder) or slow down or adjust the tempo (rubato) to emphasize important words. The performers' comprehension becomes the key to giving a musical performance, and such musical performances enhance comprehension for the listeners.

Adaptations across reading and music environments

In discussing considerations for decoding and comprehension we have described difficulties that some learners encounter when reading text or music notation. In this section, we offer suggestions for adapting materials and presentation methods to provide the best environment possible for students who need adapted instruction.

Materials adaptations

One of the most obvious adaptations for special learners is the use of adapted materials. Adaptations that make reading easier include enlarging the text or notation, rewriting poorly aligned notation, and highlighting important parts. Enlarging text or notation is easy for teachers who have access to a copying machine and may sometimes be the only adaptation needed.

Highlighting specific lines of notation or text, especially in multipart scores, is one of the simplest adaptations available. It is important that the highlighting be specific and clearly delineate the part that the student is to read. The student may need two copies of the music highlighted, one for the text and one for the musical notation.

Highlighting can be done in a variety of ways. The most obvious is to use a yellow or fluorescent marker for highlighting text. Such highlighting is also appropriate for notation; however, for some students, drawing connecting lines between noteheads (perhaps using a fine-line red pen or marker) may help reading in a different way. Teachers can experiment with different types of highlighting until they find what works best.

Simplification

Another option is to simplify the reading task. One possibility is to alter the visual discrimination load by rewriting vocal or instrumental parts. By rewriting, the teacher may be able to improve the alignment of notation and text or make a specific part easier to read. Instrumental parts are traditionally written separately for each individual instrument. However, when seated, two players of the same instrument will usually share one piece of music. Some students may do better reading a separate copy placed directly in front of them instead of sharing and reading from the side. Altering the visual task by getting the music closer and in better alignment may simplify the reading task. After practicing this way, the student may be able to adjust to shared music during performances and still read correctly. Other students may favor one side or the other visually and are only able to read when sitting to the left or the right of the music, but not vice versa. Simple adjustments of how the music is presented may make a big difference in reading success.

Using icons or graphic cues

Instrumental music usually has separate parts written specifically for each instrument, but this is not usually the case for vocal music. Pieces of choral music usually look identical, no matter what part is being sung or played. All the vocal and accompaniment parts are written on the same piece of music. For some students, separating individual parts could be helpful. Writing a separate part or using a highlighter to focus attention on the specific part to be sung may simplify the reading task and improve student performance.

To read correctly, some students may simply need their own copy of the printed music; others may need their own single part written out. However for some choral students, the multiple lines are actually helpful. Most music for younger learners has simple rhythm patterns, with notes that match the beat (mostly quarter or eighth notes). These rhythms may be read with good accuracy. Frequently, though, young readers will have trouble with notes that are longer than the beat (e.g., half notes, dotted half notes, whole notes). They often will not hold these notes long enough. However, in many cases there is either another singing part or accompaniment part that does follow the beat. To make reading easier, students can draw vertical lines on the beat so they see how different parts align across the beat or how many beats to hold notes that sound longer. Using icons (such as longer and shorter horizontal lines written above or below the notation line) may also help with pattern recognition. In addition, graphic aids can help students not only visualize in units smaller than the measure but also begin to see how the different vocal and accompaniment lines are interrelated. This is most important when rhythms are complex or syncopated. When rehearsing, complex rhythms will be thoroughly dissected aurally and sometimes even kinesthetically; but most learners need to aid their memory with graphic additions in their scores.

Pacing

For another adaptation, the teacher can alter the pacing. The teacher may adjust the pacing of a lesson by speaking, singing, or playing at a slower speed, especially when working with new music. Instead of using a recording that has an unreasonably fast, unusually slow, or inconsistent tempo, the teacher may sing a piece a cappella, using a moderate and consistent tempo that is more suitable for young readers. Most classroom reading teachers use this technique when children are presented with new materials.

Using a slower or moderate tempo is common when ensembles are sight-reading new music. A slower underlying beat is usually given with percussion or the tapping of a pencil or baton by the conductor. However, we may actually need to use slower or adjusted tempos more often than we do when teaching younger children. Our tendency to use quick tempos on recordings for children can actually make processing more difficult. Here are a few suggestions to remedy this tendency. Initially, children can be exposed to a new song through a movement activity. As the music is heard on a recording, students respond to movements modeled by the teacher or visuals that enhance the text of individual phrases or sections. One example is to have the children respond at the section level. In children's songs, most sections are two to four phrases long (eight to sixteen measures in length). By having children move to the beat or meter with two different motions, such as side-to-side windshield-wiper hand waves contrasted with push-pull arm movements, they will experience the music (beat or meter) before they are asked to read it. When the children are finally asked to read the music notation, they are somewhat familiar with the musical line and the words. Gradually, the reader should be offered opportunities to read without hearing the music first.

"Sound before sight" for reading tasks is a common practice in the regular classroom. Many children first listen to books that they are then given an opportunity to read. Reading aloud to children followed by visual exposure to the text is an excellent technique to help beginning readers.

Task analysis and separation

Another technique used in adaptive teaching is task analysis. In this technique, multisensory or multistep tasks are broken into smaller activities. For example, introduce a song with illustrations that can be shown phrase by phrase, with or without the text. We suggested activities of this nature in Chapters 3 and 4. Having phrase illustrations as well as the text may help young readers be successful reading even if they are primarily reading the pictures. Other ways to break down text decoding into smaller tasks include visual-aural matching; presentation of pictures and text in a left to right, top to bottom format; and identification of repeated words and illustrations.

Sometimes, the teacher may want to go a step further by breaking the song apart with pictures for individual phrases that are shown by the teacher at the appropriate time in the song. Then the individual pictures may be distributed among the students who hold them up when they see or hear their phrase.

There are many ways to use manipulatives in prereading activities. Special education teachers and reading specialists may provide additional suggestions for specific students or groups of students. They may even be willing to assist with the development of materials for the music setting, since students are highly motivated and enjoy music. These specialists may "preteach" students if given copies of the music that will be taught. Planning is critical for this arrangement. A good place to start might be with songs chosen for a school music program or special unit since they are known several weeks before being taught in music class.

Scaffolding

Using formats that are structured to move from less difficult to more difficult tasks is a form of scaffolding. Mediated scaffolding is described by Meyen, Vergason, and Whelan as "personal guidance, assistance, and support that a teacher, peer, materials, or task provides a learner" (1996, p. 36). Adapting music materials, pacing, and tasks and including visual aids can be done in a scaffolding manner to adjust tasks for learners who need adaptations.

Teachers may assist young readers in specific tasks either in groups or individually. By breaking larger tasks into smaller parts, learners have opportunities for small successes that encourage them. As students are successful in guided practice, they begin to learn reading routines that they can then employ independently. Frustration is kept to a minimum so students continue to practice reading, whether it is text or musical notation. There is not a single best way to use scaffolding. Teachers who work carefully with individuals and groups will gradually find activities or routines that they are comfortable using in the specific learning environment.

Repetition

Repetition is important to learning. Classroom reading teachers typically have a specific set of materials, called basal readers, that are used over and over with young readers. Each teacher has favorite books and materials that are used repeatedly in the classroom. Some become favorite materials because children find them easier to decode. Student's reading success reinforces the teacher's use of those materials. As the teacher uses the same materials over time, routines, fun activities, and extra materials develop. Music teachers also have favorite songs, activities, and routines that are repeated year after year for students of various ages or stages of development.

Similarly, ensemble directors may use the same materials over and over, especially with younger learners. The use of materials, activities, or routines that are repeated with slight variations to increase task difficulty is another form of scaffolding. Repetition is important not only for developing good tone production in music, but also for developing good skills and habits in reading. The key is for the materials to be of sufficient interest and quality that their repetition remains enjoyable for both students and teachers. Repetition is one of the simplest adaptations available. "Let's read (or sing or play) it again" may be a hint that young learners give their teachers to let them know they need that adaptation. Developing a more limited repertoire that students can actually read may provide students with stronger skills than if they experienced a wide variety of materials without developing strong reading routines.

Modeling

It is critical that the teacher directly model reading, playing, and singing. Direct instruction is an effective method of teaching. It is also helps students avoid "errorful knowledge construction" (Meyen, Vergason, and Whelan 1996, p. 119). By modeling best practices for decoding text or music, teachers help students learn the reading strategies that are most beneficial to long term success in reading. Peer modeling can also help. By letting older students model music and text reading, younger readers may have better individualized learning opportunities. With either direct instruction or peer modeling, the modeling should not result in simple rote production. Older or more proficient students might model how they solve problems when reading notation or text. As younger or less proficient students gain independence in music and text reading, they are likely to seek more challenging materials. Challenging these learners is important to keep them enthusiastic about reading and music. There are many ways to do this.

Enhancements in reading and music environments

Some students are excellent at both decoding and comprehension. Such excellence may be for text reading only, music notation reading only, or a combination of both. Students who have strong phonological skills generally will enjoy reading. They also may enjoy playing with language through writing journals, poetry, and stories. Students who have mastered musical notation will usually enjoy sight-reading new music. These children often seek opportunities to improvise or compose. Students for whom musical sounds make sense are sometimes described as "having tones in their heads" (Gardner 1983, p. 108). They enjoy manipulating sound and will either improvise or compose their own music. These students will often seek their own enhancements for learning. The following are suggestions to assist learners for whom reading text or music is enjoyable and an area of proficiency.

Text reading enhancements

Providing books about music can extend text reading in either the music or classroom setting. For example, biographies of musicians and composers provide excellent reading enhancements as do magazines about the music industry. Avid readers may enjoy giving brief reports on their readings. Another enhancement is to allow fluent readers to be narrators, or to read directions or background information aloud while the teacher sets out materials, finds a recording track, or passes out instruments. Such opportunities can encourage independent readers and save teacher voices simultaneously.

Another idea is to write directions for small group projects. Allowing small groups to decode the written instructions can demonstrate the importance of reading for task completion. It may be possible for a group of independent readers to go to a separate location and complete a task independently while the teacher works with students who need more help. It is not always necessary to have students do identical tasks. Music teachers have a tendency to design reading activities that are exactly the same for all students. Classroom teachers, whose time is generally more flexible, may be able to help music educators with ideas to develop different tasks for different types of readers and learners.

Writing enhancements

Creating parodies, new words to familiar music, is another way that teachers can enhance students' literacy skills. Students with good literacy skills will often create their own parodies. Allowing these students to share their creations privately before or after class, or during lunch or recess time, supports their emerging skills. If parody texts are appropriate for group sharing, both the creator and student listeners may learn from allowing questions and comments. When music teachers assist in this, care must be taken that any critique of the parody is based on the appropriateness of the fit between the text and the musical line rather than on the choice of topic for the parody or the vocabulary. Students who risk sharing their creations with others should be encouraged to continue producing those independent creations, not fear criticism of their work.

Music reading enhancements

Being able to sing or play music by sight is rewarding. Most learners feel a sense of accomplishment when they can read music notation. Such skills are central to developing as an independent musician. Students who have good music reading skills generally will have more opportunities for playing in small ensembles, leading their section, or just playing for their own pleasure. Being able to read music provides options for entertainment and mental stimulation that complement text reading. People with the ability to read (whether text or music notation) can advance their own learning. As stated numerous times in this text, literacy learning occurs along a continuum. The most important enhancement may be simply to provide good teaching for both text and music.

Improvisation and composition activities provide other ways to enhance music literacy skills. Students who have strong musical skills often seek an outlet for their creative energy. We all are aware of musicians who play by ear or who improvise well but do not read music proficiently. Students who improvise easily may benefit from recording their improvisations. Assisting students to notate their improvisations may encourage them to develop their reading skills. It is quite rewarding to see one's creations in a permanent form. Such is also the case for students who want to compose. Some students compose by ear and then need assistance to write down their compositions. Other students may be guided to compose by writing music according to prescribed rules and then checking it by having someone play what they wrote. Note that computer aided composition programs may allow students to compose independently and check the sound without reading the music themselves. It is important that teachers allow the student or peers to actually read the musical composition to tie the importance of reading to the value of composing.

Every aspect of reading in the music environment is important and can be enhanced or adapted for different learners. Remember that individual perceptual skills are the foundation of reading ability. Being aware of the components of reading will help teachers make appropriate adaptations and enhancements across the spectrum of reading and music literacy.

Final comments

The above adaptations are not presented in any hierarchy, and this book is not written with the idea that there are readers and nonreaders or musicians and nonmusicians. Our philosophy is that there is a continuum of learning reading and music for all learners. It is from this philosophy that we propose considerations and adaptations that allow teachers to vary the difficulty of reading and music tasks along the road to literacy. Placing illustrations or icons in the correct order to show phrases of a song is a literacy task that is of equal value to sight reading a multipart cantata. A student's level of independence and satisfaction may be one of the best indicators of success. We offer these considerations, adaptations, and enhancements to give every learner the opportunity to move along.

Section III:
Children Construct Their Own Knowledge

Chapter 8

Listening, Viewing, and Speaking: Building Blocks for Language and Literacy

Artistic literacy involves more than just associating a work with personal experiences or stories. Full appreciation involves an awareness that comes from direct viewing and listening. This helps us to think critically or evaluatively about the arts, to communicate subtle aesthetic impressions and feelings, and to expand our vocabulary so we can talk about the formal elements of the arts.

Children's cultural and artistic literacy develops from a very early age and can be enhanced in a number of ways:

- By providing opportunities for them to create and present artworks
- By viewing, listening, and speaking, and in the case of older children, reading and writing in the artistic domains

—Susan Wright, *The Arts, Young Children, and Learning*, pp. 132–133

Children are born to seek information and develop amazing skills for processing auditory and visual information. Such skills are needed for language development. Recent studies indicate that while both hearing and seeing are important, babies and preschoolers prefer auditory stimuli over visual. Preschoolers literally "tune into sounds" (Sloutsky 2003). Such research gives even more support to music in the schools, particularly where there is a need to encourage language and literacy.

The basic skills of listening, viewing, and speaking are central to literacy but are not the same as decoding or comprehension skills. Literacy learning can be integrated across the curriculum through activities that develop good listening, viewing, and speaking skills. For example, the Kansas State Department of Education (2000) has defined specific standards (including benchmarks and indicators) for listening, viewing, and speaking skills as well as for research (information retrieval) and technology (media production). The standards and their benchmarks are shown in figure 8.1.

Figure 8.1
Kansas Standards for Listening, Viewing, Speaking

Listening

1. The effective listener is attentive.
2. The effective listener identifies/recognizes verbal and nonverbal cues accurately.
3. The effective listener understands the message.
4. The effective listener remembers and applies content of the message.
5. The effective listener analyzes/evaluates the message.
6. The effective listener participates appropriately in small groups.

Viewing

1. The effective viewer is attentive.
2. The effective viewer identifies/recognizes verbal and nonverbal cues accurately.
3. The effective viewer understands the message.
4. The effective viewer remembers and applies content of the message.
5. The effective viewer analyzes/evaluates the message.

Speaking

1. The effective speaker considers variables in the speaking situation (audience, purpose, occasion, and context) that affect the composition of his/her message.
2. The effective speaker participates in a variety of communication opportunities.
3. The effective speaker produces a coherent message.
4. The effective speaker uses appropriate content for the purpose, audience, occasion, and context.
5. The effective speaker demonstrates control of delivery skills.
6. The effective speaker participates appropriately in small groups.
7. The effective speaker recognizes the role of evaluation in oral communication.

From Kansas State Department of Education Curricular Standards for Listening, Viewing, Speaking, and Related Research and Technology. (Specific indicators for each standard and benchmark can be found at http://www.ksde.org.outcomes/speaking.pdf.)

In the 1990s, Kansas (as well as many other states) restructured communication standards to focus on reading and writing. As a result, reading and writing standards were separated from other communication standards and expanded. (As reading and writing took center stage, they became the major ways to assess student literacy. Today, the No Child Left Behind Act uses reading achievement as a central measure of educational success.) To complement the reading and writing standards, Kansas developed specific Listening, Viewing, Speaking (LVS) Standards. In earlier Kansas standards, listening, viewing, and speaking were included in the communication standards. In practice, LVS skills are still usually grouped with reading and writing to create educational practices generally defined as language arts.

While separating reading and writing standards from communication standards may seem to reduce the importance of the LVS standards, it may be that this separation actually provides a wonderful opportunity to strengthen the foundations of any good language arts program. When teachers consider the separate skills associated with the development of listening, viewing, and speaking, they are drawn to the parallels and differences associated with such skills. By examining LVS skills, the value of each skill in both receptive and expressive language is highlighted. Each skill facilitates language arts learning in some way.

The term "language arts" consists of the noun "arts" and the adjective "language" modifying "arts." This does not go unnoticed by arts educators. Teachers of theater and speech are frequently included in the ranks of language arts educators. It is our belief that music teachers, in addition to other arts educators, are excellent supporters of the language arts.

To consider the importance of LVS skills in music and reading classrooms, we need to consider the value of teaching such skills in general. Giving students opportunities to practice their receptive (listening) and expressive (speaking) language skills is a critical component of any language arts program. Students who have poor receptive and expressive skills frequently need a speech-language pathologist. Children who have significant problems with auditory comprehension (listening) are at risk for language delays and subsequent educational difficulties. Students who have learning disabilities related to reading often reveal visual discrimination disorders (viewing) when they are given comprehensive evaluations. Remediation for any of these students often starts at the most basic levels of listening, viewing, and speaking. These include attending skills (turning toward sounds and movements) for listening and viewing and gesture or any verbal utterance for speaking.

At the opposite end of the spectrum are students who have advanced receptive and expressive language skills. These students generally do well in school. Students who demonstrate particularly strong skills in visual and spatial ability, listening tasks, and verbal expression are the students who participate in gifted education. It can be inferred, then, that it is important for all educators and speech therapists to help students develop LVS skills. It is our philosophy that each education professional plays a part in establishing an environment for learning and literacy. Arts educators need to understand their role in establishing literacy as much as classroom teachers, reading specialists, and speech-language pathologists.

Rote teaching cannot produce comprehensive literacy. Appendix IV includes a table of activities and media associated with various art forms across categories of listening, viewing, speaking, information retrieval, and media products. This appendix may be helpful in generating ideas for lessons that integrate arts, LVS skills, and literacy.

Arts education: Language arts skills

Recently, Susan Wright, in *The Arts, Young Children, and Learning*, devoted a chapter to literacy in the arts (2003). In this chapter she describes artistic literacy:

> In the broad sense, literacy means well educated. To be literate means being able to participate in rich personal experiences and to use written signs or symbols, such as music notation, as a way to encode a variety of events. But noting in the arts is not the same as sign recognition. Some aspects of the arts have no notation, such as painting. (p. 130)

Wright goes on to describe additional aspects of arts literacy. In her description she references Rice (1990) and states:

> Complete artistic literacy, therefore, is not just a set of isolated analytical and verbal-based skills associated with describing formal elements of the arts. Purely descriptive forms of analysis do not adequately provide a *sense* of artworks. We cannot simply *see* paintings, sculptures, and other art works, or *view* theater or dance, or *hear* musical performances and describe these through words alone. In making sense of performances or art exhibitions, people can only fully understand the necessary schema or knowledge not only to see, view, and hear, but also *interpret* artworks—interpret the diverse subject matter and the abstracted function of the work. (p. 131)

Arts experiences help children expand both their verbal and artistic languages. Each of the arts is particularly well suited to contribute to the development of a specific listening, speaking, or viewing skill. Music involves learning a specific language, the language of musical terms and notation, as well as developing sophisticated listening skills. A foundation skill for visual art is "aesthetic scanning" (Villeneuve 1992), a method for viewing works of art. Skills developed through visual arts experiences give children a sequence for viewing all things. Theater is considered the primary venue for the development of speaking skills, yet musicians, artists, and dancers all "speak" through their art forms.

Some arts experiences isolate listening and viewing skills. Music can be appreciated when listening is the focus; visual art can be viewed in silence. However, theater and dance very easily allow for the simultaneous use of listening, viewing, and speaking skills. Dance is most frequently presented for the eye and the ear. Theater (except for mime) is most certainly an exhibit of all three skills.

The arts provide an excellent vehicle for developing communication skills, including literacy. We will now consider LVS skills in the context of music and reading education.

Listening, viewing, and speaking skills in the music classroom

In music education there are many opportunities to use LVS skills. The next three sections describe common LVS activities that can be used in a music setting. Each benchmark for the Kansas LVS Standards lists suggested elements and concepts focused on the arts. In addition, there are suggested activities with a special emphasis on National Standard 8: Understanding the relationships between music, the other arts, and disciplines outside the arts (Consortium of National Arts Education Associations 1994). Being able to apply learning in different environments and using skills in new situations are important measures of success for all learners. While the emphasis in this section is on using LVS skills in music, applications to all arts are easy to find and should be included in a well-rounded literacy program.

Listening

Good music teaching helps students tune in to the major elements of sound: source, intensity, frequency, and time. Establishing a schema for listening may be one of the best gifts a music teacher can give his or her students. Well planned listening lessons provide opportunities for students to develop skills that will support all types of literacy and encourage lifelong learning.

Listening standards are applicable to learning in all subject areas. The suggestions in this section are directed primarily to music.

Benchmark 1. The effective listener is attentive.

Suggested activity. Music elements are presented in a listening selection. Students are guided to listen for specific examples of

- Medium (timbre or tone color): the sound sources, instruments, voices, environmental sounds
- Form (structure): same, different, repetition, contrast, sections, phrases, sequence
- Pitch (melody): same, different, repetition, contrast, up, down, step, skip, pattern
- Pitch (harmony): intervals, consonant, dissonant, repetition, contrast
- Time (duration and groupings): beat, meter—duple, triple
- Time (duration of individual sounds): rhythm—short, long, pattern, same, different, repetition
- Time (duration changes): tempo—fast, slow, accelerando, ritardando
- Intensity (volume, dynamics): loud, soft, crescendo, decrescendo
- Articulation (manner of production): staccato, legato, marcato
- Texture (number and types of sounds): monophony (a single line, unison), homophony (moving in relation to an important line or melody), polyphony (lines or melodies among several parts that are generally equal in importance such as canon, fugue, and countermelodies)

Application examples. The suggestions below focus on understanding form. Only one element or concept at a time should be presented. Similar activities can be designed for each of the elements described under Benchmark 1.

Benchmark 2. The effective listener identifies/recognizes verbal and nonverbal cues accurately.

Students represent form by moving or manipulating visuals that correspond to the number of different sections in a listening selection. Students hold up pictures that match the words for individual phrases in a song.

Benchmark 3. The effective listener understands the message.

Working individually, students represent form by showing how many sections, phrases, or patterns are heard. They use movement or choose or draw an iconic representation that describes the form (number of sections, same and different phrases, etc.).

Benchmark 4. The effective listener remembers and applies content of message.

Students represent form by moving, playing instruments, and so forth, to define the different sections or patterns in a piece. For example, students play maracas when they hear the chorus of a song and stop when they hear or sing the verse. Or, they stand in a circle and tap toes on the verse, then walk in a circle on the chorus.

Benchmark 5. The effective listener analyzes/evaluates the message.

Students represent form by using a symbol system. Students write alphabet letters to show the musical form. For example: ABA, ABACA (rondo), AAB.

Benchmark 6. The effective listener participates appropriately in small groups.

Students represent form by the group creation of a dance based on the form of the listening selection. Another example, form is represented by a group collage of geometric shapes to show the number of sections and where they are the same or different.

The listening activities suggested above contribute to literacy development by helping learners discriminate between same and different auditory stimuli, as well as by encouraging learners to associate and describe sound with another form of representation such as visual or kinesthetic.

Viewing

This section on viewing highlights integrating visual arts with the other arts. Students are encouraged to compare vocabulary, elements, and concepts that are common to more than one of the arts (art and music, art and literature, art and theater, art and dance). We emphasize the activities associated with LVS Standards in music education classes that can help develop literacy. There are parallels between listening and viewing for both the benchmarks and the suggested activities. Human neural anatomy uses largely parallel sensory pathways for auditory and visual processing; therefore, pairing listening and viewing activities can be extremely beneficial.

Benchmark 1. The effective viewer is attentive.

Suggested activity. Elements of visual art may support elements and concepts in music. When presented with examples of printed music, graphic representations of music, illustrations, or visual art that illustrate a specific element of music, students are guided to look for the specific element. These examples are primarily two-dimensional viewing, but viewing three-dimensional stimuli such as sculpture, mime, dancers, theater sets, actors, movements, or gestures is just as valuable.

- Medium (timbre or tone color): the sound sources, instruments, voices, environmental sounds. The medium can be viewed symbolically through the written music or observed by watching musicians who are playing, singing, or moving to create sound. Environmental sounds also may be identified by viewing their sources (waterfall, hammer hitting a nail, etc.).
- Form (structure): same, different, repetition, contrast, sections, phrases, sequence. Visual stimuli may be used to represent the form that is heard. Also, a visual design may be used as the stimulus to create a sound or musical composition.
- Line: same, different, repetition, contrast, up, down, step, skip, pattern, horizontal, vertical. Again, visual stimuli may be used to represent sounds that are heard—whether written as symbols (notation) or graphic representations (contour lines, icons, etc.). Sounds may be produced in response to visual stimuli. For example, conductors rely on musicians' ability to interpret line by following the conductor's hand or baton.
- Texture: thin, thick, repetition, contrast, smooth, rough, varied. Auditory texture may be represented visually or sounds may be produced to represent the texture of a visual design.
- Design and space of the form (similar to time): groupings can have symmetry (duple), asymmetry (triple), perspective, realism, abstraction. As elements are combined and arranged, a composition evolves. Composition may occur across time (as in musical composition, theater, dance, film, or moving sculpture) or may be static (as with drawings and sculptures that do not move).
- Design and space of the individual components (similar to duration of individual sounds): rhythm—short, long, same, different, repetition, pattern. These same elements are observed in works from all art media (music, dance, film, visual art, theater).
- Intensity (contrast): light, dark, muted, clear. These terms are used by all artists, but may have different meanings depending on the medium. Intensity is a term used to describe specific perceptual aspects (loudness, light, color, etc.) but it can also convey emotional response to the viewer or listener of a work of art or to the energy expended by the artist.
- Articulation (brush stroke or art medium manipulation): Again, this term has a variety of meanings for different arts. It is important that learners experience articulation as it relates to speech, music, visual art, and movement.

Application examples. (Notice the parallels between listening and viewing.)
Benchmark 2. The effective viewer recognizes/identifies the cues in visual messages transmitted through objects, images, sounds, and words.
Students represent form by moving or manipulating visuals.
Benchmark 3. The effective viewer understands the visual message.
Working individually, students represent form by moving, choosing, or drawing an iconic representation associated with what is viewed.
Benchmark 4. The effective viewer remembers and applies the content of the visual message.
Students represent form by moving, drawing, sculpting, and so forth in response to a heard, viewed, or felt experience.
Benchmark 5. The effective viewer analyzes/evaluates visual messages.
Students represent form using symbol systems or language.

This next benchmark is not in the Kansas LVS Standards, but we think it is an appropriate addition for pragmatic reasons, its usefulness in study skills, and as a parallel to the listening skills benchmarks.
Benchmark 6. The effective viewer participates appropriately in small groups.
Students represent form by group creation of a graphic design based on heard or viewed stimuli.

Speaking

While the speaking standards may seem most applicable to theater and language arts, there are aspects of each benchmark that are appropriate to all art forms. Performance skills in music and dance and exhibition skills in art and design are also forms of speaking in that they are forms of communicating with others. Mastering speaking skills (whether through spoken words or artistic expressions) is vitally important for students to truly become successful in an environment, whether the environment is educational, occupational, or social.

Application examples
Benchmark 1. The effective speaker considers variables in the speaking situation (audience, purpose, occasion, and context) that affect the composition of his/her message.
  ■ Apply appropriate pragmatic skills based on the situation.
  ■ Demonstrate ability to describe information related to knowledge or feelings.
Benchmark 2. The effective speaker participates in a variety of communication opportunities.
  ■ Develop art expressions or speeches for a variety of events or locations.
Benchmark 3. The effective speaker produces a coherent message.

- Use clear articulation, semantic content, and syntax.
- In art, music, drama, or dance, use the individual expressive elements and composition (structure or combination of the elements) to convey information or emotion.

Benchmark 4. The effective speaker uses appropriate content for the purpose, audience, occasion, and context.

- Use appropriate and specific vocabulary and language structure to convey meaning that fits the purpose, audience, occasion, and context.
- In the arts, use appropriate subjects or themes, elements, composition, and medium techniques.

Benchmark 5. The effective speaker demonstrates control of delivery skills.

- Control articulation, semantics, syntax, pragmatic presentation, body language, volume (intensity), fluency, pause behavior, pacing, and total talking time.
- In the arts, control the artistic and perceptual elements or media used.
- Control space, time, flow, weight, intensity, and texture. Also demonstrate awareness of presentation or style such as display of art (framing, arrangement), musical presentation (articulation, pitch accuracy, general musicality), dance (balance, control, flow), or drama (poise, projection, character development).

Benchmark 6. The effective speaker participates appropriately in small groups.

- Use skills such as attending, turn-taking, maintaining topic, consensus, adaptation to others, negotiation skills, acceptance of others' opinions.
- In the arts, use cooperation or ensemble to establish complementary design elements in a group.
- Show evidence of a gestalt experience; the ability to compromise with others to form an artistic whole, using improvisation, imitation, assimilation of ideas in a final product or performance.

Benchmark 7. The effective speaker recognizes the role of evaluation in oral communication.

- Listen to feedback and evaluate the merit of that feedback.
- Use self-reflection to improve communication.
- In the arts, show the ability to adapt based on audience response and self-evaluation.

Listening, viewing, and speaking skills in the reading classroom

Arts teachers and reading teachers follow many of the same tenets in working to develop LVS skills in their students. Can children gain proficient LVS skills simply by experiencing them in different situations, including music and reading? The answer is "yes" and "no." For "yes," we can point to hundreds of people throughout history who were self-taught artists, musicians, writers, readers, and so forth. They seem to have an artistic or linguistic "know-how" (Gardner 1983). But for "no," people who learn informally or through incidental learning may not have the "know-that" that Gardner also defines. (In his book, *Frames of Mind*, Gardner, 1983, references the work of Jeanne Bamberger who used the terms "know-how" and "know-that" to describe two contrasting ways in which children process music, p. 110.) Based on these ideas, know-how could describe musicians who play by ear and can imitate what they have heard but cannot read music notation. Readers using a similar process can decode (sound out) words but do not gain information from their reading.

Know-that incorporates the decoding along with comprehension and literacy skills developed to higher level of formality, which allows someone to truly understand a specific code system for an area of intelligence. The musician with know-that ability may actually become more comfortable and proficient with the analysis of music than with his or her performance skills.[1]

Some children gain a level of proficiency in their skills simply by experiencing listening, viewing, and speaking in different situations, including music and reading. For those few individuals, exposure is enough. However, for most learners, simply being exposed is not enough. There is a need for direct instruction. Very few people can learn a language or become literate at the highest levels simply by hearing or viewing; speaking (doing) must also be included. Howard Gardner's definition of intelligence includes the use of a specific vocabulary, "agreed upon code systems which are used by those who embrace that intelligence area" (1983, p. 108). But how do individuals develop an understanding of these languages and vocabularies within different intelligence areas? They develop this understanding through direct and well-planned instruction by highly qualified teachers who plan, model, instruct, and assess so that their students will have the experiences they need to develop both the know-how and the know-that that lead to true literacy. True literacy blends decoding and comprehension abilities into systematic and natural ways of interacting with the world.

Reading teachers, music teachers, and other arts educators who incorporate direct instruction in listening, viewing, speaking; decoding and comprehension; and writing will have the greatest effect on literacy development in their students. Literacy development is a team effort that deserves the attention of all educators, but every educator need not employ the same methods. Arts educators should not be asked to abandon their curricular standards or their successful arts education activities in favor of periods of silent reading or sustained writing. Rather, it is through varied approaches provided by teachers in all curricular areas that students truly become literate.

Endnote

1. In our opinion, children need to be given opportunities to develop both know-how and know-that. That is why there is a real need to balance course offerings between performance classes and appreciation, history, and theory courses. We encourage individual instructors to work with other educators and artists to provide balance. As teachers, most of us are usually more comfortable with either performance-based or academic-based course formats. We may have a tendency to look for ways to structure all of our classes like our preferred venue. However, it is important that we provide students with know-how and know-that within the same course, or if we can't, provide outside resources that complement our own best efforts.

Chapter 9

Writing in the Music Classroom

> In order to assess any kind of performance well, we have to get inside it, see it from the inside out, truly get in touch with all the details and particulars. Surely, this is true of writing.
> —Vicki Spandel and Richard Stiggins, *Creating Writers: Linking Writing Assessment and Instruction*, p. xi

Writing is often used to rehearse skills and learning, thus strengthening both writing skills and content knowledge. It forces us to think clearly and express our thoughts and beliefs articulately. Writing requires cognitive abilities as well as emotional connection to the topic and to the audience. It also requires basic fine motor skills. It connects cognition and emotion in a way that enhances and expands thinking and therefore learning. Patricia Wolfe suggests that writing can be used to strengthen brain synapses, thus reinforcing learning: "Writing activities ... challenge students to clarify, organize, and express what they are learning" (2001, p. 171). Current research points to the need for teachers to connect positive emotions to academic learning. Writing can be one way to support this connection by requiring students to think about their feelings and knowledge and communicate this understanding to others.

Writing is a motor activity and requires control of a number of muscles. "As a general rule, allowing children to have multisensory input and to be motorically active while learning is important" (Bergen and Coscia 2001, p. 57). This is particularly important for young children, but is clearly critical to writing for students at all grade levels. Since writing is a motor activity, it is likely that adding more writing experiences, particularly in areas that are emotionally charged such as music, will increase learning.

Music teachers do not usually like the idea of having students take out pencil and paper and write about music. Writing during music class cuts into the precious minutes available for rehearsal and seems to contradict the philosophy of learning by doing. Some music educators have found, however, that carefully placed opportunities for student writing can dramatically increase students' vocabularies and improve their ability to evaluate musical performances and articulate their knowledge about music. In fact, some teachers find that well-placed writing time actually helps the rehearsal, promotes more focused individual effort, and encourages greater self-reflection by students.

In this chapter we will present the Six-Trait Analysis of Writing Model as a way to evaluate both the quality of students' written work and the quality of musical composition. We will examine the different genres of writing that can be explored as part of a music class and instructional strategies for special education, English for Speakers of Other Languages (ESOL), and general population students. Finally, we will suggest ways to include writing in the music classroom.

Writing genres

Writing is used to share ideas and information, to persuade, to explain, and to describe. Writing genres are ways to describe writing for different purposes. Students need to understand the purpose of each style to increase their ability to communicate thoughts, beliefs, and opinions. Teachers, then, need to understand the different forms and purposes of written genres to teach students the how and the why behind them. Figure 9.1 shows how the various categories can be used in the music classroom.

Figure 9.1
Writing Genres: Music Classroom Applications

Writing Genre	Expository	Narrative	Descriptive	Persuasive	Technical
Music Application	Analytical writing that describes theoretical or historical aspects of the music.	Creative-thinking stories based on ideas and thoughts generated by listening to or performing music.	Narration that describes what is heard in the music in more descriptive than technical terms.	Writing used to persuade others of the quality or viability of music.	Writing about how to perform the technical aspects of the music.

Expository writing

"Expository writing gives directions, explains a situation or event, or tells how a process happens" (McCarthy 1998, p. 5). This type of writing is used frequently in schools and is usually specific to the subject. For example, students may write about the cause of a historical event or a scientific process. Expository writing is often formulaic, with a clearly stated main idea supported by essential facts presented in a clear and orderly fashion. The writing is geared toward a specific audience. Writers must have the ability to think logically and sequentially so that the directions or descriptions of events are clear to the reader.

Narrative writing

Narrative writing tells a story—a good one if the writer is imaginative or skilled. People are born storytellers, but they must learn to write their stories. Narrative stories must be organized and have a main idea or plot with characters, a storyline, descriptive examples and words that expand the story, and, usually, a culminating event. Narrative writing requires the ability to select words that express the main idea or plot of the story as well as the emotions behind the story.

Descriptive writing

Sometimes considered a subset of narrative writing, descriptive writing uses words and phrases that create a specific sense or feeling in the reader. Poetry, metaphors, and stories are examples of descriptive writing. Readers can feel they are part of a story if reading a good descriptive paragraph or essay. Descriptive writing can be a separate genre, but is also a part of other genres. In expository writing, for example, the depiction of a battle in the Civil War or a butterfly in flight might be descriptive as well as expository. To write well in this genre, students need to have an expanding vocabulary, an ability to synthesize information, the ability to focus on critical elements of a main idea, and experiences that increase their understanding of the world.

Persuasive writing

Persuasive writing gives an opinion that is supported by facts. Many students are quick to offer their opinions on a wide variety of subjects, but opinions are not persuasive unless they are reinforced by facts and supported by reasons that provide a rationale to believe them. Persuasive writing, therefore, requires students to think analytically and synthesize information to create a basis for a written opinion.

Technical writing

"Technical writing is communication written for and about business and industry, focusing on products and services—how to manufacture them, manage them, deliver them, and use them" (Gerson n.d., p. 1). Examples of technical writing include memos, instructional manuals, reports, and professional letters. To communicate clearly and effectively in this style, the writer must use words precisely. Students need a clear understanding of the topic so that they can distill the essence and present the facts in an objective manner. This requires analytical and sequential thinking.

Prompts

Prompts are starting points for writing, often provided by the teacher. Prompts can be generated by a class brainstorming session as well. In a music classroom, when students are asked to write about music, they often need a prompt to ignite their imagination or give them direction. Here are some prompts that can be used in the music classroom along with suggestions for some types of writing that could be used with music. More examples can be found in Appendix III.

Expository writing

Using music vocabulary we've learned:
- Describe the form of this music.
- Under what historical circumstances did the composer write this music?
- Compare and contrast the organizational principles of Brahms' *Requiem* with Mozart's *Requiem.*
- Some types of writing that could be used with music: biography, oral history, photo or audio essay, editorial, profile, report, music review or critique.

Narrative writing

With music as the motivation, write a narrative using these prompts:
- What do you think of when you hear this music? Tell a story.
- A song that means a lot to me is …
- When I play this music I feel like …
- Some types of writing that could be used with music: family story, play, poem, tall tale, postcard or letter, journal.

Descriptive writing

With music as the motivation, write a description using these prompts:
- Describe how the music sounds to you. Use at least four of the adjectives listed on the board.
- I enjoy listening and performing this music because …
- Some types of writing that could be used with music: travelogue, parody, parable, metaphor, autobiography, postcard or letter, journal.

Persuasive writing

Using music vocabulary we've learned, convince your classmates of the following:
- The concert by the Play Along Band was worth the price of the ticket.
- Jazz music is more fun to listen to than rock.
- Saturday night our band will play the final concert of the year. You should bring your family and attend.

■ Some types of writing that could be used with music: an editorial, dialogue, report, review or critique, letter or postcard.

Technical writing

Using music vocabulary we've learned:
■ Describe how to properly hold your instrument.
■ Describe what is happening to the singers when they begin singing sharp.
■ Describe how you could improve your part in this piece.
■ Some types of writing that could be used with music: journal, user's manual (explanations, directions), essay.

Using verbs in writing

"Understanding how to use verbs is to understand the subject. Accurate, interesting writing depends on strong verbs" (Benjamin 1999, p. 67). Verbs energize and create a tone or voice in our writing. The verbs listed in figure 9.2 provide a starter list for music students.

In addition, most teachers find Bloom's Taxonomy of Education Objectives (see figure 5.7) to be very helpful in providing verbs and ideas for prompts to use in questioning (assessment) and writing strategies.

Figure 9.2
Verbs to Motivate Composition or Improvisation Projects

design	intone	decorate	unite	match
arrange	calm	adorn	touch	resonate
compile	excite	make elegant	convey	reverberate
compose	mesmerize	twang	exaggerate	ricochet
invent	depart	emphasize	strengthen	reposition
order	shift	digress	jam	cause

The six-trait model of writing

Research conducted by Paul Diederich led to the development of an evaluation model for writing (1974). Diederich's research identified and described the most important traits of writing, based on responses from teachers, writers, editors, business people, and other readers. The research yielded five key traits, listed here in order of apparent influence (Spandel and Stiggins 1997): ideas, mechanics (usage, sentence structure, punctuation, and spelling), organization and analysis, wording and phrasing, and flavor (voice, tone and style, and personal qualities).

Over the years, researchers expanded Diederich's work, including Alan Purves (1992), who identified the specific characteristics of each trait. Combined with that and responses from teachers across the country, Spandel developed the six-trait model of writing (Spandel and Stiggins 1997, pp. 29–36). The traits are as follows:

1. *Ideas.* Clarity, detail, original thinking, and textual interest
2. *Organization.* Internal structure, logical sequencing, captivating lead, and sense of resolution
3. *Voice.* Liveliness, passion, energy, awareness of audience, involvement in the topic, and capacity to elicit a strong response from the reader
4. *Word choice.* Accuracy, precision, phrasing, originality, love of words, and sensitivity to the reader's understanding
5. *Sentence fluency.* Rhythm, grace, smooth sentence structure, readability, variety, and logical sentence construction
6. *Conventions.* Overall correctness, attention to detail, and editorial touch

These traits are essentially descriptions of what we value in writing. They allow us to assess the quality of a written piece based on specific criteria. Writing teachers then use an analytic scoring guide to rate the quality of each trait. More specific analytic guides have been developed by individual states and writing specialists for each genre of writing and various grade levels. Figure 9.3 is a general scoring guide that can be used for all genres and grade levels. Please note: For a given piece of writing, one or all six of the traits might be assessed. Examples of student work scored using the guide can be found in Appendix II.

Writing for students who are developmentally delayed
Cognitive aspects

Students who have cognitive delays may find both reading and writing difficult. Simple adaptations may allow students to be successful writers. The following adaptations can be used to aid students with cognitive difficulties when they write. The activities are appropriate for all classrooms and are organized according to the six-trait writing model.

1. *Ideas*
   - Students who have cognitive disabilities may have particular problems generating original ideas. To keep students from having trouble at the beginning of the writing process, allow them to choose from several topics, themes, main characters, and writing genres or let them create their own. Those students who have original ideas will gravitate toward using them, while those students who struggle will not be paralyzed.
   - Use visual aids to help generate ideas. These may be photographs of specific people (composers, performers, musical ensembles), places (different countries or

Figure 9.3
Analytic Scoring Guide for Writing

Trait	Level 5: Strong	Level 3: Developing	Level 1: Beginning
Ideas The heart of the message, the main thesis, impression, or story line of the piece, together with documented support, elaboration, anecdotes.	The paper is clear, focused, purposeful, and enhanced by significant detail that captures a reader's interest. ■ Makes a vivid impression. ■ Makes a clear point. ■ Doesn't bog reader down in details. ■ Writer selectively and purposefully uses knowledge, experience, examples, and/or anecdotes to make the topic understandable and interesting. ■ Details consistently inform, surprise, or delight the reader.	The writer has made a solid beginning defining a key issue, making a point, creating an impression, or sketching out a story line. More focus and detail would breathe life into this writing. ■ Can see where writer is headed, though may be lacking some details. ■ Reader grasps big picture, but yearns for more specific elaboration. ■ General observations outweigh specifics. ■ Perhaps too much information; more selectivity.	The writing is sketchy or loosely focused. The reader must make inferences to grasp the point or piece together the story. The writing reflects more than one of these problems: ■ Writer needs to clarify the topic. ■ Reader often feels information is limited, unclear. ■ Facts or details do not add up to a coherent whole. ■ May be hard to identify the main theme or story line. ■ Everything seems as important as everything else.
Organization The internal structure of the piece. It is both skeleton and glue. Begins with a purposeful, engaging lead and wraps up with a thought-provoking close. In between, the writer takes care to link each detail or new development.	The order, presentation, or internal structure of the piece is compelling and moves the reader purposefully through the text. ■ Organization showcases or enhances the central theme. ■ Details fit right where they are placed, enlivened by a surprise or two. ■ Inviting lead draws the reader in; satisfying conclusion. ■ Pacing feels natural and effective. ■ Organization flows smoothly. ■ Strong sense of direction and balance. ■ Main ideas stand out.	The structure guides the reader through the text without undue confusion. ■ Sequencing seems reasonably appropriate. ■ Placement of details seems workable though not always deft. ■ Predictable moments outweigh surprises. ■ Introduction and conclusion are recognizable and functional. ■ Transitions are usually present but sometimes reinforce obvious connections. ■ Structure sometimes dominates and makes focus on ideas and voice difficult. ■ Piece has a developing sense of balance, but does not have strong momentum.	Ideas, details, or events seem loosely strung together. Reader struggles to discover a clear direction or purpose. ■ No identifiable structure. ■ No real lead sets up what follows. ■ Missing or unclear transitions force the reader to make giant leaps. ■ Sequencing feels more random than purposeful, often leaving the reader adrift ■ Writing does not build to a high point or turning point.

Figure 9.3 (Continued)

Trait	Level 5: Strong	Level 3: Developing	Level 1: Beginning
Voice The presence of the writer on the page. When the writer's passion for the topic and concern for the audience are strong, the text virtually dances with life and energy, and the reader feels a strong connection to both writing and writer.	Writer's energy and passion for the subject drive the writing, making the text lively, expressive, and engaging. ■ Tone and flavor of the piece fit the topic, purpose, and audience well. ■ Writing belongs to this writer, no one else. ■ Writer's sense of connection to the reader is evident. ■ Narrative text is open, honest, and revealing. ■ Expository or persuasive text is provocative, lively, and designed to prompt thinking and to hold reader's attention.	Writer has not quite found his or her voice but is experimenting. Moments here and there amuse, surprise, or move the reader. ■ Writer often seems reluctant to "let go" and holds individuality, passion, and spontaneity in check. ■ Writer only occasionally speaks or invites the audience in. ■ Writer often seems right on the verge of sharing something truly interesting, but backs away.	■ Writer does not seem to reach out to the audience or to anticipate their interests and needs. ■ Writing takes no risks and does not involve or move the reader. ■ Writer does not yet seem sufficiently at home with the topic to personalize it for the reader.
Word Choice Precision in the use of words— wordsmithery. The love of language, a passion for words, combined with a skill in choosing words that create just the moods, impression, or word picture the writer wants to instill in the heart and mind of the reader.	Precise, vivid, natural language paints a strong, clear, and complete picture in the reader's mind. ■ Writer's message is remarkably clear and easy to interpret. ■ Phrasing is original, even memorable, yet the language is never overdone. ■ Lively verbs lend the writing power. ■ Striking words or phrases linger in the reader's memory, often prompting connections, memories, reflective thoughts, or insights.	Language communicates in a routine, workable manner; it gets the job done. ■ Most words are correct and adequate, if not striking. ■ Energetic verbs or memorable phrases occasionally strike a spark, leaving the reader hungry for more. ■ Familiar words and phrases give the text an "old comfortable couch" kind of feel. ■ Attempts at colorful language are full of promise, even when they lack restraint or control.	Writer struggles with a limited vocabulary, searching for words or phrases to convey the intended meaning. ■ Vague words and phrases convey only the most general sorts of messages. ■ Redundancy inhibits clarity and creativity. ■ Cliches and tired phrases impair precision. ■ Words are used incorrectly. ■ Reader has trouble understanding writer's intended message.

places where music might be heard), or things (instruments, musical elements).
■ Allow students to cut photos from magazines or catalogs to stimulate their own ideas. Allow students to browse computer graphics that may provide material for writing.
■ Let students use music examples or sound bites from compact discs, sound-effects recordings, or improvised music to generate ideas for writing.

Figure 9.3 (Continued)

Trait	Level 5: Strong	Level 3: Developing	Level 1: Beginning
Sentence Fluency Finely crafted construction combined with a sense of rhythm and grace. It is achieved through logic, creative phrasing, parallel construction, alliteration, absence of redundancy, variety in sentence length and structure, and a true effort to create language that literally cries out to be spoken aloud.	An easy flow and rhythm combined with sentence sense and clarity make this text a delight to read aloud. ■ Sentences are well crafted, strong with varied structure that invites expressive oral reading. ■ Purposeful sentence beginning often shows how a sentence relates to and builds on the one before it. ■ The writing has cadence —hear beat in your head. ■ Sentences vary both in structure and length, making the reading pleasant and natural, never monotonous. ■ Fragments, if used, add to the style.	The text hums along with a steady beat. ■ Sentences are grammatical and fairly easy to read aloud, given a little rehearsal. Some variation in length and structure enhances fluency. Some purposeful sentence beginnings aid the reader's interpretation of the text. Graceful, natural phrasing intermingles with more mechanical structure.	A fair interpretive oral reading of this text takes practice. ■ Irregular or unusual word patterns make it hard to tell where one sentence ends and the next begins. ■ Ideas are hooked together by numerous connectives to create one gangly, endless "sentence." ■ Short, choppy sentences bump the reader through the text. ■ Repetitive sentence patterns grow distracting or put the reader to sleep. ■ Transitional phrases are either missing or so overdone they become distracting. ■ The reader must often pause and reread to get the meaning.

■ Hold group discussions and problem solving sessions that center on current events, school issues, occupations, transportation, entertainment, and daily activities to stimulate ideas that are more relevant to individual students. Students who have cognitive disabilities will initially have better ideas when they write about literal people, places, and things rather than ideas and relationships. Abstract thinking may prove difficult for these students, therefore writing about themes may be especially difficult.

■ Some students may actually have more initial success with technical or descriptive writing. Allow students to work in pairs with one student doing an activity and the other writing about that activity. Or, have students brainstorm about the musical elements they hear in a particular music example and then describe how or why a composer used those elements to tell his or her musical story. This can be a bridge to telling a story.

■ Allow students to create found-sound stories or use percussion instruments to tell a story. Model the use of instruments to add sound effects to a story they already

Figure 9.3 (Continued)

Trait	Level 5: Strong	Level 3: Developing	Level 1: Beginning
Conventions Punctuation, spelling, grammar and usage, capitalization, paragraphing. Does not include layout, formatting, or handwriting.	Writer has excellent control over a wide range of standard writing conventions and uses them with accuracy and (when appropriate) creativity and style to enhance meaning. ■ Errors are so few and so minor that a reader can easily overlook them unless searching for them specifically. ■ Text appears clean, edited, and polished. ■ Text demonstrates control of a range of conventions appropriate for writer's age and experience. ■ Text is easy to mentally process; nothing to distract or confuse a reader. ■ Only light touch-ups would be required to polish the text for publication.	Writer shows reasonable control over the most widely used writing conventions and uses them consistently to create text that is adequately readable. ■ There are enough errors to distract an attentive reader somewhat; however, errors do not seriously impair readability or obscure meaning. ■ Writing clearly needs polishing. ■ Moderate editing would be required to get text ready for publication. ■ Paper reads much like a rough draft.	Writer demonstrates limited control even over widely used writing conventions. ■ Errors are sufficiently frequent and/or serious as to be distracting; it is hard for the reader to focus on ideas, organization, or voice. ■ Reader may need to read once to decode, then again to interpret and respond to the text. ■ Extensive editing would be required to prepare the text for publication.

Adapted from Vicki Spandel and Richard Stiggins. *Creating Writers: Linking Writing Assessment and Instruction.* 2nd ed., pp. 45–57. Published by Allyn and Bacon, Boston, MA. Copyright © 1978 by Pearson Education. Reprinted/adapted by permission of the publisher.

know. Then allow them to find or create their own sound effects. The students can then write their own version of the story. This is especially helpful for auditory learners.

2. *Organization*
   ■ Assist students by providing literal reminders of organization. For example, students may use photos, shapes, or key-word cards that can be arranged to show time sequence, cause and effect, compare and contrast characteristics, or theme and variations.
   ■ Provide students with examples of musical form through listening or dance or movement and then assist students to use similar forms for writing organization.
   ■ Help students understand the importance of repetition and contrast in both music and language compositions. Help students find different ways to say the same

thing. Then help them describe an opposite concept, emotion, or action. Using movement and visual art examples as well as music examples can be helpful.

3. *Voice*
   - Use photos, sounds, situations, and problems to give students a literal perspective for voice. Let a student create a mask, a paper doll cut from magazine pictures, or a clay figure puppet to provide a model when working on voice. Give students opportunities to have the character be the speaker and listener and to change from first person to third person.
   - Allow students to act out an idea to experience voice. Record the acting and allow students to evaluate the aspects of voice, then write in the same way or a different way.
   - Allow students to personify objects such as musical instruments, musical elements, or composers and write from that perspective.

4. *Word choice*
   - Provide students with word cards to expand vocabulary. Let students draw from a stack of vocabulary words to be used in writing.
   - Have students collect words to make a personal dictionary.
   - Provide specific and colorful phrases that can be used in a writing composition. For example, have students compose simple pentatonic music phrases and add words to the phrases to use in their written compositions.
   - Use activities such as writing haiku to help students gather a set of related words that can be expanded in a writing sample.
   - Show phrases from advertisements and then ask students to convey the same idea with their own words. Or, use the words from the ad in a new way.

5. *Sentence fluency*
   - Have students read their own compositions aloud to a peer (not to the whole class) so they can check the fluency.
   - Have the peer read the other student's composition aloud without having heard it first, then allow the student to rewrite the composition so it is easier for the reader.

6. *Conventions*
   - Sometimes, allow the student to use a computer program for grammar check as well as spell check.
   - Ask students to leave a writing assignment at school over the weekend so they can edit it on Monday after time away from the material.
   - Allow peer editing experiences in teams, so that two editors work on a writing sample for another team rather than one-on-one editing.

Physical aspects

Students who have physical disabilities may or may not have cognitive difficulties. For students who have physical disabilities but not cognitive disabilities, you can help the writing process in several ways:

- Use a "writer" to take dictation for the student. This may make a huge difference in conveying information. If it takes a long time to write one word, the student may forget what he or she wanted to say because of the laborious process.
- Use a tape recorder. The student can submit the verbal composition, or can then recopy his or her ideas at a slower pace without losing valuable ideas.
- Use Dragon or other voice activated software with typing capabilities for students who do not have speech articulation problems. This allows students to write at the same speed they can speak.
- Use word cards that can be arranged to make sentences if a student has difficulty physically writing. Or provide sentence fragments for main characters or main ideas. For example, you might give a student sentence fragments such as: The rhythm of the music was _____. Then provide a series of word cards that can be chosen to complete the sentence (even, uneven, syncopated, derived from the rhythm of the words, a recurring motive). These types of fragments could allow students with physical disabilities to "construct" writing instead of hand writing sentences. This lets the student be more independent but still involved in the process.

Language and experiential aspects

While the student's primary need may be help with the physical act of writing, other issues may result from a student having a physical disability because of limited life experiences or a different perspective of the world (from a wheelchair, a hospital bed, etc.).

1. *Ideas*

Students who have physical disabilities may have had different experiences. They should be encouraged to write stories based on their personal experiences. They may not have done certain common activities such as skating, biking, swimming, or running. They may, however, have unique perspectives and ideas from being in a hospital regularly, seeing life from a wheelchair, or solving problems about reach or mobility. Such ideas may provide unique perspectives for the writer.

A variety of successful composers and musicians have or had physical disabilities. Allowing students to read about these musicians may inspire those who have physical disabilities to describe their own life experiences.

2. *Organization*

People with physical disabilities may not have organized their own environments, instead being assisted by parents, nurses, or aides. As a result, they may have had limited choices about how to organize their time, belongings, or environments. Providing students with examples of music organization or organizational devices from other arts (elements of form or style) can help. Focusing on aspects of repetition and contrast in movement, art, music, and writing may assist students in their ability to organize.

3. *Voice*

Students who have physical disabilities may have had good or bad experiences. Teachers should be aware that voice is the area where the student's emotions may show. For people with disabilities, these emotions may be stronger than normal, or they may have been suppressed. It is critical that the teacher validate the voice that is used by the student. This is one area where the arts can allow students with physical disabilities to present their ideas. The voice of the student's writing may reveal frustration, anger, or love where the arts are concerned. Students who have minimal opportunities to physically interact with the world because of illness or disability may have strong associations with musicians or artists.

4. *Word choice*

Students who have physical disabilities may have trouble using a printed dictionary, so they may limit their word choices to ones they know how to spell or that are short and therefore easier to write.

Students with physical disabilities may not have experienced the difference between a skip and a jog. They may not choose the best verbs or adverbs because of their limited experiences with certain motor activities. However, they may have excellent skills for listening and describing what they hear or see.

Again, the use of word cards or a closed set of vocabulary that can be learned for writing may assist these students.

5. *Sentence fluency*

Students who have physical disabilities may not have experienced fluent movement. Some are not able to speak fluently. However, these same students may have excellent and "fluid" ideas, thinking, and language. For some students, writing is actually the best mode of communicating fluently with others.

6. *Conventions*

Students who have physical disabilities are aware of the guidelines and attention to detail that make their physical world easier to access. Doorways that are not the correct width create barriers. Uneven sidewalks, Braille signs not placed at a consistent level in a building, and items not returned to their appropriate places all create an environment hard to access. Drawing parallels between accessible environments and accessible language and writing can give students a different perspective on the use of conventions (rules) in their language.

Music may provide examples of conventions. Give students a music example that has no time or key signatures, no accidentals, and an inappropriate cadence (this can even be a familiar melody that has been altered). Ask them to play or sing it. Help them realize that it is difficult because it doesn't follow the rules. Then, provide the same piece that has been corrected. Let them realize that editing makes reading music easier. Follow with an example of text. Help them see the same type of conventions have meaning in music, music text, and text only.

Give students the chance to edit their peers' text and music writing. Let students edit their own and others' writing. Provide your own writing samples that have mistakes (for example, a letter to parents about the upcoming music field trip) and let the students find and evaluate the errors. Not only does it show them the value of conventions, it also gives them a sense of contributing to the letter that needs to go home.

Remember that adaptations for learning are important for all students, not just those who have disabilities. Any idea that helps a student improve music making may have an application for reading and writing. One key idea is to provide choices and numerous guided opportunities to practice. Successful reading and writing experiences (in text, music, or music text) provided by a supportive teacher carry over to new settings. Positive experiences in a music setting may set the stage for positive experiences in other educational settings. Students who have disabilities may gravitate toward the arts because the arts can have more than one way to look at the world and more than one correct answer. Adapting for their special needs helps teachers and students pursue artistic joy and excellence.

Writing for English Speakers of Other Languages (ESOL)

English as a Second Language (ESL) Standards for PreK–12 students were written in 1997 by the organization Teachers of English to Speakers of Other Languages (TESOL). Throughout the document are goals for oral and written language skills, both in the learner's native language and in English. The document includes a glossary of instructional techniques that may be useful to music educators and includes the following:

- Big books. Version of a book (or music for a music class) in which the print has been enlarged so that all students can follow along together (TESOL 1997, p. 163).
- Cooperative learning. Tasks that involve students working together to solve a problem or working toward a mutually defined goal (p. 164).
- Debriefing. A process in which the teacher asks students to relate what they have learned before they leave the class. This activity can include asking students to answer questions or to perform a portion of music correctly before leaving the room. This insures that students understand what the teacher has communicated (p. 164).
- Expert groups jigsaw. A cooperative learning activity in which different groups of students learn different portions of the content material and then teach what they have learned to others (p. 164).

We would add a few additional suggestions:

- K-W-L chart. A three-column chart designed to set a purpose for learning, access what students know already (K), realize what they want to know (W), and discover what they have learned (L).
- Language-experience approach. A strategy in which something the children have experienced and discussed is dictated by the students, recorded by the teacher, and used as a text for reading instruction. In the case of music instruction, the teacher could use this technique to create lyrics for preexisting melodies.

The six-trait model of writing for music composition

Music educators sometimes struggle to find ways to evaluate the quality of student compositions. With the six-trait model, a music teacher can narrow the evaluation to one or more traits using language specific to music composition. Defining such criteria as creativity is difficult, to be sure. However, if one views creativity through the lens of the trait "voice," it may be possible to eliminate some of the subjectivity in this area. Figure 9.4 shows each of the six traits and how they might be used as a criterion for evaluating music compositions. Please note that this scoring guide is intended for instrumental music only, not music with lyrics or text. The analytic model shown here is based on the Analytic Scoring Guide in figure 9.3. Examples of compositions assessed by the six-trait model can be found in Appendix II.

Teacher role in using the six-trait model

- Familiarize students with the traits and rubric prior to use.
- Use only the traits that are necessary to effectively evaluate student work.
- Have another teacher use the rubric to evaluate your students' work.
- Encourage students to evaluate their own work using the rubric.
- Communicate with the language arts teachers in your building so that they are aware of your work.
- Inform parents and administrators about your students' writing assignments and how they are being assessed.
- Give an in-service for the teachers in your building. Create some interesting prompts and have them write a short passage, then, using the rubric as an assessment, have them evaluate their own work.

Other writing in music class
Journals

Journals are booklets, notebooks, or folders in which students keep personal reflections about what they have learned and done in music. They can range from a

Figure 9.4
Analytic Scoring Guide for Music Composition

Trait	Level 5: Strong	Level 3: Developing	Level 1: Beginning
Ideas The heart of the music, the main themes—the predominant musical elements that are the foreground of the listening experience. The parts of the music that speak to the listener together with other appropriate and supportive musical elements.	The music is clearly focused, purposeful, and enhanced by nuances that capture the listener's interest. ▪ Makes a vivid impression. ▪ Clear presentation of musical elements is evident. ▪ Doesn't bog the listener down in excess or unnecessary sounds. ▪ Music consistently surprises and delights the listener.	The composer has made a solid beginning defining the main music ideas, creating an impression, or using distinctive musical elements. ▪ More focus and detail would breathe life into this music. ▪ Perhaps too many musical sounds; more selectivity may be needed.	The music is loosely focused. The listener must make inferences in order to grasp the point or piece together the musical ideas. ▪ Composer needs to clarify the themes or musical ideas through more purposeful use of selected musical elements. ▪ Listener often feels the musical expression is limited, unclear. ▪ May be hard to identify the main theme. ▪ Everything seems as important as everything else.
Organization The formal structure of the piece. It is both skeleton and glue. Begins with a purposeful, engaging lead and wraps up with a thought-provoking close. In between, the composer takes care to link each detail or new development.	The order, presentation, or internal structure of the piece is compelling and moves the listener purposefully through the music. ▪ Organization showcases or enhances the central theme. ▪ Details fit right where they are placed, enlivened by a surprise or two. ▪ Inviting lead draws the listener in; satisfying conclusion. ▪ Pacing feels natural and effective. ▪ Organization flows smoothly. ▪ Strong sense of direction and balance.	The structure guides the listener through the music without undue confusion. ▪ Placement of details seems workable though not always deft. ▪ Predictable moments outweigh surprises. ▪ Introduction and conclusion are recognizable and functional. ▪ Transitions are usually present but sometimes reinforce obvious connections. ▪ Structure sometimes dominates and makes focus on ideas or voice difficult. ▪ Piece has a developing sense of balance, but does not have a strong momentum.	Ideas, details, or events seem loosely strung together. Listener struggles to discover a clear direction or purpose. ▪ No real lead sets up what follows. ▪ Missing or unclear transitions force the reader to make giant leaps. ▪ Organization feels more random than purposeful, often leaving the reader adrift. ▪ Writing does not build to a climax.

Figure 9.4 (Continued)

Trait	Level 5: Strong	Level 3: Developing	Level 1: Beginning
Voice The presence of the composer in the music. When the writer's passion for the music is strong, the music virtually dances with life and energy, and the listener feels a strong connection to both composer and composition.	Composer's energy and passion drives the music, creating lively and engaging expression. ▪ Tone and flavor of the piece fit the themes, purposes, and audience well. ▪ Composition belongs to this composer, no one else. ▪ Composer's sense of connection to the listener is evident. ▪ The music is open, honest, revealing, provocative, lively, designed to prompt aesthetic enjoyment, and to hold listener's attention.	Composer has not quite found his or her voice but is experimenting. Moments here and there amuse, surprise, or move the listener. ▪ Composer often seems reluctant to "let go" and holds individuality, passion, and spontaneity in check. ▪ Composer only occasionally speaks or invites the audience in. ▪ Composer often seems right on the verge of sharing something truly interesting but backs away.	▪ Composer does not seem to reach out to the audience or to anticipate their interests and needs. ▪ Writing takes no risks and does not involve or move the listener. ▪ Composer does not yet seem sufficiently at home with how to express him or herself musically or personalize it for the listener.
Element Choice Precision in the use of the elements of music. The love of musical details, a passion for aesthetics combined with a skill in choosing sounds that create just the moods, impression, or images the composer wants to instill in the heart and mind of the listener and performers.	Precise, vivid, natural musical language paints a strong, clear, and complete picture in the listener's mind. ▪ Composer's message is remarkably clear and can be interpreted by an individual listener. ▪ Musical language is original, even memorable, and use of individual elements is never overdone. ▪ Use of a variety of musical elements lends the writing power. ▪ Striking musical expression lingers in the listener's memory, often prompting connections, memories, reflective thoughts, or insights.	Musical language communicates in a routine, workable manner; it gets the job done. ▪ Most phrases and expressions are correct and adequate, if not striking. ▪ Energetic or memorable phrases occasionally strike a spark, leaving the listener hungry for more. ▪ Familiar melodies and phrases give the text an "old comfortable couch" kind of feel. ▪ Attempts at colorful musical language are full of promise, even when they lack restraint or control.	Composer struggles with a limited musical vocabulary, searching for phrases or sounds to convey the intended meaning. ▪ Vague phrases convey only the most general sorts of messages. ▪ Redundancy inhibits clarity and creativity. ▪ Cliches and tired phrases impair precision. ▪ Harmonic or melodic elements are used ineffectively. ▪ Listener has trouble understanding the composer's intended message.

Figure 9.4 (Continued)

Trait	Level 5: Strong	Level 3: Developing	Level 1: Beginning
Fluency Finely crafted construction combined with a sense of rhythm and grace. It is achieved through logical, creative phrasing, parallel construction, absence of redundancy, variety in phrase length and structure, and a true effort to create musical language that literally cries out to be performed.	An easy flow and rhythm combined with phrase sense and clarity make this music a delight to perform and listen to. ■ Phrases are well crafted. ■ Strong and varied structure invites expressive performance. ■ Purposeful beginning shows how a measure or phrase relates to and builds on the one before it. ■ The music flows along in a manner appropriate for the intended style and genre. ■ Musical expression is pleasant and natural, never monotonous.	The music moves along unimpaired by odd phrase lengths or melodic or harmonic inconsistencies. ■ Some variation in length and structure enhances fluency. ■ Some purposeful phrasing aids the performer's interpretation of the music. ■ Graceful, natural phrasing intermingles with more mechanical structure.	Irregular or unusual patterns make it hard to tell where one phrase ends and the next begins. ■ Ideas are hooked together by numerous connectives to create one gangly, endless "musical sentence." ■ Short, choppy phrases bump the reader through the music. ■ Repetitive rhythmic, harmonic, or melodic patterns grow distracting or put the listener to sleep. ■ Transitional phrases are either missing or so overdone they become distracting. ■ Listener/performer must often pause and relisten or reread to get the central meaning.

simple student-made booklet to a spiral notebook or binder with loose-leaf pages. Journals help tie together students' musical experiences and give them opportunities to construct personal meanings. They document the cognitive and metacognitive processes in the music class. There are basically five categories of journals (Cooper 1997, p. 307):

1. *Diaries.* A private record of personal observations or random jottings or a daily record of thoughts and feelings. These are shared only if the student agrees.
2. *Response journals.* Used by students to keep a record of their personal reactions to, questions about, and reflections on what they read, view, write, or listen to. May or may not be read by the teacher.
3. *Dialogue journals.* These have the same purpose that response journals do, except that the teacher (or sometimes peers) reads and responds in writing to the student's responses.
4. *Double-entry journals.* Pages are divided in two parts. On the left-hand two-thirds of the page, students make notes, list predictions, and draw diagrams during appropriate instructional times. On the right-hand side, they can write a

Figure 9.4 (Continued)

Trait	Level 5: Strong	Level 3: Developing	Level 1: Beginning
Conventions The use of appropriate musical composition conventions for given musical cultural/ethnic genres. Involves rules of composition including construction of melodic themes, harmonic, expressive, or rhythmic devices.	Composer has excellent control over a wide range of standard compositional conventions and uses them with accuracy and, when appropriate, creativity and style. ■ Errors are so few and so minor that the listener/performer can easily overlook them unless searching for them specifically. ■ Music appears clean, edited, and polished. ■ Music demonstrates control of a range of conventions appropriate for composer's age and experience. ■ Music is easy to mentally and aurally process; nothing to distract or confuse the listener/performer. ■ Only light touch-ups would be required to polish the work for publication.	Composer shows reasonable control over the most widely used musical conventions and uses them with consistency to create music that is adequately readable. ■ There are enough errors to distract an attentive performer somewhat; however, errors do not seriously impair readability or obscure meaning. ■ Writing clearly needs polishing. ■ Moderate editing would be required to get music ready for publication. ■ Music reads much like a rough draft.	Composer demonstrates limited control even over widely used music composition conventions. ■ Errors are sufficiently frequent and/or serious as to be distracting; it is hard for the performer/listener to focus on ideas, organization, or voice. ■ Listener may need to "read" to decode, then again to interpret and respond to the music. ■ Extensive editing would be required to prepare the music for publication.

Adapted from Vicki Spandel and Richard Stiggins. *Creating Writers: Linking Writing Assessment and Instruction.* 2nd ed., pp. 45–57. Published by Allyn and Bacon, Boston, MA. Copyright © 1978 by Pearson Education. Reprinted/adapted by permission of the publisher.

response to their own words. Or, if the journal is being treated as a dialogue journal, the teacher would respond on the right-hand side.

5. *Learning log.* Daily records of what students have learned. Teachers may or may not respond to these journals, or they may be treated as a dialogue journal between the teacher and students.

Prompts for journals

Wrap-ups. Summarize main points of a lesson such as a listening lesson, evaluation of a concert, self-reflection of personal or ensemble performance techniques, and so forth.

Key terms. Write the definitions of key vocabulary words or use them in a descriptive or expository writing assignment such as a critique, observation, or essay.

Before and after. Write a before and after statement relevant to a music topic. Can be used as a pre- and post-activity or assessment—how students performed when they began and where improvement occurred.

Current issues. Link music learning, such as historical background, lyrics, or musical styles, to a controversial issue in our society.

Interdisciplinary language. Students find connections between terminology in one curriculum area of study and another through themes or concepts.

Questions. Ask thought provoking questions about music topics or use question and statement starters.

(These prompts come from Amy Benjamin's *Writing in the Content Areas,* 1999, pp. 107–115.)

Forms of writing development

Scribbling forms. Children are exploring what happens when a pencil, crayon, or marker moves across a surface.

Linear, repetitive forms. These are scribbles in a semistraight line and are made of repetitious shapes or forms.

Letter-like forms. The marks on the paper are beginning to look like letters, but are not letters. Forms may be circular or lines in segments.

Combination of letter and letter-like forms and other symbols. Children are now using some letters while continuing other letter-like forms or symbols.

Invented spelling. Children are beginning to make the connection between letters and the sounds of words. At first, the beginning letter may be used, sometimes to symbolize the entire word. Then the last sound in a word may be added. Children may fill in the word with random letters based on the length of the word or the size of the subject of the word. For example, "Daddy" may be a long word because Daddy is big.

Standardized spelling. Gradually, as they become more aware of phonic principles, children will become standard spellers. They are motivated by wanting to write like others (particularly adults).

(These forms are taken from Marjorie Fields' *Your Children Learn to Read and Write,* 1998, pp. 17–20.)

When to write about music

- After a concert
- At the end of rehearsal
- At the conclusion of rehearsing a particular piece
- Along with a listening lesson
- As part of a unit of study
- During sectionals when another part is rehearsing

Section IV:

Literacy Is Not Measured by a Single Output

Chapter 10

Assessing Music Literacy Skills

Educators in the arts always have gone beyond the bounds of traditional pencil-and-paper testing. In fact, the current interest in performance assessment in other disciplines is partially due to the effectiveness of such procedures in the performing arts.

—Scott Shuler, ed, Connecticut, State Board of Education, *The Arts: A Guide to K–12 Program Development,* p. 190

Just as defining literacy has its challenges, so does assessing literacy. In *Literacy Assessment and Its Implications for Statistical Measurement,* Soares discusses the critical need for literacy assessment, but expresses concern about how such assessment will be constructed, given the lack of a precise, universal definition of literacy (1992). Soares states,

Initially, a central point must be stressed: The assumption that literacy cannot be assessed and measured in an absolute manner must be clear. As it is not feasible to "discover" a definitive and unequivocal definition of literacy, or the *one best* way of defining it, any literacy assessment or measure will be relative, depending upon *what* (which reading and/or writing skills and/or literacy social practices) is being assessed or measured, *why* (for what purposes), *when* (at which time), and *where* (in which socioeconomic and cultural context) is it being assessed or measured and *how* (by which criterion) is it assessed or measured. (1992, p. 25)

It is within these parameters, then, that we present examples of assessments of musical literacy.

Early childhood assessment

Assessment is "the process of observing, recording, and otherwise documenting the work children do and how they do it" (Bredekamp and Rosegrant 1992, p. 22).

The information gathered should be used to make decisions, mainly educational decisions, that affect the child. Assessing young children is always interesting, often difficult, and occasionally (maybe even frequently!) rewarding, when assessment results are used to improve learning and support teacher decisions. By following certain assessment guidelines, teacher and child can perform their best. Here are some guidelines:

- The teacher should have an in-depth knowledge of child development and content area.
- The assessment should match the reason for assessment.
- The assessment should be aligned with curriculum content.
- The assessment should be beneficial to the student.

Early childhood assessment is strongly based on teacher observation. A requirement for the teacher, therefore, is to have a strong knowledge of child development. Knowledge of the content area is also important. Even if the child is being assessed in the social-emotional domain, the teacher needs knowledge of the content area to correctly interpret assessment results.

A key guideline is using an assessment that matches the purpose for which the child is being assessed. For example, assessing a child's areas of strength and need is different from assessing a child for his or her knowledge level in a certain subject (such as mathematics or music). Bredekamp and Rosegrant, in their definitive book on assessment and curriculum, *Reaching Potentials: Appropriate Curriculum and Assessment for Young Children*, Vol. 1 (1992, p. 22), suggest that there are several different reasons to assess young children:

1. Planning instruction and monitoring progress
2. Communicating progress to parents
3. Identifying children in need of special services or intervention
4. Evaluating how well the program is meeting its goals

All of these reasons are valid, and assessments to meet those needs must be done throughout the school year. However, teachers typically use the first two (and, when appropriate, the third) more frequently than the fourth.

Aligning assessment with curriculum content is critical to getting good results to determine the effectiveness of instruction and its effect on an individual child. Assessment is inseparable from good instruction. To select appropriate instructional strategies, classroom materials, or even organize the classroom, teachers use knowledge of their students that is, in part, based on assessment results. Curriculum decisions are also based on assessment information. Initial assessments (at the beginning of the year) provide the teacher with an understanding of what his or her students know and can do. Subsequent assessments monitor each child's progress so that the teacher can adjust and modify classroom experiences to meet the needs of each and every child in the class.

Finally, members of the early childhood community believe that assessment should do no harm. Assessment data should be used to help children improve their learning, show what they can really do, and benefit them as they progress through school and life. Assessments that are developmentally inappropriate do not help the teacher support the child's learning and thus do not benefit either the child or the teacher. Early childhood assessment should be collaborative and include the teacher, the child, and the family as well as other relevant people such as the principal, preschool teacher, and the appropriate therapist. The information gathered from formative assessment and monitoring children's progress is invaluable to teachers and other adults working with children daily.

Teachers guide student learning based on their knowledge of the child's development and knowledge level. This information comes from assessing each child continuously. A variety of assessment procedures embedded in instruction are required to obtain this knowledge. Such assessment can be informal, such as a teacher's quick note based on a short observation or a conversation with another teacher or a parent, or more formal, including planned collection of student work or a structured observation based on expected child development.

Remember that assessments should be given multiple times in a year. Assessment results that reflect only a single point in time can easily misrepresent a child's learning. Development in the elementary school years is often uneven and sporadic. That means that one shot assessment may not accurately represent that child's learning or knowledge level.

Assessing music literacy

The four basic types of assessment are teacher observation, performance assessment, work samples, and interviews. Due to the parallels with the communication arts, we present examples of how to assess music literacy as it intersects with reading in the assessment types. Though the assessments described are geared for younger children, they reflect our premise that *the ultimate goal of music education is to foster conceptual understanding of music.*

Teacher observation

By far the most common assessment for young children is recorded teacher observation. The observations should be within the context of regular classroom activities and embedded in the actual curriculum. Some procedures and concerns that teachers should be aware of with observation assessment are summarized below:

- *Time.* Be realistic about the amount of time spent observing and recording. Even a few minutes per class period can produce important data.
- *Assessment indicators and criteria.* In observation assessment settings, teachers should identify what demonstrable skills and knowledge they are targeting prior to the observation. Considering the many ways children demonstrate what they

know and can do is important. Be sure that children have adequate opportunities to learn the skill and that it has been carefully taught before observation.

- *Fair assessments.* Children should only be assessed on what they have been taught and assessment should occur more than once. The context in which the child is demonstrating a particular skill is key. The observer should always reserve judgment about a child and not generalize impressions from a single encounter. Children, like adults, often react differently in different situations.
- *Validity and reliability.* Assessment indicators should align with predetermined curriculum standards and objectives. In other words, the assessment is based on what is being taught (validity). The observation ratings should be discussed and agreed upon by all observers before the assessment (reliability). They should never be based on personal opinion.

Performance assessment

Performance assessment is based on observation and professional judgment that requires students to produce work or engage in direct demonstration of their skills, understanding, or knowledge (Hansen 2002, p. 6). Timothy Brophy's excellent text, *Assessing the Developing Child Musician,* is an important source of information and authentic, field-tested music assessments and assessment procedures. Brophy states,

> Fundamental aural discriminations should be regularly assessed through performance demonstration, particularly in the elementary grades when these are a primary focus of the curriculum and are developing most rapidly within the students. These fundamental discriminations facilitate or underlie musical performance and thinking, and serve as the prerequisites for higher-level musical understanding. A child's understanding of a musical concept depends upon the acquisition of one or more of these fundamental aural discriminations. (2000, p. 90)

Brophy says that the most efficient technique for recording observations of children's "procedural understanding" (p. 110) is to prepare rubrics with specified criteria and achievement levels (p. 72). In other words, develop specific descriptions of what the child will do to demonstrate understanding (criteria) and specific descriptions of the levels of achievement. For example, if a child responds to a sound that is high or low (single criterion), that one demonstrable skill could be assessed by yes or no, + or − , (bi-level achievement). Hearing gradations between high and low will evolve as auditory and visual discriminations are developed through experience and instruction. Remember, the ability of a child to accurately identify the elements of sound, frequency, intensity, time, and timbre is fundamental to moving up the literacy continuum in music as well as reinforcing skills for reading.

Figure 10.1 suggests ways to measure auditory and visual processes. These skills represent discrete tasks decoding both text and music. Note that these skills are commonly

Figure 10.1
Assessments of Auditory and Visual Processes Important in Music Reading and Music Learning

Auditory analysis Aurally identifies same-different pitch, skips-leaps, within a musical line.	**Visual analysis** Visually identify specific note types or durations within a measure of music or icons.
Auditory association Match auditory sample to the sound source through kinesthetic response.	**Visual association** Locate, identify, and demonstrate/respond to dynamic markings in music.
Auditory attention Respond to music or rhythmic patterns verbally or kinesthetically.	**Visual attention** Remain engaged with music symbol or iconic reading activity (age appropriate).
Auditory blending Identify patterns by sound in melody and rhythm.	**Visual blending—proximity** Visually locate patterns of melody or rhythm in music.
Auditory discrimination Identify high-low pitch, loud-soft, long-short, sound sources, meter, etc. through responding, creating, or performing.	**Visual closure/completion/projection** Fill in the missing beats in music or iconic symbols.
Auditory figure—ground Respond to an accompanied melody or rhythmic pattern through movement.	**Visual figure—ground** Identify a rhythmic or melodic pattern or highest-lowest pitches in a line of music or iconic symbols.
Auditory memory—sequential memory Recall and perform a song by memory.	**Visual memory—sequential memory** Recall and perform a song by looking at the music or iconic symbols.
Binaural fusion Demonstrate pitch matching or high-low discrimination.	**Visual continuation** Visually identify a phrase or patterns of a piece of music or draw the lines representing melodic contour.
Binaural separation Perform alone or own part while others accompany.	**Visual separation** Visually follow an individual line of music above or within accompaniment.
Localization Identify the name of an instrument playing the melody in an ensemble.	**Visual—spatial functions** Demonstrate consistency in responding to music symbols in different music literature.

taught in music settings, though they are equally as important in reading text as in reading music. Remember, these task-specific skills are important to children's ability to decode text—a critical component in their ability to read with fluency and comprehend text.

If a child has problems with any of these skills, consider the following interventions: observe the child demonstrating the skill in a different context, model the correct response, or directly teach the skill. Music and reading teachers sometimes make the assumption that with maturity or more of the same kind of instruction, children will overcome deficits in their learning. In some cases, this may be true, but, teachers should be alert and sensitive to the abilities of all children and be prepared to supply further instruction and interventions if needed. One wonders if children who seem to lack talent in music would benefit from the instructional interventions mentioned above at an early age, just as children with difficulties in reading do.

Interviews

Teachers use one-on-one interviews to determine the extent of their students' knowledge of a given curriculum area. The interview can be recorded or the teacher can note impressions later. In a music setting, individual interviews are difficult given time limitations. However, if teachers are conducting auditions or singing checks, they should incorporate a few pertinent questions that might reveal a child's knowledge base.

Examples of performance assessments
Project Spectrum music assessment

Several effective models for recording a child's skills are presented in *Project Spectrum: Preschool Assessment Handbook* (Gardner, Feldman, and Krechevsky 1998). "Project Spectrum is a nine-year research and development project, based on the theories of Howard Gardner of Harvard University and David Feldman of Tufts University" (Gardner, Feldman, and Krechevsky 1998, p. 1). The first phase of the project was to develop tools to evaluate the cognitive abilities of preschool children. Kindergarten and first grade children were the focus of assessment tools for cognitive abilities in the second phase. In the project, seven cognitive domains were identified and corresponding activities and assessments developed. The domains include movement, language, mathematics, science, social, visual arts, and music. In music, two assessment activities are of particular interest: the singing activity and the music perception activity. In these, some of the auditory and visual processing skills described in figure 10.1 are addressed. While these activities were designed for preschool children, they can easily be modified for older children.

The singing activity

This activity records a child's ability to demonstrate auditory attention (paying attention to auditory signals for an extended time), auditory memory (recalling and performing specific musical stimuli), and auditory discrimination (discriminating among and within specific musical elements). There are four parts to this exercise:

1. The child sings a favorite song and the teacher records overall impressions of performance, including enthusiasm. (See observation sheet, figure 10.2.)
2. The child sings "Happy Birthday" completely through and then trades phrases with the teacher. The child is evaluated for four measures on rhythmic accuracy and on three measures for pitch accuracy. (See observation sheet, figure 10.3.) The child is also evaluated on the ability to respond to contour patterns.
3. The child sings a new song that has been learned in class and reinforced over four or five sessions. The child is evaluated on the ability to reproduce words, phrases, contour, and rhythm (see observation sheet).
4. During this activity, a child who has responded well to the above activities is taught a new and more challenging song. The child is evaluated according to the speed with which the song is learned. Additionally, the teacher can choose to evaluate the accuracy of the text, rhythm, and contours or the child's ability to match pitch or observe a key change in the song.

Figures 10.2 and 10.3 are the two forms used to assess the performance of each child. The alternate scoring form does not require analysis of each individual phrase in the song. The *Project Spectrum: Preschool Assessment Handbook* describes the specific criteria and rubrics for evaluating the performances.

The music perception activity

The auditory discrimination and auditory memory skills of the child are specifically assessed in this activity. The activity is divided into five parts:

1. Song recognition. The child is assessed on his or her ability to recognize excerpts from well-known tunes. (See figure 10.4.)
2. Error recognition. The child is assessed on his or her ability to identify incorrect versions of a familiar tune such as "Row, Row, Row Your Boat." (Three versions were used.)
3. Play and match. The child is assessed on his or her ability to match the pitches of a familiar tune. In this exercise the child is presented with five differently pitched tone bells of equal size and shape. The child is asked to match pitch with the bells that are played by the teacher. The child is allowed to play the bells until they find the one that matches. Then two bells are used to match pitch with intervals of a second, third, fourth, and fifth.
4. Listen and match. The child discriminates pitches on bells heard from behind a screen so that the focus is on the sound source. In this exercise, the child is given a D, G, and C′ bell (in that order). The teacher plays corresponding bells behind a screen. Care is given to play the notes consistently so that dynamic level is not

Figure 10.2
Singing Activity Observation Sheet

Child _____ Age _____ Date _____ Observer _____

I. Favorite Song:

Song Chosen: _____

Comments: (Note attention to rhythm, pitch, level of musical challenge, etc.)

II. Birthday Song

	Number of Units	Grouping	Pulse	Clarity	Rhythm Subtotal	Contour	Key	Interval	Pitch Subtotal	Total
Phrase 1										
Phrase 2										
Phrase 3										
Phrase 4										

Responsive Singing

	Number of Units	Grouping	Pulse	Clarity	Rhythm Subtotal	Contour	Key	Interval	Pitch Subtotal	Total
Phrase 2										
Phrase 4										
TOTAL										

Comments:

III. Music Memory:

Comments: (What does the child remember from the song? Words? Tune? Number and order of phrases? Contour? Also note level of scaffolding.)

Figure 10.3
Alternate Birthday Song Observation Sheet

Child _____ **Age** _____ **Observer** _____

Song _____ **Date** _____

Yes= 2 points

No= 0 points

N/A= if singing is inaudible or child does not participate in activity

1. Rhythm

	Yes	No	Score
Child includes the correct number of notes (number of units)	_____	_____	_____
Child makes a distinction between long and short notes (groupings)	_____	_____	_____
Child keeps a regular and consistent tempo throughout song (pulse)	_____	_____	_____
Child sings notes on appropriate beat (clarity)	_____	_____	_____

Rhythm Subtotal _____

2. Pitch

Child's general direction of phrases is appropriate (contour) _____ _____ _____

Child makes a distinction between the different phrases of the song _____ _____ _____

Child is able consistently to jump from one note to another and end
  up in the right place (interval) _____ _____ _____

Child sings most of the song in tune _____ _____ _____

Pitch Subtotal _____

3. General

Child sings the song exceptionally well, is in tune and
  rhythmically correct _____ _____ _____

Child is expressive; accenting words, reflecting a mood
  in her rendition, or both _____ _____ _____

General Subtotal _____

TOTAL _____

Comments:

Figure 10.4
Music Perception Observation Sheet

Child _____   Observer _____
Age _____   Date _____

Part I. Song Recognition
Check at which point child recognizes song.
4 pts.=   recognizes song in first phrase
3 pts.=   recognizes song in second phrase
2 pts.=   recognizes song after hearing first two phrases twice
1 pt. =   recognizes song after hearing all four phrases

Recognizes in: 1st phrase   2nd phrase   1st and 2nd phrases twice   4th phrase

Melody 1

Melody 2

Melody 3

Subtotal ☐

Part II. Error Recognition   **Comments:**
Place a check next to each version that child
accurately identifies as correct or incorrect (3 pts. each)

_____   Incorrect version 1
           (E-flat in first measure)

_____   Incorrect version 2
           (change in triplets in third measure)

_____   Correct version

_____   Incorrect version 3
           (mistake in second measure—starts on F instead of E)

Subtotal ☐

Figure 10.4 (Continued)

Part III. Play and Match   **Comments**

Check if child identifies matching pair (3pts. each)

First pair
(C, C)

Second pair
(F, F)

Third pair
(D, D)

Fourth pair
(A, A)

Subtotal: [　　　]

Part IV. Listen and Match   **Comments**

Check if child identifies matching bell (3 pts. each)

(1) (G, G)

(2) (D, D)

(3) (E, E)

(4) (C, C)

Subtotal: [　　　]

TOTAL: [　　　]

Part V. Free Play—Comments:
(unscored)

---

perceived to be a factor. The child determines which bell the teacher is playing by playing all three of his or her bells and then choosing.

5. Free play. The child plays freely on bells. The child is not formally assessed on this activity, but observed on his or her approach and technique of playing.

When considering the significance of the results of these assessments, music teachers must realize that auditory and visual perception skills are significant for decoding text and music. These skills are also fundamental to developing future conceptual understanding of reading and music. Of great interest would be a study that compares these skills—whether a child with identifiable deficiencies in auditory or visual processing in music also experiences the same deficiencies in reading. Also intriguing would be a study that demonstrates improved achievement in reading given instructional interventions for these skills in a music setting.

Assessment in an early childhood arts program

In another example of an observation assessment, the Kansas Arts Commission decided to use part of their at-risk program funds to assess the effect of artist-in-residence programs for pre-K children at early-childhood centers in Kansas. In this pilot project, seven early-childhood centers created long-term arts programs that involved professional artists and lead early-childhood teachers. The director, artists, and lead teachers from each site attended a workshop in basic assessment, specifically observation techniques. These team members were given a common assessment tool based on the ten indicators of the grant, spread over the four observable outcomes. (See figure 10.5.)

Because the program at each site was dramatically different, the team members were asked to define what the indicators (criteria) meant at their location and set the achievement levels "not yet," "in progress," and "proficient." The assessment tool adapted performance indicators from *Work Sampling System, Omnibus Guidelines* (Jablon et al. 1994).

The people who assessed the children (about ten at each site) were asked to perform a pre-assessment the first day of the program and a posttest observation at the end of the program.

Analysis of the data collected from the seven sites revealed significant correlations between each of the ten indicators and the programs. Many of the indicators on this assessment are considered school-readiness indicators by the National Association for the Education of Young Children (NAEYC).

Steps to quality assessments

Creating assessments is a fluid and interactive process. Many teachers find themselves determining activities and assessments simultaneously, while still supporting the goals of a district curriculum or state and national standards. In Appendix V, the reader

Figure 10.5
Arts in Early Childhood Program Assessment

Child's Name (remove name at completion of program) _____ **Age/Gender** _____ **Ethnicity/SES (if applicable)** _____ **Organization/ Location** _____	1st _____ 2nd _____ Observation Date _____		
	Not Yet Needs full assistance with targeted behavior.	**In Progress** Beginning to demonstrate targeted behavior, though needs some assistance.	**Proficient** Independently demonstrates targeted behavior.
Learning in the Arts Artistic Learning 1. Demonstrates creative solutions for arts activities.	1. ☐	☐	☐
2. Shows eagerness and curiosity in arts activities.	2. ☐	☐	☐
3. Demonstrates understanding of targeted arts vocabulary and concepts.	3. ☐	☐	☐
4. Responds to arts activities by demonstrating targeted motor skills.	4. ☐	☐	☐
Behavioral Change Approach to Learning 5. Follows classroom rules and routines.	5. ☐	☐	☐
6. Follows directions that involve an age appropriate sequence of actions.	6. ☐	☐	☐
7. Shows initiative and self-direction.	7. ☐	☐	☐
8. Demonstrates age appropriate ability to transfer arts skills in daily living activities (e.g., measurement, categorizing, recognizing patterns).	8. ☐	☐	☐

Figure 10.5 (Continued)

	1st _____ 2nd _____ Observation		
	Date _____		
Social Change	**Not Yet**	**In Progress**	**Proficient**
Interactions with others			
9. Interacts appropriately with peers when engaged in arts activities.	9. ☐	☐	☐
10. Cooperates and interacts appropriately with teachers and artist.	10. ☐	☐	☐

Created by Dee Hansen and Gayle M. Stuber for the Kansas Arts Commission.

will find examples of tasks and assessments that demonstrate this alignment, as well as examples of assessments for higher-order skills and cognitive processes. As assessments are developed, consider these steps:

- Determine overall outcomes.
- Align outcomes with appropriate national, state, or local standards.
- Determine the specific tasks (indicators) that children will do to demonstrate their skills or knowledge.
- For each indicator, describe the levels of achievement for each task.
- Determine the most appropriate assessment tool (rubric, checklist, etc.).
- Make sure students clearly understand the evaluation criteria and achievement levels.

Each of these steps is important in determining the short- and long-term learning goals of any classroom. If we are to move children to high levels of conceptual understanding in music, we must constantly monitor where they are in their learning, either formally or informally.

Final thoughts on assessment

We must balance assessment and teaching. Overemphasis on testing can interfere with meaningful instruction and learning. Testing in reading and mathematics, considered by some to be the most important indicators of children's literacy, has led to many concerns among arts educators. When the definition of literacy is reduced to success on reading and mathematics tests, a comprehensive education is lost, thus diminishing the importance of the arts and other curricula in education.

In closing, we would like to offer you these comments on school accountability:

> While academic achievement should be a critical component of education reform, we must not forget that in the long run we are in the business of educating human beings, not producing test scores.
>
> We must provide for meaningful, goal-directed group activities, self-evaluation in the quest for quality, and the creative expression intrinsic to all arts disciplines to assure a learning environment that nurtures the essence of the human spirit. (Dee Hansen, from a recent workshop)

Codetta

Our goal in this book has been to encourage educators to think about music in a broad context. We believe that children must experience and learn music as part of their lives and their journey toward literacy. At the same time, we know that music educators can assist peers and administrators with reading accountability issues through shared vocabulary and teaching strategies. We close this book with the thoughts of Paul Young, past president of the National Association of Elementary School Principals, who spoke eloquently and passionately at MENC's 2003 Summer Leadership Conference in Reston, Virginia. For *The Music and Literacy Connection,* he offers these words,

Imagine this! Every middle school student in America playing a musical instrument (and sticking with it!). There would be an improvement in attendance rates, motivation, discipline, attitude, self-esteem, and sense of belonging. Student achievement rates would soar. Parent involvement would be high. High schools would never be the same. No child would feel as though they were being left behind!

Research clearly shows that music students also perform well in other academic areas. School leaders who are desperately looking for new ideas and programs to improve failing schools should immerse students in the study of music. It's a time-proven route to success. Drive past any American high school on a football Friday night. Look at the size of the marching bands during the halftime shows. Show me a failing school where hundreds of kids are participating in the marching band. Bet you can't find one.

Much of what educators desire in school improvement already exists in a study of the arts. Think, dream, be creative, and invest in musical instruments and highly qualified music teachers. Empower them to do their magic (and enrich the lives of kids) and watch your school improve!

Authentic Exercises

Using music to teach decoding skills

By Debra Gorden Hedden, associate professor of music education, University of Kansas, Lawrence.

In these exercises, decoding skills are practiced through music activities. They contain many examples of visual and auditory processes being developed and reinforced.

Read multiple verses (Grade 1)

The reading teacher has taught the children to follow the "rule" of reading each consecutive line. In music, students must break that rule to read multiple verses. One successful strategy for this has three parts:

1. Review a song that is familiar to the children, such as "Sesame Street," before placing the words in front of the class.
2. Present an enlarged version of the song with two verses printed below the music, but use a highlighter to mark the first verse. Then finger-trace the words while teaching the students to follow the text and "jump" lines to follow the verse. After teaching them to do this, stop tracing the lines and allow the children to read on their own. In subsequent classes, trace the second verse (without highlighting).
3. Eventually, the highlighting can be removed so that the class reads the first and second verses without assistance.

Create patterns (Grade 2)

Students can understand patterns by both reading completed verses in a song and creating additional ones. A song that lends itself well to this is "Honey, You Can't Love

One." The four-line verses end with rhyming words: one–fun; two–true; three–me. The class can then be given the pattern—sixteen syllables, syllables nine and sixteen must rhyme—to create their own verses. If children practice clapping the rhythm of the last two lines, then they can easily create this pattern.

Compose an alphabet rap (Grade 2)

Students can improve reading and writing skills by composing an alphabet rap. The teacher provides a model, such as "A is for apple, it's good to eat; B is for boy whose name is Pete." The students offer suggestions and dictate the text, going through the entire alphabet. They can also provide spellings and then read and perform their entire composition.

Read text and dynamic markings simultaneously (Grade 3)

It is easier to teach students to read text and dynamic markings simultaneously if there is an obvious reason for the markings to change. Since the children will need to read and interpret the dynamic markings while reading the text, dual symbol systems are being decoded. One song that can be used to teach this is "Old Woman's Courtship." The song presents a story of a young man and old woman. The young man asks the old woman to darn his stockings and card wool and spin it for him. She feigns a hearing impairment until he asks more quietly
to court and marry her. She loudly exclaims that she hears him.

Read first and second endings (Grade 3)

Teaching students to read first and second endings can be quite challenging. One way is to use a large chart of a familiar song such as the refrain from "Jingle Bells." The first ending might be color-coded in yellow while the second might be in blue. If teachers finger-trace the words and prepare the class to read the endings, students are guided in reading both text and music symbols.

Read two symbol systems simultaneously (Grade 4)

Students can practice both reading and performing using classroom instruments. If students are reading a verse while simultaneously reading chord symbols such as C or G^7, on chording instruments like Autoharp or ukulele, they are reinforcing their ability to read two symbol systems simultaneously.

Read two- and three-part music (Grade 5)

Students learn to read two- and three-part music by following specific lines throughout the text. They must learn to jump lines to remain on their part and read the text related to that part. Students can use symbols to mark their lines (★ ■) or highlighters.

Conduct research (Grade 5)

Students can research particular composers or pieces being presented in the music classroom. They should consult books and online resources to gather and present information in a report. During the course of the year, students might construct a timeline, visually presenting composers' names, important dates in the composers' lives, and important musical contributions.

Write a parody (Grade 5)

Students study a text in terms of rhyme scheme, syllabic structure, number of syllables per line of text, and form so that they can produce a parody. "The Battle Hymn of the Republic" is an excellent model for creating parodies. The class first learns the song to study its historic significance and meaning. The teacher then provides guidance in analyzing the rhyme scheme (first three phrases rhyme, last doesn't), syllabic structure of each line (typically fourteen to fifteen syllables per line), and form (verse and chorus or AB); as a group, the students are then guided through the group creation of a parody on an appropriate subject. While the form of the song remains intact, the text is changed. The students write the new text and perform the parody by reading their composition. Later, in pairs, the students then embark on creating their own parody by using the structure of the same piece.

Create a commercial (Grade 6)

Students can create a commercial, complete with a jingle, music, lyrics, script, and sound effects, all of which they write in a score. They decide on a product to advertise, prepare the entire commercial, and then rehearse and perform it. Reading skills are well integrated into all parts of this exercise.

Creat musical games (Grade 6)

Students might create musical games with terms, definitions, and instructions for their peers. Playing with language in written and oral forms provides reading opportunities for the class.

Determine phrasing (Grades 3–6)

Students can visually preview a song by looking for phrases to determine where they should breathe when singing. By locating punctuation marks and reading the phrases in unison before singing, they practice reading the text and learn to drop their voices at the end of the phrase as they do when they read sentences.

SOUNDS MAKE

Oral Language, Steady Beat, Gross Motor Coordination

EVERYDAY SOUNDS

Explain to students that all music has rhythm. Many people like to move to the rhythm in music. But rhythm is heard not only in music; it is all around us. It is also fun to move to "everyday sounds!"

Invite students to say these "everyday" sounds, and coordinate their speaking with each movement.

Say: beat beat beat beat
Move: hand tapping on the chest

Say: tick tock tick tock
Move: tilt head to the left, tilt head to the right

Say: bounce bounce bounce bounce
Move: hand tapping the floor

Say: drip drip drip drip
Move: index finger tapping the opposite hand

Mathematical Groupings, Steady Beat

GROUPING SOUNDS

Explain to students that in music, sounds are organized into groups and patterns. Lead students in exploring the five different groupings below, A through E. Clap each grouping for the students, inviting them to listen and repeat what they hear. As the leader, you must keep a steady beat. To play each rhythm evenly, establish the beat by counting, "1-2-3-4" before you demonstrate each example.

When you see ![clap], clap your hands and say "clap." When you see the word "rest," hold your hands out to the side and quietly say "rest."

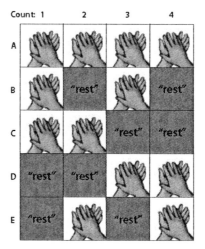

After the exercise, remind students that rhythm is created when sounds are organized into groups. When you repeat each group of sounds, it makes a pattern. Also tell students that when they listen to music, they may enjoy listening for simple rhythms that they can recognize and remember.

RHYTHM!

WORDS HAVE RHYTHM

Count:	1	2	3	4
A	Bee	Bee	Bee	Bee
B	Bee	Bee	Bum-ble	Bee
C	Bum-ble	Bum-ble	Bee	Bee
D	Hon-ey	Bear	Fluf-fy	Cat
E	Yel-low	Duck	Fur-ry	Bat
F	Bum-ble	Bee	Bee	Bee

Explain to students that when people speak, their words make different rhythms. Lead students in exploring the five different word phrases (A through F) in the chart above. Clap each phrase for the students and invite them to listen and repeat what they hear. As the leader, you must keep a steady beat. To play each rhythm evenly, establish the beat by counting, "1-2-3-4" before you demonstrate each example.

To make these rhythms, clap once for each syllable. For example, you will clap one time when you say the word, "bee" and clap two times when you say the word "bum-ble."

PRACTICING WORD RHYTHMS

To practice more word rhythms, use the insert page titled "Words Make Rhythm." On this insert are four word phrases with pictures underneath the syllables in each word.

Follow these four steps for using each word example on the insert:

▶ Read aloud the first word phrase, emphasizing the syllables in each word to give the words rhythm. Invite students to repeat the word phrase.

▶ Read aloud the word phrase as you clap the syllables. Invite students to copy your example.

▶ Read aloud the word phrase and, as you speak, use your finger to tap the picture below each syllable. Your finger tapping will create a rhythm. Students copy your example, speaking and tapping on the desk or floor.

▶ Finally, tap the pictures with your finger as you silently say the words in your head. Invite students to copy your example, tapping the rhythm without speaking the words.

MORE WORD RHYTHMS

To further develop students' awareness of word rhythms, read aloud and discuss stories with rhythmic language.

Student Work

The following composition projects are Julie Linville's, developed for her elementary music classes.

First-grade class composition project
Procedure

1. Brainstorm a list of items and activities associated with a given topic and write this list on the board.
2. Sort the list into categories within the topic (on the board).
3. Have the class choose one category for the composition.
4. Write one phrase using an idea from the chosen list (7–8 beats long). Have students make several suggestions and come to a consensus with the choice the class is happy with.
5. Have students name words that rhyme with the last word of the first phrase and write them on the board.
6. Have the class choose one rhyming word to use for a second phrase and then offer ideas for that phrase (7–8 beats long). As a class, choose the one that works best with the first phrase.
7. Add the rhythmic notation to the two phrases on the board. Students are given a copy of the words as well for them to copy the rhythm as it is written on the board.
8. Choose notes using *sol*, *mi*, *la*, and *do*, with the first phrase ending on *sol* and the second ending on *do*.
9. Write the composition in standard notation on the staff. Students are once again given a paper with the words and staff already prepared and are to copy the standard notation from the board.
10. Perform the composition.

List of items associated with winter

snow	snowman	Frosty
snowball fight	sledding	ice skating
cold	Christmas	Christmas tree
lights	wreath	presents
Jesus	Santa Claus	Mrs. Claus
Rudolph	reindeer	sleigh
Hanukkah	menorah	dreidel
eight days	candles	

List of winter items sorted into categories

Weather	**Christmas**	**Hanukkah**
snow	Christmas tree	menorah
snowman	lights	dreidel
snowball fight	wreath	eight days
sledding	presents	candles
ice skating	Jesus	
Frosty	Santa Claus	
cold	Mrs. Claus	
	Rudolph	
	reindeer	
	sleigh	

First phrase

I like sledding down the hill in the snow.

Rhyming words

bow	blow	doe	foe
flow	go	grow	glow
Joe	low	mow	no
know	pro	row	sew
so	stow	show	slow
toe	though	throw	woe
yo			

Second phrase

I like to sled fast, not go slow!

Fast, Not Slow!

Mrs. Haynes' first-grade class

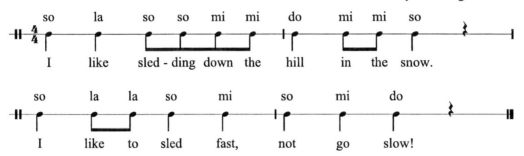

so   la   so so mi mi   do   mi mi   so

I   like   sled - ding down the   hill   in   the snow.

so   la   la   so   mi   so   mi   do

I   like   to   sled   fast,   not   go   slow!

Fast, Not Slow!

Mrs. Haynes' first-grade class

I   like sled-ding down the hill in the snow.   I like to sled fast,   not go slow!

Fourth- and fifth-grade composition project

After her students had been playing recorder for a few months, Julie Linville developed this project as a way to incorporate composition into her curriculum as well as to include several music standards in one project. The project took eight thirty-minute class periods to complete. Students first used the circles to create a rhythm with the correct number of beats in a measure. (The circles are divided into quarters with the top left being beat one, the bottom left beat two, and beats three and four the top and bottom right quarters.) After writing their rhythm in the circles, the students rewrote it in standard notation. Then the students assigned pitch letter names to the notes in the rhythm. The directions required the first phrase to end on *sol* and the final on *do*.

"Shih Tzu" was the first project completed by Bethany. To check progress and growth, the project was presented again a year later. "Bel Aire" is the final product produced by Bethany.

Domain project focus
The students will compose an eight-measure song to be performed on recorders.
Domain: composition

National Standards to be addressed
2. Performing on instruments, alone and with others a varied repertoire of music
4. Composing and arranging music within specified guidelines
5. Reading and notating music

Links to local curriculum
1. Exhibit knowledge of rhythm through melodic and rhythmic performance
2. Demonstrate melody through singing and playing
5. Increase knowledge of music's place in the past and present and develop skills to become a discriminating consumer of music

Project materials
Circle-rhythm worksheets, manuscript paper, recorders

Grades
Fourth and fifth

Timeline
8 class periods

Teaching strategies. direct instruction, graphic organizers, process writing (rough draft, peer edits, teacher edits, final draft)

Activities

Worksheet for practice with note and rest values and writing linear rhythms from circle

Creating rhythms using circles and rhythm guidelines

Assigning note names according to melody guidelines

Generalize composition from circle sheet to standard notation

Individual recorder performances of compositions

Assessment/reflection

Periodic reflections—what they like, what they need to change, quality of individual
  performance

Scoring rubric for entire project

Name _____

Answer the following.

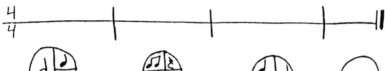

Place the following rhythms on the line. Include bar lines

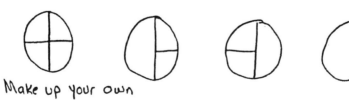

Make up your own

Name _____

Use the circles to write the rhythm for your composition. You may divide the circles
into sections like the examples in class to ensure four beats per circle. You will later
transfer this information to standard manuscript paper. Use only pairs of eighths,
quarter, half, and dotted half notes. One whole note may be used. Use only quarter
rests. You may not use two or more quarter rests in a row. Each measure (except the
one with a whole note) must use at least two different note values. You will use eight
measures in your composition. Extra circles are for fixing mistakes or extra practice.

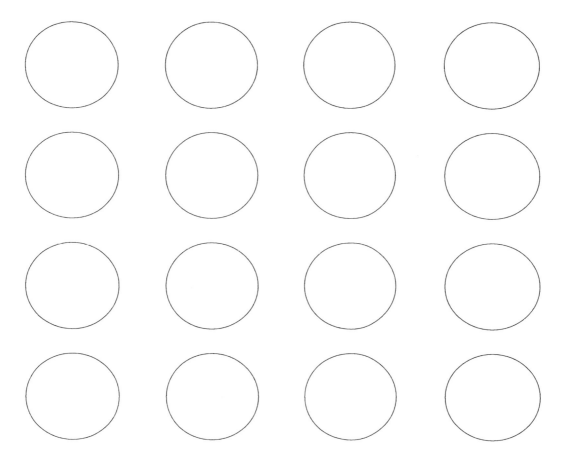

Composition Project
Name _Bethany_

title	yes	no	
composer	yes	no	
treble sign	each	once	no
time sig.	yes	no	
key sig.	each	once	no
rhythm	got it	on the way	getting started
melody	got it	on the way	getting started
circle sht.	yes	no	
rough drft	yes	no	
final drft	yes	no	
reflection 1	yes	no	
reflection 2	yes	no	
performance	got it	on the way	getting started

18/18

What I like best about my
composition is my notes

What I need to change in my
composition is size of measure

The most difficult part
composing was playing it

Bethany

I changed the eight 4p
notes to the same. It
made it better. No, I had to
many rests.

Composition project with lyrics

After moving to a new school district, Julie Linville wanted to expand her composition project across a wider age range of students. Because the students were not playing recorders then, she decided to have them write for barred instruments using the pentatonic scale. Linville added student-written lyrics so that students would be able to sing and play at the same time. This gave students the chance to use skills learned in writing in a new situation. The six-trait music composition assessment guide helped Linville present the project to students in a more efficient manner and resulted in musically stronger compositions. This project took eight 45-minute class periods.

Linville six-trait music composition assessment guide
Ideas and content (theme, expression, and dynamics)

5 Specific—varied in a way to keep the listeners' attention; expression and dynamics support main theme.

3 Some really good parts, some not there yet—player usually knows what is meant; some parts will be better when they support other elements.

1 Just beginning to understand what composer intends—themes are difficult to identify.

Organization (form)

5 Clear and compelling—order works well; has listener anticipating; recognizable pattern.

3 Some really smooth parts, some need work—order of composition makes sense most of the time.

1 Not shaped yet—order is jumbled and confused.

Voice (timbre)

5 Really individual and powerful—instrument choice fits personality; sounds original.

3 Individuality fades in and out—instrument choice fits sometimes.

1 Not yet me—not comfortable matching instrument to desired sound.

Word choice (melody/harmony)

5 Extremely clear, visual, and accurate—just the right melody direction and harmony in the right places.

3 Correct but not striking—gets message across but doesn't capture the imagination or attention.

1 Confusing melody and harmony—melody difficult to follow; harmony doesn't follow standard progressions.

Sentence fluency (rhythm)

5 Varied and natural—clear and easy to play; rhythm follows natural rhythm of words.

3 Routine and functional—follows rules for rhythm but sounds choppy or awkward.

1 Needs work—difficult to play/sing even with practice.

Conventions (symbols, accurate manuscript)

5 Mostly correct—few errors; wouldn't take long to get it ready to publish.

3 About halfway home—number of bothersome mistakes to clean up before publishing.

1 Editing not under control yet—many mistakes, particularly with pitch and rhythm accuracy and following general music theory rules.

Six-trait writing assessment guide

Ideas and content

5 Focused, clear, and specific—full of the details that keep a reader's attention and show what is really important about the topic.

3 Some really good parts, some not there yet—reader usually knows what is meant, some parts will be better when they tell more about what's important.

1 Just beginning to figure out what to say—hard for reader to understand what author means or paper is about.

Organization

5 Clear and compelling direction—order works well and makes reader want to find out what's coming next.

3 Some really smooth parts, others need work—order of paper/story makes sense most of the time.

1 Not shaped yet—order is jumbled and confused.

Voice

5 Really individual and powerful—lots of personality, sounds different from the way anyone else writes.

3 Individuality fades in and out—thoughts and feelings only show up sometimes.

1 Not yet me—not comfortable sharing thoughts and feelings.

Word choice

5 Extremely clear, visual, and accurate—just the right words for just the right places.

3 Correct but not striking—gets message across, but doesn't capture the imagination or attention.

1 Confusing, misused words and phrases abound—"What does this mean?"

Sentence fluency

5 Varied and natural—clear and delightful to read aloud.

3 Routine and functional—some sentences choppy and awkward, most are clear.

1 Needs work—difficult to read aloud, even with practice, lacks "sentence sense."

Conventions

5 Mostly correct—few errors; wouldn't take long to get it ready to publish.

3 About halfway home—number of bothersome mistakes to clean up before publishing.

1 Editing not under control yet—first reading to decode, second reading to get the meaning.

Mackenzie's music composition project,
spring 2003, second grade

Directions

1. Review six traits for music composition.
2. Brainstorm topics.
3. Brainstorm ideas within a topic.
4. Write one phrase, two measures long.
5. List rhyming words with last word of first phrase.
6. Write second phrase, two measures long.
7. Dictate rhythm of phrases.
8. Assign melody notes—*do, re, mi, sol, la.*
9. Second phrase must end on *sol.*
10. Fourth phrase must end on *do.*
11. Write in standard notation.
12. Edit and revise at each step.
13. Final draft.
14. Perform on barred instruments or hand chimes.

Brainstorm topics for writing lyrics to a song—at least 10 ideas.

Jump rope   the piano

basketball   tennis   Daseball
Soccer   dance   Cards
Skatebording   iceskateing

Choose one topic and brainstorm ideas related to the topic.

dance   I hear music ballet
tap and jazz, resitel, friends
teacher

I jump in the air with my jazz shoes on.

First phrase

I jump in the air with my | jazz shoes on.

Rhyming words

don   bawn
con   Pawn
dawn   Ron
fawn   gone
gone   Shawn
Jon   Yawn

Second phrase

I feel ready and I | dace till dawn
good

Do first two phrases rhyme? yes

Are first two phrases related? yes

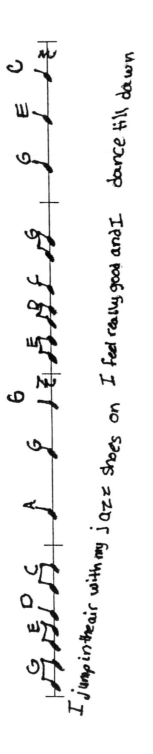

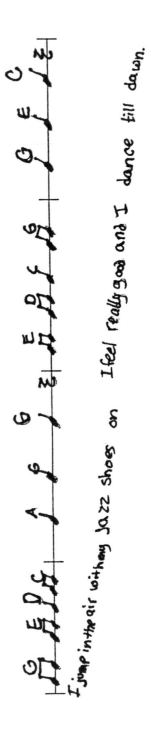

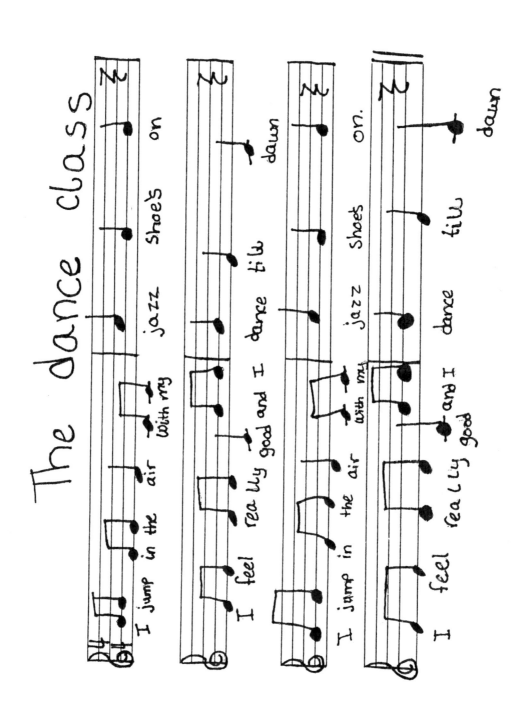

6 Trait Music Composition

Ideas and Content (theme, expression, and dynamics)
(5) specific—varied in a way to keep the listeners attention; expression and dynamics support main theme
3 some really good parts, some not there yet—player usually knows what is meant; some parts will be better when they support other elements
1 just beginning to understand what composer intends—themes are difficult to identify

Organization (form)
(5) clear and compelling—order works well; has listener anticipating; recognizable pattern
3 some really smooth parts, some need work—order of composition makes sense most of the time
1 not shaped yet—order is jumbled and confused

Voice (timbre)
5 really individual and powerful—instrument choice fits personality; sounds original
NA 3 individuality fades in and out—instrument choice fits sometimes
1 not yet me—not comfortable matching instrument to desired sound

Word Choice (melody/harmony)
5 extremely clear, visual, and accurate—just the right melody direction and harmony in the right places
(4) 3 correct but not striking—gets message across but doesn't capture the imagination or attention
1 confusing melody and harmony—melody difficult to follow; harmony doesn't follow standard progressions

Sentence Fluency (rhythm)
(5) varied and natural—clear and easy to play; rhythm follows natural rhythm of words
3 routine and functional—follows rules for rhythm but sounds choppy or awkward
1 needs work—difficult to play/sing even with practice

Conventions (symbols, accurate manuscript)
5 mostly correct—few errors; wouldn't take long to get it ready to publish
(4) 3 about halfway home—number of bothersome mistakes to clean up before publishing
1 editing not under control yet—many mistakes, particularly with pitch and rhythm accuracy and following general music theory rules

$$\frac{23}{25}$$

(4.6)

E

Carter's music composition project, spring 2003, fourth grade

Directions

1. Review six traits for music composition.
2. Brainstorm topics.
3. Brainstorm ideas within a topic.
4. Write one phrase, two measures long.
5. List rhyming words with last word of first phrase.
6. Write second phrase, two measures long.
7. Write third phrase, two measures long, related to first two.
8. List rhyming words with last word of third phrase.
9. Write fourth phrase, two measures long.
10. Dictate rhythm of phrases.
11. Assign melody notes—*do, re, mi, sol, la.*
12. Second phrase must end on *sol.*
13. Fourth phrase must end on *do.*
14. Write in standard notation.
15. Edit and revise at each step.
16. Final draft.
17. Perform on barred instruments or hand chimes.

Brainstorm topics for writing lyrics to a song—at least 10 ideas.

Sports pizza   bike riding
video games snow cones singing   cornbread
scrapbooking tools Skateboarding gocarts
TV football games Cheese Mcdonalds
earl pickled okra bacon   popcorn
basketball pigs party extreme sports
dance ice skating Easter Island cotton candy
travel soccer   pickles
read ice cream motorcross Irish peopl
Music DVD's   chickens dogs
Swim   beans   speed skating
baseball burrito   tuna
Skiing corn bread leperchauns

Choose one topic and brainstorm ideas related to the topic.

Swimming

smell - clorine
hear - the splashing of water
feel - the slippery side of the pool
taste - water and clorine
see - patterns on the bottom of the pool

You dive and do flip turns
with long strokes

First phrase

Swimming is cool you dive
and flip.

Rhyming words

Flip   Clip
Trip   Zip
Nip   Wip
lip
Rip

Second phrase

Swimming is hard when you
rip

Do first two phrases rhyme? yes

Are first two phrases related? yes

Third phrase

Though when you rip it's
hand to dive.

Rhyming words

Jive   five
chive   ? ?
Live   arrive
Hive   strive

Fourth phrase But you cann dive when
you swim five

Do phrases three and four rhyme? Yes

Are phrases three and four related? yes

Do they relate to phrases one and two? yes

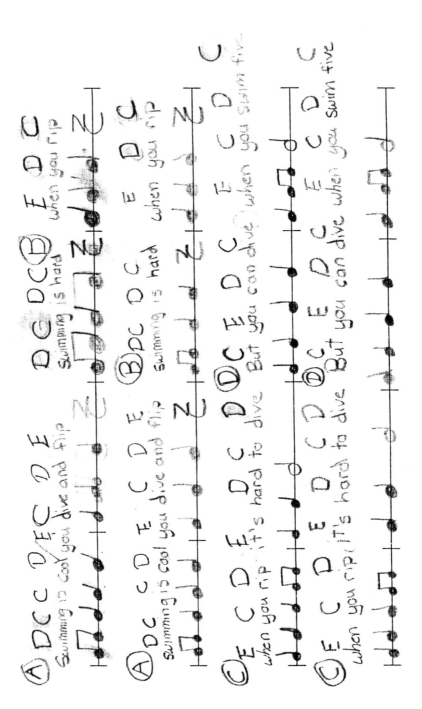

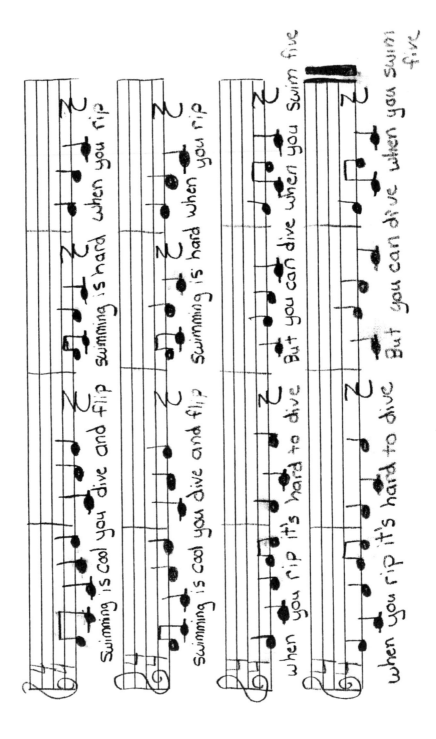

Carter

6 Trait Music Composition

Ideas and Content (theme, expression, and dynamics)
- 5 specific—varied in a way to keep the listeners attention; expression and dynamics support main theme
- 3 some really good parts, some not there yet—player usually knows what is meant; some parts will be better when they support other elements
- 1 just beginning to understand what composer intends—themes are difficult to identify

Organization (form)
- 5 clear and compelling—order works well; has listener anticipating; recognizable pattern
- 3 some really smooth parts, some need work—order of composition makes sense most of the time
- 1 not shaped yet—order is jumbled and confused

Voice (timbre)
- 5 really individual and powerful—instrument choice fits personality; sounds original
- 3 individuality fades in and out—instrument choice fits sometimes
- 1 not yet me—not comfortable matching instrument to desired sound

Word Choice (melody/harmony)
- 5 extremely clear, visual, and accurate—just the right melody direction and harmony in the right places
- 3 correct but not striking—gets message across but doesn't capture the imagination or attention
- 1 confusing melody and harmony—melody difficult to follow; harmony doesn't follow standard progressions

Sentence Fluency (rhythm)
- 5 varied and natural—clear and easy to play; rhythm follows natural rhythm of words
- 3 routine and functional—follows rules for rhythm but sounds choppy or awkward
- 1 needs work—difficult to play/sing even with practice

Conventions (symbols, accurate manuscript)
- 5 mostly correct—few errors; wouldn't take long to get it ready to publish
- 3 about halfway home—number of bothersome mistakes to clean up before publishing
- 1 editing not under control yet—many mistakes, particularly with pitch and rhythm accuracy and following general music theory rules

22
___
25

(4.4)

F

Kayla's music composition project, Spring 2003, fourth grade

Directions

1. Review six traits for music composition.
2. Brainstorm topics.
3. Brainstorm ideas within a topic.
4. Write one phrase, two measures long.
5. List rhyming words with last word of first phrase.
6. Write second phrase, two measures long.
7. Write third phrase, two measures long, related to first two.
8. List rhyming words with last word of third phrase.
9. Write fourth phrase, two measures long.
10. Dictate rhythm of phrases.
11. Assign melody note—*do, re, mi, sol, la.*
12. Second phrase must end on *sol.*
13. Fourth phrase must end on *do.*
14. Write in standard notation.
15. Edit and revise at each step.
16. Final draft.
17. Perform on barred instruments or hand chimes.

Brainstorm topics for writing lyrics to a song—at least 10 ideas.

sports, video games, scrapbooking,
TV, eat, basketball, dance, travel
read, music, swim, baseball, skiing, bike riding,
singing, skateboarding, cheese, bacon,
extreme sports, Easter Island, pickles, dogs
motorcross, chickens, speed skating Irish People
tuna, ice skating, soccer, ice cream cotton candy
DVD's, beans, burrito, cornbread, snow cones
McDonalds, popcorn, leperchauns, tools, football games

~~~~~ = maybe want to do

Choose one topic and brainstorm ideas related to the topic.

• have to have good rythm
• be able to count to 8
• be able to count music

Dance

• sweating
• yourself in the mirror
• tap shoes
• yourself dancing like flying through the air
• ballet (boring).
• jazz
• music
• feel good
• have to be in shape
• have to be together with your team
• have to stay with the music

First phrase

A I jump on the floor ready to tap.

Rhyming words

pap
cap
dap
gap

Second phrase

After the taps start everyone
claps &

Do first two phrases rhyme?
yes

Are first two phrases related?

Yes they both
have to do with
dance

Third phrase

You hear the loud music and
watch all the fast taps

Rhyming words
prancen

Fourth phrase

The dance is over and everyone
claps

Do phrases three and four rhyme? yes

Are phrases three and four related? yes

Do they relate to phrases one and two? yes

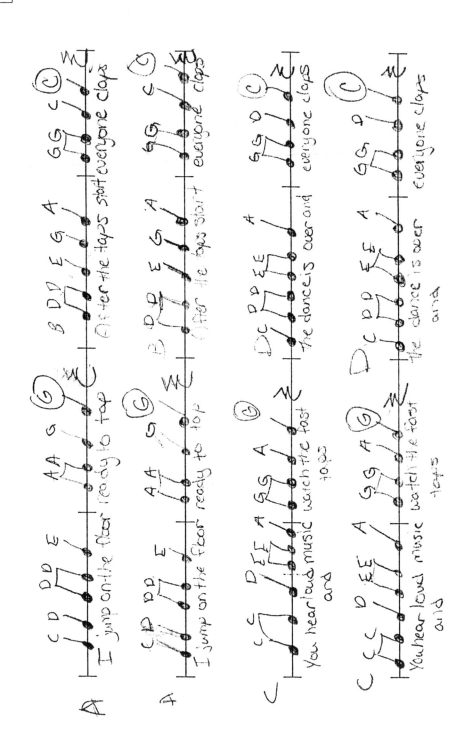

Dancing

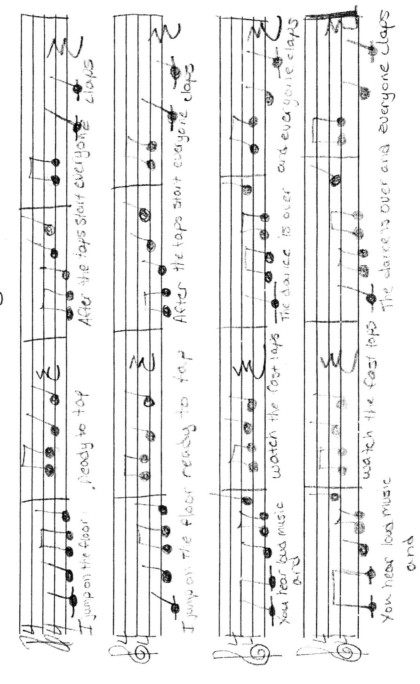

6 Trait Music Composition

Ideas and Content (theme, expression, and dynamics)
- 5 specific—varied in a way to keep the listeners attention; expression and dynamics support main theme
- 3 some really good parts, some not there yet—player usually knows what is meant; some parts will be better when they support other elements
- 1 just beginning to understand what composer intends—themes are difficult to identify

Organization (form)
- 5 clear and compelling—order works well; has listener anticipating; recognizable pattern
- 3 some really smooth parts, some need work—order of composition makes sense most of the time
- 1 not shaped yet—order is jumbled and confused

Voice (timbre)
- 5 really individual and powerful—instrument choice fits personality; sounds original
- 3 individuality fades in and out—instrument choice fits sometimes
- 1 not yet me—not comfortable matching instrument to desired sound

Word Choice (melody/harmony)
- 5 extremely clear, visual, and accurate—just the right melody direction and harmony in the right places
- 3 correct but not striking—gets message across but doesn't capture the imagination or attention
- 1 confusing melody and harmony—melody difficult to follow; harmony doesn't follow standard progressions

Sentence Fluency (rhythm)
- 5 varied and natural—clear and easy to play; rhythm follows natural rhythm of words
- 3 routine and functional—follows rules for rhythm but sounds choppy or awkward
- 1 needs work—difficult to play/sing even with practice

Conventions (symbols, accurate manuscript)
- 5 mostly correct—few errors; wouldn't take long to get it ready to publish
- 3 about halfway home—number of bothersome mistakes to clean up before publishing
- 1 editing not under control yet—many mistakes, particularly with pitch and rhythm accuracy and following general music theory rules

Lesson Unit and Extensions:
Advanced Conceptual Learning

Choral singing and problem-solving domain project

This project, designed by Martha Gabel, elementary general music teacher at Bentwood Elementary School in Olathe, Kansas, uses a two-part song to help students learn to evaluate their own choral performances and use the problem-solving process to generate a plan to improve. The project was designed and refined over several school years as part of her involvement as a trainer in the Music PROPEL workshops in Kansas. PROPEL uses Howard Gardner's "Arts PROPEL" terminology of the Domain Project to represent a long-term music "domain" project that extends over many days or weeks. The project addresses many music standards but also satisfies state initiatives in problem-solving and assessment.

Objective statement

The student will:
- Use and apply appropriate singing skills
- Sing in two-part harmony
- Apply pitch and rhythm reading skills
- Identify and apply a variety of musical symbols
- Use an age-appropriate musical vocabulary when discussing music
- Critically listen to and evaluate a performance of a song
- Apply the problem-solving process to identify areas for improvement within a performance and to list possible strategies for improvement

Domain
- Singing
- Reading
- Listening
- Evaluating

Dimensions within the domain
- Singing
  - Pitch
  - Posture
  - Breath support
  - Tone
  - Harmony

- Reading
  - Rhythm/pitch
  - Musical symbols and terms

- Listening
  - Vocabulary
  - Critical listening

- Evaluating
  - Developing criteria for assessment

National Standards
1, 5, 6, 7

Olathe outcomes/objectives
- Imitate supported and nonsupported tones (6.1.1)
- Demonstrate accurate beginning and ending consonants (6.1.2)
- Perform in an ensemble responding appropriately to the conductor's cues (6.1.3)
- Independently sing harmony in a two-part arrangement while other students sing the melody (6.1.4)
- Read, notate, and perform rhythms using: quarter note, quarter rest, eighth note pairs, half note, half rest, dotted half note, whole note, whole rest, sixteenth notes, dotted rhythms in 2/4, 3/4, and 4/4 (6.5.1)
- Identify various musical symbols and terms (6.5.3)
- Use appropriate musical terms to identify: dynamics, tempo, meter, form, and

timbre in a variety of musical examples (6.6.2)

- Develop and apply criteria for evaluating the quality of his/her own and others' performances and compositions (6.7.1)
- Use musical terminology to describe and evaluate preferred musical works heard or performed (6.7.2)

Materials

- Use any song. I focus on two-part harmony, but this could easily be used with unison pieces as well.
- Videocamera/tape/VCR/TV
- Materials from packet

Grade level and timeline

- Sixth grade
- 7 or 8 thirty-minute class periods

Prior to project

Select a two-part song that your students have been working on and are fairly familiar with. I do a small unit where we focus on two-part harmony and sing several songs demonstrating different types of harmony (rounds/canons, melody/counter-melody, partner songs, etc.). As we work through the unit, I select one of the songs to extend into this project. (I select one that they have not memorized as one of my goals is to discuss how to hold music appropriately while singing.)

Day 1

1. Use think/pair/share to discuss the elements of a "good choral performance." From this discussion, generate a list of "performance criteria" (see sample).
2. As a class, write definitions for each criteria listed so that everyone has the same general understanding of what each item looks like and/or sounds like.

Day 2

1. Make a video recording of the class performing the selected song.
2. Remind students of the "performance criteria" they selected and how they defined each item.
3. As students watch the video, have them use the Choral Performance Evaluation #1 to assess their class performance on the selected criteria. (The performance rubric is in this packet of materials.)

Day 3

1. Review the four problem-solving steps. As a class, discuss how these steps can be applied to many things outside of math. Generate some examples within discussion.

2. Discuss how we will apply this model as we work to improve the performance of our song.
3. Pass out the Music Problem Solver along with the Choral Performance Evaluation #1 to each student. Have each student look through his/her evaluation and select one area, that if improved, would have the greatest impact on the overall performance. As students write that "problem" on the problem-solver, they should be very specific about what is happening and why it is a problem.
4. Put students into groups of twos or threes and have them brainstorm solutions and/or strategies that might be used to fix the "problem" each student identified. Those solutions/strategies should be written on the bottom section of the problem solver.

Day 4

1. As a class, share the "problems" identified by each student and organize them according to the performance criteria. (I usually make a big chart on my whiteboard with each of the criteria listed and students identify where their "problem" should be listed.)
2. As a class, select two "problems" to solve.
3. Brainstorm strategies that might be used in a rehearsal situation to fix the problems and make a list. (Students who identified this problem should share some of the strategies they listed on their problem solver.)
4. Guide students to plan a rehearsal using some of the strategies listed to address the identified problems.

Day 5

Follow the rehearsal planned by the class during the previous class time. While rehearsing, be sure to check with students to see if they feel their planned strategies are working or if they need to make some adaptations.

Day 6

Make a video recording of the class performing the selected song once again.

Day 7

1. Have students watch the recording of their first performance followed by the recording of their second performance (might need to do this a couple of times).
2. Students will use the Final Performance Evaluation to assess their class performance and whether or not they improved in the areas selected. They will also use this as a self-assessment on singing skills.

Day 8

Depending on whether your students keep journals in music or not, this would be a great ending for the unit. I do give a few starters to help students make the best use of their time.

Choral Performance Evaluation #1

Name _____

Use the 4-point performance rubric to evaluate your class performance on each area listed below. Briefly tell why you selected each rating.

Performance Criteria/Definition	Rating/Reasoning
Good Posture: back away from chair, back straight, facing forward, shoulders slightly back, feet on floor	
Open Mouth: mouths open, facing forward, understand the words, jaw relaxed, back teeth apart	
Appropriate Music Holding: book in front, not in face, not on lap … in middle	
Good Singing Tone: blend with others, correct pitch, open tone, not shouting … singing voice, supporting tone … energy	
Correct Pitch: singing the right note at the right spot in the music, hitting the pitch in the middle … not sliding or scooping	
Correct Rhythm: keeping a steady tempo, correct duration, rest on the rests	
Good Part Balance: both parts sound equal in loudness	

Problem-Solving Steps

1. **I**dentify the problem

2. **C**hoose a strategy

3. **A**nswer the problem

4. **N**ow it makes sense

Music Problem Solver

Name _____

Song Title: *You're a Grand Old Flag*

1. Identify the problem (What did you hear or see that needs to be fixed?):

2. Choose a strategy (How are we going to fix it?):

Final Performance Evaluation

Name _____

Listed below are the 2 problems your class identified from the 1st performance. Listed unde
them are the solutions and rehearsal strategies your class selected. Use the 4-point performance
rubric to rate your class in these areas on your 2nd performance. Indicate your reasoning for
this rating and whether or not you think the solutions and rehearsal strategies your class selected
worked. Do you have any other solutions and rehearsal strategies that you feel might have
worked better?

Problem 1	
Solutions/Rehearsal Strategies Used	
Rating	4 3 2 1
Reasoning	
Other Solutions to Try	

Problem 2	
Solutions/Rehearsal Strategies Used	
Rating	4 3 2 1
Reasoning	
Other Solutions to Try	

Personal Self-Evaluation

Please consider your personal performance when answering the following questions.

A. Name the performance criteria on which you feel you did the best. What made it the best?

B. Name the performance criteria on which you feel you need the most work. How do you plan to improve in the area?

C. Considering all of the performance criteria, rate yourself on the work you did during this unit.

   4   3   2   1

   Why is this rating appropriate?

D. Rate yourself regarding the effort you put forth during this unit.

   4   3   2   1

   Why is this rating appropriate?

Reflection Journal Starters

- During the unit, I learned …

- My plan to become a better singer is …

- Singing in harmony is …

- During this unit, I was the most successful at …

- During this unit, I had the most difficulty with …

- I will use what I have learned during this unit to …

- In the future, I plan to …

Twelve-bar blues composition: Domain project for upper elementary and middle school general music

This project was developed by Greg Gooden when he taught in the Buhler, Kansas, school district. Gooden currently teaches in Salina, Kansas, and is a music education instructor at Sterling College in Sterling, Kansas. Greg is also a trainer for the Kansas Music PROPEL workshops. The project coincides with school participation in the national DARE (Drug Abuse Resistance Education) program. DARE is a nation-wide drug prevention program implemented by local law enforcement agencies.

Project focus

The students will develop musicianship through the creation, performance, and evaluation of an original twelve-bar blues composition that reflects the core values of the DARE program (DARE Twelve-Bar Blues Composition).

Domain

Composition skills
Notation skills
Listening skills
Improvisation skills

National Standards for Music Education (Grades 5–8)

1. Singing, alone and with others, a varied repertoire of music
2. Performing on instruments, alone and with others, a varied repertoire of music
3. Improvising melodies, variations, and accompaniments
4. Composing and arranging music within specific guidelines
5. Reading and notating music
6. Listening to, analyzing, and describing music
7. Evaluating music and music performances
9. Understanding music in relation to history and culture

Materials

a. *Junior Jazz II: Beginning Steps to Singing Jazz.* Two-part collection by Kirby Shaw (Hal Leonard 08741143) with accompaniment cassette.
b. *Junior Jam Session.* Orff arrangements by Laurie Zentz with demonstration and accompaniment cassette (West Music Co.).
c. *Share The Music* (1995). Fifth-grade texts and CDs.
d. Boomwhackers. Diatonic "tube" instruments (West Music Co.).
e. *The Boomwhacker Beat Bag* and accompaniment CD by Bradley L. Bonner (West Music Co.).

f. *Big Mouth Blues.* Recorder collection and CD by Jim Tinter (West Music Co.).

g. *Volume 24—Major and Minor in Every Key* and *Volume 42—Blues in All Keys,* Jamie Aebersold.

h. Autoharps, piano keyboards, barred (Orff) instruments, resonator bells, guitars, assorted percussion instruments, recorders.

i. Staff paper, Musical Composition Tips handout, CD/cassette player, any handouts created about the history of jazz and specifically the blues, Performance Assessment Task handout.

j. *Music Alive* magazine issues (October, November, and December 1999, and January 2000) and accompanying CDs.

k. "Joe Turner Blues." Orff arrangement by Bob DeFrece (workshop).

What grade levels or classes will be involved?

Upper elementary and middle school (I used it for sixth grade.)

Timeline

I would suggest a nine-week project. It depends on how many experiences you provide and how much jazz (blues) history you discuss prior to the actual project.

Teaching strategies

Critical listening
Problem solving
Student accountability
Higher-order thinking
Communication skills
Aesthetic awareness
Composition and orchestration
Decision making

Activities

(There were many experiences provided prior to the actual project. Last year the students learned about the I, IV, and V chords and had several playing experiences on Autoharps and barred instruments.)

The preliminary experiences for the domain project were:

a. Reading, discussing, and listening to music examples from *Music Alive* magazine's four-part series "Exploring the Blues":

Part 1: "The Birth of the Blues" (October 1999)
Part 2: "Early Female Singers" (November 1999)
Part 3: "The Birth of Blues Guitar" (December 1999)

Part 4: "Who's New In Blues" (January 2000)

b. Handouts: History of Jazz, Ten Basic Elements of Jazz, and What Is Jazz? (teacher lecture/discussion).

c. Learning to play all parts and perform the Orff selection "Orffin' Blues." (This was the piece where we first experienced the twelve-bar blues form!)

d. Learning to perform "Blues Whackers" on the boomwhackers. (This, too, introduced us to the twelve-bar blues form and to call-and-response.)

e. Learning to perform and improvise "Big Mouth Blues" on our recorders. (We discovered riff, swing rhythm, flat 3 blues note, and improvisation.)

f. Learning to sing all the selections from *Junior Jazz II* in two parts. (These selections addressed smears, fall-offs, blue notes, scat singing, etc. in addition to other things mentioned in the above pieces.)

g. The students improvised to the Jamey Aebersold CDs on the keyboard using the C major scale. (Ideas from a workshop given by Marcia F. Dunscomb from Florida International University, Miami at Friends University, Wichita, Kansas, in the summer of 1999.)

h. We also covered lessons in the fifth grade *Share the Music* text in Unit 6 on "Good Morning Blues" and "Joe Turner Blues." Using resonator bells, we played chord roots (blocked chords on the beat) as an accompaniment to both selections. We also played an arpeggiated accompaniment.

These preliminary activities were followed with the actual project as described on the Performance Assessment Task handout.

Assessment and reflection

The class, each performing group, and the teacher will provide verbal and/or written assessment. All students will write a reflection for their portfolio at the end of the project, specifically commenting on what worked, what didn't work, and what they would do different next time.

Performance assessment task
Background

The blues is a type of jazz music created by African American musicians in the United States in the early 1900s. It uses a twelve-bar (measure) form that is improvised. Common topics contained in the lyrics are love, personal misfortune, or loneliness. The musicians sing the blues to take the blues away.

Task

You are a jazz musician in the year 2000. On Saturday night, you will represent

Kansas at the National DARE Convention in Washington, D.C. Our DARE officers asked you to create an original blues composition to be presented as part of the evening entertainment. If your song is a hit, a national recording contract will be presented to *you*! Your recording will air all over the United States as the official DARE song. Other recording contract opportunities also exist because executives from all major recording companies will be present. The concert will be presented at the Kennedy Center for the Performing Arts.

Audience

Your audience will include law enforcement officials from all over the country and world famous jazz musician Wynton Marsalis.

Purpose

Your task is to compose a twelve-bar blues song that will highlight the core values that are taught in the DARE program at our school. (Your lyrics may be about self-esteem, respect, peer pressure, substance abuse, saying *no*, making choices, behavior types, etc.—any values that are taught in DARE.)

Procedure

1. Give yourself and your partners appropriate jazz names. Also, give the group a name.
2. Use the twelve-bar blues form

    I   I I I
   IV IV I I
   V IV I I

3. Use the key of C major, F major, or G major and the I, IV, and V chords in the key you choose.
4. Write the lyrics. They must be about the DARE program core values! Make sure you have three phrases in each verse. Remember, phrases 1 and 2 use the same lyrics, and phrase 3 is a response to the previous phrases. Try to make the end of phrase 3 rhyme with the last word in phrases 1 and 2. You must write three verses. Try saying your words in a rhythm as you strum the chords on an Autoharp or play them on a keyboard or a barred instrument. Chant them until the words and accompaniment seem to fit together. Remember, there should be some space between each phrase (like in "Joe Turner Blues") for an improvised solo.
5. Create a melody. Since blues is a predominantly improvised form, see if you can improvise a melody for your lyrics as you strum the chord progression on the Autoharp. Gradually sing the words on pitches you hear in the chords. Figure out which words should be sung as blue notes. What blue notes will you use (flat 3, 5, 7, or more than one)? Use

a keyboard to find the notes you sang in your melody. Follow the musical composition tips as you notate your melody on staff paper. Be careful as you notate the rhythm!

6. Arrange the performance to be creative. You could add an introduction or a coda (ending). Decide which instruments you will use and play. Consider using any instruments in addition to the chordal accompaniment. Determine how the lyrics should be sung (solo, duet, trio) and who will sing them.

7. Rehearse, then perform your blues for the class.

8. Finally, assess your blues composition and the performance.

Performance task assessment list: Original twelve-bar blues

Element	Points Possible	Self	Teacher

A. Creating a twelve-bar blues

1. The lyrics contain appropriate themes that convey the feelings and emotions characteristic of the blues. (DARE values) _____ _____ _____

2. The lyrics are in three phrases phrase one and two being the same. _____ _____ _____

3. A twelve-bar blues form is used. _____ _____ _____

4. Blue notes from the blues scale are used in the melody. _____ _____ _____

5. The song is original and authentic. _____ _____ _____

6. The pitches of the melody are correctly notated on staff paper. _____ _____ _____

B. Performing a twelve-bar blues

1. Appropriate instruments were used in the performance. _____ _____ _____

2. The ensemble stayed together. _____ _____ _____

3. Improvisation was used between phrases. _____ _____ _____

4. The group was prepared. _____ _____ _____

Structuring musical concepts

Structuring Musical Concepts and Sequencing Levels of Artistic Process are designed to be used with Figure 6.5, Levels of Conceptual Understanding in Music, in Chapter 6. It is helpful to place the Chapter 6 figure next to these charts. The purpose of these two charts is to further define sequential music learning aligned with Bloom's Taxonomy. Aurelia Hartenberger designed these charts to assist teachers in her school district with the scope and sequence of their lessons as well as to maintain alignment with music standards. At the top of each column, one of Bloom's Taxonomy levels is listed. Each music element that she has defined as being basic to music education—frequency, time, intensity, and timbre—is listed at the knowledge level. Musical concepts that grow from those basic concepts are then described in terms of the range of Bloom's Taxonomy objectives.

Hartenberger also offers a graphic organizer that captures the Sequencing Levels of Artistic Processes. Beginning with the simplest level, naming, the concentric circles move sequentially to higher levels of music skills, knowledge, and pursuits.

Structuring Musical Concepts
Aurelia Hartenberger, 2003

Level 1	Level 2	Level 3	Level 4	Level 5	Level 6	
Knowledge	Comprehension	Application	Analysis	Synthesis	Evaluation	
SCIENCE OF SOUND (Verifiable facts)	Interpret/Classify	ELEMENTS OF EXPRESSION Construct/Organize	Distinguish/Categorize	Design/Theorize	CONCEPTUAL LENS Judgment	NON-MUSICAL Themes/Concepts
FREQUENCY	PITCH (Intervals/Range)	MELODY	Patterns (Repetition/Imitation)	Genres Style Design/Form	Expression Performance Aesthetics	Cultural Identity; Beliefs/Values; Historical Perspectives: Events; Function/Purpose; Relationships; Environment; Mental and Emotional Wellness (Mood/Attitude); Social Health (Cooperation/Conflict); Insight (Perceptions); etc.
			Phrases/Cadences			
			Forms/Designs (Ostinato)			
		TONALITY/ MODALITY	Scales/Ragas			
			Transposition			
		HARMONY	Chords			
			Cadences			
		TEXTURE	Monophonic/Homophonic/ Polyphonic/Heterophonic			

Level 1	Level 2	Level 3	Level 4	Level 5	Level 6	
Knowledge	Comprehension	Application	Analysis	Synthesis	Evaluation	
SCIENCE OF SOUND (Verifiable facts)	Interpret/Classify	ELEMENTS OF EXPRESSION Construct/Organize	Distinguish/Categorize	Design/Theorize	CONCEPTUAL LENS Judgment	NON-MUSICAL Themes/Concepts
TIME	DURATION Temporal organization of sound and silence					Cultural Identity
						Beliefs/Values
		BEAT				Historical Perspectives: Events
			Tempo			Function/Purpose
			Meter (Symetrical/Asymmetrical)	**Genres** **Style** **Design/Form**	**Expression** **Performance** **Aesthetics**	Relationships
			Talas			Environment
		RHYTHM				Mental and Emotional Wellness
			Patterns (Repetition)			(Mood/Attitude)
			Articulation			Social Health
			Syncopation			(Cooperation/Conflict)
			Quantizing			Insight (Perceptions)
			Forms/Designs			etc.

Level 1	Level 2	Level 3	Level 4	Level 5	Level 6	
Knowledge	Comprehension	Application	Analysis	Synthesis	Evaluation	
SCIENCE OF SOUND (Verifiable facts)	Interpret/Classify	**ELEMENTS OF EXPRESSION** Construct/Organize	Distinguish/Categorize	Design/Theorize	**CONCEPTUAL LENS** Judgment	**NON-MUSICAL** Themes/Concepts
INTENSITY	**VOLUME** Degrees of loudness	**DYNAMICS**				
			Gradual (Crescendo/Diminuendo)			Cultural Identity
			Terrace			Beliefs/Values
			Accents (Sforzando/Rinforzando)			Historical Perspectives:
		ACOUSTICS		**Genres** **Style** **Design/Form**	**Expression** **Performance** **Aesthetics**	Events
			Acoustical/Amplification			Function/Purpose
						Relationships
						Environment
						Mental and Emotional Wellness (Mood/Attitude)
						Social Health (Cooperation/Conflict)
						Insight (Perceptions) etc.

Level 1	Level 2	Level 3	Level 4	Level 5	Level 6	
Knowledge	Comprehension	Application	Analysis	Synthesis	Evaluation	
SCIENCE OF SOUND (Verifiable facts)	Interpret/Classify	**ELEMENTS OF EXPRESSION** Construct/Organize	Distinguish/Categorize	Design/Theorize	**CONCEPTUAL LENS** Judgment	**NON-MUSICAL** Themes/Concepts
TIMBRE	**TONE COLOR** Quality of sound					
		ARTICULATION	Generator of Sound: Membranophone/Chordophone Idiophone/Aerophone/ Electrophone			
			Classification and Register: Soprano, Alto, Tenor, Bass			Cultural Identity
			Family of Instruments: Woodwinds/Brass Percussion/Strings			Beliefs/Values Historical Perspectives: Events Function/Purpose Relationships Environment
		VOICING/ INSTRUMENTATION	Balance—Accompaniment/Solo	**Genres Style Design/Form**	**Expression Performance Aesthetics**	Mental and Emotional Wellness (Mood/Attitude) Social Health (Cooperation/Conflict) Insight (Perceptions) etc.
			Transcriptions/Arrangements			
			Medium: Band/Choir/Orchestra/ Ensemble			
		TONE QUALITY	Resonance			
			Blend			
			Diction: Enunciation/Vowel Placement			
			Intonation			
			Style: Belcanto/Coloratura/ Basso profundo			

By Aurelia Hartenberger, music coordinator, Mehlville School District, Missouri, and MENC Southwestern Division president.

SEQUENCING LEVELS OF ARTISTIC PROCESS
Aurelia Hartenberger

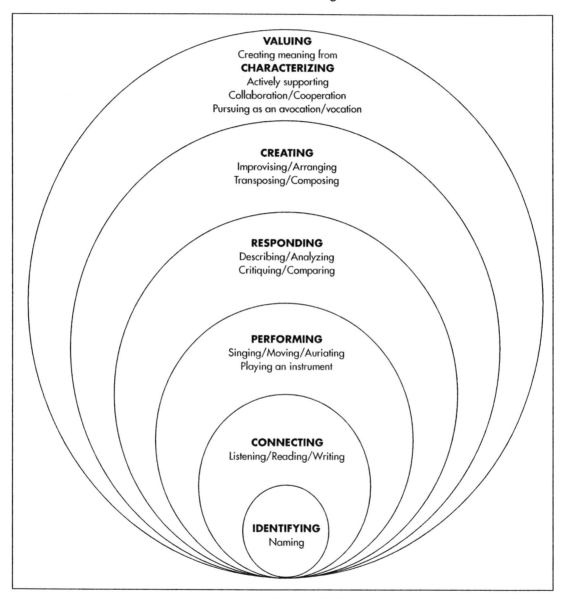

By Aurelia Hartenberger, Music Coordinator, Mehlville School District, Missouri,
and MENC Southwestern Division president.

Cross-Curricular Connections

Because many schools target reading comprehension in the school improvement process, the following charts were designed by Dee Hansen to help connect common text reading comprehension strategies and common instructional strategies and activities across the arts. The first column of each section defines the reading strategy (finding the main idea, sequencing, summarizing, etc.) and then describes the parallel processes in drama, music, visual art, and dance.

The matrix was designed to help teachers, artists, and therapists establish a common vocabulary and set of sample activities for using the arts to develop Listening, Viewing, and Speaking skills. The matrix lists primary art disciplines and their major concepts and elements along the vertical axis. The horizontal axis shows the primary skills for communication that are included in the Listening, Viewing, and Speaking Standards.

Reaching Comprehension: Common Reading Strategies and Examples of Parallel Arts Strategies

Reading Strategy	In Reading	In Drama	In Music	In Visual Art	In Dance
Finding the main idea	Find critical facts and details in narrative (stories) or expository (informational) literature.	Determine the plot through critical facts and details.	Identify themes, melodies, or motifs through repeated rhythmic and melodic patterns, tonal centers, etc.	Determine what the artist was communicating through synthesizing critical sensory, formal, and technical properties of the art.	Determine what the choreographer was communicating by discussing the elements and principles of movement (time, space, and energy).
Sequencing	Identify the beginning, middle, and end of a story.	Determine the sequence of events in a play or dramatic reading. Discuss the development of characters as the plot unfolds.	Determine the form through repetition of cadential patterns, melodic and rhythmic structure, phrase structure, climatic points (golden mean), etc.	Identify the organizational principles such as thematic design, symmetry, balance, unity, repetition, and value. Also, discuss the step-by-step process of creating the art.	Determine the form through repetition and patterns of movement, tension and relaxation, stillness and motion.
Summarizing	Pull together information in a meaningful way through written or oral presentations.	Present a synopsis of a dramatic text through interpretation and reflection in oral or written expression.	Analyze compositional elements, discuss historical context, create an original piece in the style of a given composer or style period.	Present an analysis of art through interpretation of critical elements including historical, stylistic, and cultural influences.	Present an analysis of a dance by exploring the choreographic solutions used to convey the meaning.
Making predictions	Reach conclusions and predict outcomes based on prior knowledge combined with new knowledge.	Predict different endings by rewriting events in the plot. Determine outcomes of character's actions in different historical settings.	Explore the effects of key changes or changes of modality, meter, style, and tempo on existing music.	Create multiple solutions to specific visual art problems. Change basic art elements: line, shape, color, value, texture, and space.	Create, plan, and organize responses to music, art, literature through movement. Change original meaning by altering dance elements.

Reaching Comprehension: Common Reading Strategies and Examples of Parallel Arts Strategies
(Continued)

Reading Strategy	In Reading	In Drama	In Music	In Visual Art	In Dance
Using imagery	Use their imaginations to create pictures in the mind about what they have read or studied and then communicate what they see.	Create a flowchart of events in a play. Imagine a play in a different time period. Paint a picture of character they study.	As they rehearse music, imagine elements of nature (birds soaring, a thunderstorm, etc) to transform note playing into music making.	Mindmap ideas for a work of art. Use a Venn diagram to compare and contrast the works of different artists. Design and paint a mural that depicts local history.	Video tape the movements of animals in order to stylistically dance their movements. Create shapes with their bodies as part of choreographing a dance.
Writing	Construct meaning through written expression. Reread and write about story or create a new story based on given story elements.	Write scripts, plays, and character lines. Reflect impressions or analysis in journals or in essays.	Compose and arrange music. Reflect evaluations of performances or write about music in journals for persuasive writing assignments.	Write about the expressive properties of art in journals and demonstrate the writing skills of voice and ideas.	Write out choreography of a dance by using Laban or self-created symbols. Write how social, cultural, and political aspects influence dance.
Retelling	Respond to stories by retelling, role playing, drawing pictures, and storyboards.	Read and retell plays or dramatic literature by discussion, role playing, writing and improvising.	Listen to and describe musical performance. Move to music, sight-read and reread for precision, improvise using an existing melodic or rhythmic motif.	Observe and describe visual art, discuss art critically, write about the properties of art. Create art in the style of a work by a famous artist.	Respond to dance by written or oral presentations. "Retell" a dance in student's own choice of movements.

From Dee Hansen. 2002. Part of tARgeTS. KSDE 9–12.

Listening, Viewing, Speaking Standards and Related Arts Matrix

Music	Listening	Viewing	Speaking	Information Retrieval	Audiovisual Products
Timbre (source) Intensity Pitch/harmony Duration Texture Form (repeat/contrast) Style	Elements ■ Timbre (source) ■ Intensity ■ Pitch/harmony ■ Duration ■ Texture ■ Form (repetition/contrast) ■ Style	■ Notation ■ Vocabulary ■ Historical photos or art ■ Live performances	■ Describe elements ■ Describe feelings ■ Perform ■ Improvise ■ Compose ■ Parodies ■ Rhymes, poems, haiku with music	■ Compare and contrast ■ Categorize ■ Record own music ■ Find recordings ■ Notate ■ Find videos ■ Live concerts	■ Ads or jingles ■ Parodies ■ Music videos ■ Critiques ■ Interviews ■ Music on synthesizer ■ Computer compositions ■ Edit sounds
Art Color Line Form Texture Contrast Perspective Organization Medium	■ Commentary ■ Interviews with artists ■ Follow instructions ■ Retell information	Elements ■ Color ■ Line ■ Form ■ Texture ■ Contrast ■ Perspective ■ Organization ■ Medium	■ Describe ■ Compare ■ Contrast ■ Instruct others ■ Define ■ Interpret ■ Critique	■ Library art ■ Internet samples ■ Visit Web sites ■ Contact museums ■ Create a display	■ Graphics ■ Clip art ■ Computer "paint" ■ Collage ■ Any art medium: draw, paint, sculpt, design, photograph, mat, arrange, edit images
Dance Weight (heavy-light) Space (direct-indirect) Time (sudden-sustain) Flow (bound-free) Planes (vertical, horizontal, saggital)	■ Interpret dance elements ■ Follow instrutions ■ Move to music ■ Interpret environmental sounds ■ Sequence	■ Mirror movements ■ Group choreography ■ View others dancing ■ View self—mirror ■ View	■ Describe ■ Compare ■ Contrast ■ Instruct others ■ Define ■ Interpret ■ Critique ■ Accompany movement with vocal output	■ "Notate" a dance ■ Video retrieval or editing ■ Interview ■ Film ■ Research the history of a dance or dancer	■ Create a dance video ■ Choreograph a dance, ■ Write directions for a learned dance ■ Create costumes or props for a dance
Drama Time (pace) Space (staging) Light/sound Voice/action Ensemble	■ Retell the story ■ Interpret a piece of music, nursery rhyme, poem, environmental sounds	■ Sets, costumes, character expressions	■ Voice, pacing, character development, fluency, focus, projection	■ Find primary sources ■ Research a character	■ Improvisation ■ Play writing ■ Costume, set, technical design ■ Advertising
Creative Writing Content/ideas Organization Voice Word choice Fluency Conventions	■ Respond to a story, music, or environmental sounds in writing	■ Illustrate a book, or write the story to a book of illustrations or photos	■ Interpretive reading, choral reading, rap	■ Research a person, place, or event for a written piece	■ Use a word processor, PowerPoint, etc.

From Elaine Bernstorf. Handout at a Kansas Speech-Language-Hearing Association Convention session, October 13, 2000.

Suggested adaptations for students in special education

The following narrative contains suggestions for adaptations that may be needed for special education students. In addition, students with English as a second language may also benefit from similar adaptations.

Definitions

Definitions and descriptions associated with special education terminology are continually being updated and changed. The federal law revised in July 1997 is the Individuals with Disabilities Education Act (IDEA)—Revised. Each state has its own State Plan for Special Education. A copy is always available in school district offices for special education. This document is the best source of information regarding directives for special education in any state. Descriptions of criteria for special education placement, descriptions of special education services, and procedures are included in this document. The music educator is encouraged to consult this document for specific information. Individual districts may also have working definitions for various special education offerings and may have specific documents to describe procedures for special education placement and services provided to students with disabilities. Music teachers are encouraged to consult these documents for specific definitions.

Music teachers are also encouraged to consult members of the child study team for information. The child study team generally includes the school psychologist, social worker, counselor, speech pathologist, nurse, and an administrator. Speech pathologists are excellent resources for music educators because they are familiar with auditory processing as well as speech and language disorders. These types of disorders may have the most impact on the music setting.

Characteristic behaviors

Students who have specific types of disorders may have characteristic behaviors. It is important that teachers avoid the tendency to stereotype students based on the students' label of "disability." For example, individual students with autism, hearing impairment, or mental retardation may respond similarly in certain situations even though their disorders are quite different in nature. The nature of each of these disorders requires the music teacher to reduce layers of stimuli to avoid auditory confusion or overstimulation. Structured and slower paced presentation of materials and use of multiple repetitions of activities would be appropriate. In addition, these students may need visual representations of information in order to learn concepts that are presented.

Music teachers may want to contact music professionals who work with students with disabilities on a regular basis. Another source of information is the local or state chapter of the Council for Exceptional Children. Finally, the reader is encouraged to search for Web sites using specific special education categories. Numerous societies and organizations for specific disabilities now exist. Many of these organizations have information on the World Wide Web. These sites generally provide address information and updates regarding new research for the disability. They also provide the most current definitions of the disorder and often describe treatment suggestions.

Adaptations to consider

1. Consider simplification of vocabulary.

Music experiences include the perception of sound. Specifically, these perceptions include the sound source (timbre or tone color), intensity (dynamics), frequency (pitch), duration (beat, meter, rhythm, tempo), structure (form), and number of sources (texture).

The inclusion of all musical concepts and elements from the standards are appropriate for all students. Some students may have difficulty with activities which require specific language or vocabulary skills. These students may need to experience musical elements through participatory (nonverbal) activities such as moving, playing instruments, and manipulating visuals of specific musical concepts rather than language specific activities such as singing difficult words or verbalizing with more difficult musical terms.

2. Provide alternate demonstrations of understanding.

For students with cognitive or language difficulties, authentic assessments of learning may include audio- or videotaping participation in music activities rather than written tests. A variety of activities for learning musical concepts and for demonstrating understanding should be included. Students should be given options for responding. Such options may include choosing between several visuals of pitch contours or rhythmic patterns rather than verbalizing "the melody ascends by steps" or even "the music goes up by steps." Some students are able to demonstrate understanding of musical concepts even when unable to verbalize understanding. It should be noted that some students may demonstrate or even verbalize understanding of concepts but not play or sing with great accuracy. Other students may have strong memory or performance skills and be able to respond with skill through rote learning but not be able to demonstrate understanding of the concepts related to such performances. It is important to separate "concept learning" from "performance skill" so that a complete picture of the student's musical learning is seen.

3. Consider cognitive abilities separately from physical or performance abilities.

When students demonstrate learning concerns and cognitive difficulties, it is important to simplify language and use very obvious examples of musical concepts. In addition, repetition of activities is needed for these students. Students with cognitive disabilities may need many repetitions to understand a concept or develop a skill. Some students need exact repetitions of an activity in order to understand a concept or develop a specific skill.

Other students need repetition through varied activities. For example, the student may need to experience the same concept through different behaviors. A younger or lower functioning student may need to learn a pitch concept such as moving by steps by playing step bells, pointing to visuals, singing and verbalizing "steps" using the same song for each activity. Repetition of the same concept using different behaviors assists students by providing different modality experiences (auditory, visual, and kinesthetic) that help students who may not integrate information. Such experiences also may assist students who find it difficult to generalize conceptual understanding to new situations. Some students need to experience a concept such as syncopation in several different contexts using the same behavior. For example, students may need to play syncopated patterns on the *guiro* when such patterns are heard in several different songs or instrumental examples. By demonstrating the same concept in multiple contexts, students may begin to generalize learning to new situations.

4. Begin with the concept that is most obvious.

Students who have disabilities may have difficulty with perception. Students with certain disabilities (hearing, vision, physical) may need specific adjustments in order to perceive the concept or skill that is being presented. For example, it may help to present musical examples in an a capella format before using an example that has a thicker texture or is more complex. It may be important to sequence activities so that the most obvious concept is taught first. It is important for the teacher to actually listen to recordings that will be used so that the most audible concept is taught first. At times, introducing a short lesson using the form of the music may help familiarize students with the sound of the music in a more general sense, before other lessons that focus on more specific or subtle concepts are introduced. It is important to consider which concept is most easily perceived in auditory musical examples. It is also important to consider which concept may be the most obvious in the written music (notation). Depending on whether a specific musical example is introduced through auditory or visual means may make a difference regarding the concept to be taught initially.

5. Assist students in translating information from one modality to another.

Some students experience learning disabilities in the areas of auditory perception or visual perception. It is important to provide multiple sources of information for these students. For example, students who have difficulty with auditory perception may actually be able to "hear" a repeated rhythm pattern (such as short, short, long) if the teacher points to a graphic representation of the pattern such as (— — ———). Other students may be able to hear sophisticated nuances in the music but need movement activities (such as Dalcroze movements or Kodály hand signs) to assist in "reading" music. These students may not associate the sound and symbol without some type of accompanying movement or positioning. The use of classroom, orchestral, band, and keyboard instruments may especially help these students. It may be important to introduce some students to instrumental music programs as early as possible so that they may "feel" the music as well as "hear" it or "see" it.

6. Structure for success.

Flexibility is the key when working with students of varying abilities. This is true for students in special education, students from varying cultures, and students of varying ages or abilities. For some students who have more "know-how" than they have "know that," it may be beneficial to begin with auditory and/or participatory examples. For students who are better describers of music than performers, the more successful experiences may begin with explanations, visuals, or even notational examples of a concept. Only later may these students want to "perform" or attempt to demonstrate the concept through playing or singing.

Some students learn only when a musical concept is demonstrated as part of a whole piece of music. These students may need to have recordings of the music so that there is a complete context. Other students may need to experience specific concepts or patterns in isolation. They may need to see, hear, or play short sections or patterns out of the context of the whole piece so that they can manipulate the tempo or have a specific focus on the concept without the confusion of other sound sources.

7. Monitor students and ask for suggestions.

Teachers should teach a variety of musical concepts using excellent musical examples. A teacher who has carefully planned is able to monitor student responses and make adjustments during the lesson. Students with disabilities may actually indicate what they need to be successful. Students who need visual aids may ask if there is a picture or graphic representation (icon) of the pattern. Other students may ask to "hear" a specific passage that they have difficulty perceiving from the notation. Still other students may ask, "Can we play it?" so that they have an opportunity to experience the concept through a kinesthetic activity. It is appropriate and often important to ask students who have disabilities to suggest ways that they learn best. Most students want to learn and want to be successful. If asked, they will give suggestions for activities or aids that work best for them.

Let students who have physical disabilities choose their own way to move or play an instrument. Always demonstrate the correct way to move or play, but then allow students to demonstrate in the ways that are best for them. A student may hold, strike, strum, or blow an instrument in a way that seems unconventional or even incorrect. However, students most often do their best to move, play, or sing in the way that either (1) best demonstrates their understanding of the concept or (2) produces the most pleasant musical sound. By allowing the student to have opportunities to try different holding techniques, etc. the teacher shows that he or she values that student and welcomes the student's participation in the school music program.

8. Take time to teach through conceptual activities; avoid learning skills by rote.

When students with disabilities experience difficulty, avoid the move to rote learning. This is a caution that must be discussed. Students who are taught using rote methods may always ask for the auditory example. If students have not learned to translate musical notation into graphic icons, into specific movements (such as Kodály hand signs), or into specific hand positions on an instrument they may always ask, "Can you play it for us?"

Given the time pressures and individual differences of students, it may seem expedient to "give them a little help with the piano" or "sing along with the students to make sure they are getting it right," or "play along so that it sounds better." While these techniques may seem to help in the short term so that students can produce pleasant and accurate sounds for a school program, we must always have the goal of assisting students to develop musical independence. Students do not write perfect language compositions or read orally with perfect intonation and pronunciation without many years of experience. Reading, language, math, and science programs do not use rote imitation throughout the school career to develop "perfect" performances. We must beware of sacrificing lifelong learning and independence by avoiding mistakes or less than perfect performances.

9. Don't assume that students with disabilities have a short attention span.

Students with disabilities may appear to have a short attention span because they are unable to process the information as it is being presented. If students have an auditory processing or language processing disorder, they may appear to become distracted or inattentive if too much information is being presented in an aural or oral format. These students may try to move as a response to the music in order to create their own kinesthetic input when they cannot process the auditory-only format. Teachers may avoid the use of visuals and movement activities because they think that students will become distracted. However, when students are given structured input using multisensory examples of musical concepts, they frequently are able to focus their attention through their learning-strength areas, thereby actually enhancing their ability to pay attention.

The resulting positive experience generally encourages the students and enhances their ability to attend. A caution is in order. Students with disabilities may not be able to easily assimilate new information. They may not be able to respond as quickly as students who do not have disabilities. As a result, they may become frustrated and avert their attention to avoid the feeling of frustration. If students appear to have a short attention span it is advisable to slow the pace of the presentation, adjust the presentation to include visuals and representative movements to enhance the aural musical stimuli, and increase the number of repetitions of activities. Often, these adjustments will give the students a more successful experience with the musical activities and result in increased motivation and participation.

10. Take the time to ask other professionals for suggestions.

Time is always short for music educators. However, taking the time to gain some knowledge of a child's disability can make a significant difference in the classroom. By knowing more about a child's difficulties, adaptations can be made to avoid frustration. The use of movements to represent musical concepts can give students who have language or reading problems ways to respond nonverbally. The use of tactile aids such as puff paints, pipe cleaners, or other three-dimensional representations of sound may help students with visual perception problems.

Students who exhibit various types of behavior disorders may need specific behavior plans. Students with health impairments may need different types of adaptations. Each student who is served by a special education program has an Individualized Education Plan (IEP). In the federal law called IDEA, the IEP is defined as "a written statement for each child with a disability that is developed, reviewed, and revised in accordance with section 614 (d)." Section 614 (d) describes all of the requirements for any IEP. One of these requirements is the inclusion of "a statement of measurable annual goals, including benchmarks or short-term objectives." By taking a few minutes to read the goals and objectives for a student who may be having difficulty in the music class, the music teacher may find suggestions that can be implemented to enhance the student's learning in the music setting. Special education and support personnel are aware of the benefits of music experiences for students who have special needs. Let them help you provide the best learning opportunities possible for each student.

From Elaine Bernstorf. 1998. Part of the Kansas Curricular Standards for Music Education. Available online at www.ksde.org/outcomes/music3.html.

Curriculum Standards

The Kansas Music Curriculum Framework—Prekindergarten
NATIONAL CONTENT STANDARD 1: Singing and playing instruments

Elements	
	Achievement Standard a: use their voices expressively as they speak, chant, and sing *Exit Outcome* The student will: 1. increase variety and appropriateness of vocal expression in a variety of settings using developmentally appropriate vocal production.
Timbre	*Sequential Outcomes* The student will: 1. imitate environmental or animal sounds. 2. use vocal sounds to accompany routine activities. 3. use singing quality spontaneously during play. 4. use varying vocal timbres to express ideas and feelings. 5. Exit Outcome.
Expression: Dynamics	The student will: 1. produce contrasting loud and soft sounds. 2. produce a continuum of dynamic levels. 3. use varying vocal dynamic levels to express ideas and feelings. 4. Exit Outcome.

Elements	
	Achievement Standard b: sing a variety of simple songs in various keys, meters, and genres, alone and with a group, becoming increasingly accurate in rhythm and pitch *Exit Outcome* The student will: 1. sing familiar songs to express ideas, feelings, and events using developmentally and individually appropriate vocal skills.
Pitch	*Sequential Outcomes* The student will: 1. create/use vocal inflection in play or directed activities. 2. use pitch in spontaneous songs/vocal play. 3. gain some control of pitch and match repeated pitch patterns with increasing accuracy. 4. create repetitive vocal sound patterns (personal/group vocal routines). 5. imitate song phrases with increasing accuracy. 6. sing parts of familiar songs with increasing accuracy. 7. sing complete familiar songs. 8. Exit Outcome.
Time	The student will: 1. control production of recurring vocal sounds to accompany play or events. 2. begin to organize duration of vocal sounds to create approximations of beat, meter, or rhythms. 3. imitate vocal expressions of beat, meter, or rhythms with increasing accuracy. 4. initiate vocal expressions of beat, meter or rhythms in varying contexts at the appropriate time. 5. use duration in vocal expressions in varying contexts with increasing accuracy and vocal skill.

Elements	
	Achievement Standard c: experiment with a variety of instruments and other sound sources *Exit Outcome* The student will: 1. demonstrate understanding of cause and effect; realize that he or she is in control of the sound source and manner of production within individual fine motor skill ability.
Timbre	*Sequential Outcomes* The student will: 1. play instruments or produce sounds in varying contexts, i.e., to accompany stories, role play, body movement/sounds (clapping, tapping, stomping, patchen). 2. choose appropriate sound sources to illustrate songs, stories, ideas, and feelings in individual and group settings. 3. Exit Outcome.
Texture	The student will: 1. use instruments and sound sources with intent to produce varying textures. 2. Exit Outcome.
Articulation	The student will: 1. imitate varying methods of playing on instruments or other sound sources. 2. choose appropriate articulation/manner of playing instruments to illustrate songs, stores, ideas, and feelings in individual and group settings. 3. Exit Outcome.
Dynamics	The student will: 1. produce contrasting dynamic levels (loud-soft). 2. imitate varying dynamic levels from adult model. 3. produce varying dynamic levels on a continuum appropriate to the context. 4. Exit Outcome.

Elements	
	Achievement Standard d: play simple melodies and accompaniments on instruments *Exit Outcome* The student will: 1. play simple melodies and accompaniments on instruments with increasing accuracy and independence using individually and developmentally appropriate fine motor skills.
Pitch/ Melody	*Sequential Outcomes* The student will: 1. explore pitched instruments. 2. explore/imitate simple pitch patterns. 3. perform simple pitch patterns/melodies with assistance or adult model. 4. perform simple pitch patterns/melodies independently with increasing accuracy. 5. Exit Outcome.
Pitch/ Harmony	The student will: 1. explore harmonic expressions in specific contexts (i.e., pentatonic, whole tone, bourdon). 2. imitate harmonic expressions with adult model. 3. play simple harmonic accompaniments with increasing accuracy on appropriate instruments. 4. Exit Outcome.

The Kansas Music Curriculum Framework—Prekindergarten
NATIONAL CONTENT STANDARD 2: Creating music

Elements	
	Achievement Standard a: improvise songs to accompany their play activities *Exit Outcome* The student will: 1. improvise songs using one or more musical elements to accompany a variety of play activities.
All Elements	*Sequential Outcomes* The student will: 1. explore musical elements spontaneously during play: tempo (fast, slow, faster, slower); dynamics (loud, soft, getting louder, getting softer); articulation (heavy, light, smooth, legato, staccato); melody (up, down, step, skip, same); rhythm (short, long). 2. create musical sounds using one or more elements spontaneously during play. 3. create spontaneous music using patterns (i.e., melodic or rhythmic patterns, motifs, phrases, short songs during play). 4. create musical patterns during play that are purposeful, thematic, or convey complete ideas (songs). 5. Exit Outcome.
	Achievement Standard b: improvise instrumental accompaniments to songs, recorded selections, stories, and poems *Exit Outcome* The student will: 1. improvise own instrumental accompaniment to enhance songs, recorded selections, stories, and poems of varying styles, genres, or cultures alone or in a group.
All Elements	*Sequential Outcomes* The student will: 1. explore instrumental musical sounds during various activities (songs, recorded selections, stories, and poems). 2. create instrumental sounds (spontaneously or with assistance) to accompany specific ideas or feelings during various activities. 3. use instrumental sounds purposefully to accompany specific songs, recorded selections, stories, or poems individually or as part of a group. 4. improvise spontaneously on instruments in a structured music setting (i.e., using pentatonic, whole-tone, or non-pitched instruments) to "accompany" activities. 5. improvise using instruments to express specific musical ideas as accompaniments to songs, recorded selections, stories, and poems (i.e., non-pitched accompaniments, rhythm pattern given but pitches improvised, or pitches given but rhythm improvised). 6. Exit Outcome.

Elements	
	Achievement Standard c: create short pieces of music using voices, instruments, and other sound sources *Exit Outcome* The student will: 1. use/arrange/sequence short patterns/sections of music (repetitions, contrasts) to create short pieces of music using voices, instruments, and other sound sources at individual and developmentally appropriate levels.
Style	*Sequential Outcomes* The student will: 1. explore sounds to express ideas, feelings, and basic concepts. 2. imitate sound patterns to express ideas, feelings, and basic concepts with modeling only or assistance as needed. 3. play known sound patterns to express ideas, feelings, and basic concepts using voices, instruments, and other sources. 4. create own sound stories using spontaneous and known sound/music patterns to express ideas, feelings, and basic concepts. 5. create short sound/music stories (individually or as a group) that reflect a song structure (beginning, middle, and end; AB; rondo) with assistance as needed. Example: Teacher plays a pattern, child or children play responses to create a "song" or "piece." 6. Exit Outcome.
	Achievement Standard d: invent and use original graphic or symbolic systems to represent vocal and instrumental sounds and musical ideas *Exit Outcome* The student will: 1. create or draw known or original graphic representations, manipulatives, models, or symbols to represent vocal and instrumental sounds and musical ideas using a variety of media appropriate to developmental and individual skill levels.
All Elements	*Sequential Outcomes* The student will: 1. demonstrate awareness of visual graphics or manipulatives used to represent sound or no sound. 2. demonstrate awareness of visual graphics or manipulatives used to represent the sound source as it is heard. 3. match or choose prepared graphics or manipulatives to represent vocal or instrumental sounds or musical ideas (with modeling or assistance as needed). 4. draw own graphics or choose/arrange manipulatives to represent musical ideas, feelings, or elements. 5. respond to symbols (simple and developmentally appropriate) paired with or representing known musical elements and graphic/manipulatives. 6. create or draw known or original graphic representations, manipulatives, models, or symbols to represent vocal and instrumental sounds and musical ideas. 7. Exit Outcome.

The Kansas Music Curriculum Framework—Prekindergarten
NATIONAL CONTENT STANDARD 3: Responding to music

Elements	
	Achievement Standard a: identify the sources of a wide variety of sounds *Exit Outcome* The student will: 1. associate a specific movement, picture, graphic representation, or word as a representation of individual sounds.
Timbre	*Sequential Outcomes* The student will: 1. respond to presence or absence of sound. 2. respond differently to different sounds. 3. choose movements, pictures, or graphic representations to represent sounds. 4. Exit Outcome.
	Achievement Standard b: respond through movement to music of various tempos, meters, dynamics, modes, genres, and styles to express what they hear and feel in works of music *Exit Outcome* The student will: 1. move independently and appropriately to demonstrate what they hear and feel in response to examples of various musical elements in music of varying genres and styles using individual and developmentally appropriate gross and fine motor skills.
Form	*Sequential Outcomes* The student will: 1. respond to presence or absence of musical sounds. 2. respond differently to changes in musical elements (timbre, tempo, dynamics, pitch, duration, harmony). 3. imitate models of movement to demonstrate repetition and contrast of musical elements. 4. choose representative movements to demonstrate repetition and contrast of musical elements. 5. create own movements to demonstrate repetition and contrast of musical elements. 6. Exit Outcome.

Elements	
	Achievement Standard c: participate freely in music activities *Exit Outcome* The student will: 1. participate freely (independently or with a group) in music activities representing a variety of styles or genres at appropriate and individual skill levels.
Expression	*Sequential Outcomes* The student will: 1. respond to presence or absence of music. 2. respond in varying ways to music in the environment. 3. explore musical activities in the environment by choice (exploratory play). 4. respond to/imitate music and musicians in a group setting (parallel play). 5. respond to specific music activities or a model in a group setting (associative play). 6. participate as a member of a music making group, with assistance as needed. 7. participate freely in a variety of music activities independently or with a group (cooperative play). 8. Exit Outcome.

The Kansas Music Curriculum Framework—Prekindergarten
NATIONAL CONTENT STANDARD 4: Understanding music

Elements	
	Achievement Standard a: use their own vocabulary and standard music vocabulary to describe voices, instruments, music notation, and music of various genres, styles, and periods from diverse cultures *Exit Outcome* The student will: 1. use personal and standard music vocabulary to describe music qualities in varying musical contexts.
All Elements	*Sequential Outcomes* The student will: 1. produce a communicative intent (vocalization, gesture, physical contact) in response to music. 2. produce a consistent communicative intent (vocalization, gesture, physical contact, utterance, word) in response to music. 3. use consistent communicative intents or own vocabulary to express personal ideas, feelings, and understandings about music. 4. use their own vocabulary to describe musical ideas, feelings, and concepts. 5. show understanding of modeled music vocabulary in response to specific musical examples. 6. use modeled vocabulary to describe musical examples. 7. show understanding of (developmentally appropriate) standard vocabulary in response to specific musical examples. 8. use standard vocabulary to describe musical examples of various genres, styles, and periods from diverse cultures. 9. Exit Outcome.

Elements	
	Achievement Standard b: sing, play instruments, move or verbalize to demonstrate awareness of the elements of music and changes in their usage *Exit Outcome* The student will: 1. use personal and standard music vocabulary (appropriate to developmental level, language level, and culture) to describe music qualities in varying musical contexts.
All Elements	*Sequential Outcomes* The student will: 1. respond (vocalization, gesture, physical contact, body sound, instrument sound) to obvious changes in musical elements. 2. produce a consistent response (vocalization, gesture, physical contact, utterance, word, singing response, instrumental pattern) to represent changes in musical elements. 3. respond in a variety of ways to express personal ideas, feelings, and understandings about musical elements. 4. imitate an adult model (singing, playing, moving, manipulating objects or verbalizing) in response to elements of music and their changes in usage. 5. respond independently (sing, play, move, manipulate objects, or verbalize) to describe musical ideas, feelings, and concepts. 6. show understanding of musical elements (developmentally appropriate) and changes in their usage through a variety of musical responses individually and in a group. 7. Exit Outcome.
	Achievement Standard c: demonstrate an awareness of music as a part of daily life *Exit Outcome* The student will: 1. respond to, ask for, choose, or make appropriate music during daily activities and routines in familiar locations.
Style	*Sequential Outcomes* The student will: 1. respond to presence or absence of sound. 2. respond to presence or absence of music in the environment. 3. seek musical toys or sources of music in the environment or ask for music. 4. associate specific musical examples with activities, routines, or locations in the environment. 5. choose appropriate music for activities, routines, or locations in the environment. 6. associate appropriate musical examples with varying styles, genres, cultures, or events. 7. Exit Outcome.

Bibliography

Allen, K. E., and L. Marotz. 1994. *Developmental profiles: Pre-birth through eight.* 2nd ed. New York: Delmar Publishers.

Andress, B., ed. 1989. *Promising practices: Prekindergarten music education.* Reston, VA: MENC.

Andress, B. L., and L. M. Walker. 1992. *Readings in early childhood music education.* Reston, VA: MENC.

Bruce, C., ed. 1998. *Young children and the arts: Making creative connections.* Washington DC: Arts Education Partnership.

Consortium of National Arts Education Associations. 1994. *National standards for arts education: What every young American should know and be able to do in the arts.* Reston, VA: MENC.

MENC: The National Association for Music Education. 1994. *Opportunity-to-learn: Standards for music instruction, Grades PreK–12.* Reston, VA: MENC.

MENC: The National Association for Music Education. 1994. *The school music program: A new vision: The K–12 national standards, PreK standards, and what they mean to music educators.* Reston, VA: MENC.

Pica, R. 1995. *Experiences in movement with music, activities and theory.* New York: Delmar Publishers.

Olathe School District USD #233 Olathe, KS
3rd Grade General Music

Program Goal 3.1: Singing, alone and with others, a varied repertoire of music.

Outcomes The learner will:	Indicators/Objectives The learner will:	Key Content/Key Ideas	Instructional Strategies	Assessment
3.1.1 Sing with appropriate posture.	A. Use appropriate posture for singing.	■ Straight back, edge of seat, both feet flat on floor	■ Teacher modeling ■ Hand signs ■ Posture levels ■ Pitch ladder ■ Mirroring activities ■ Call & response ■ Listening examples ■ Small groups	■ Performance assessment ■ Rubric ■ Peer feedback ■ Teacher observation ■ Video tape ■ Written assessment ■ Self-assessment
3.1.2 Sing with accurate pitch.	A. Independently sing simple songs with accurate pitch.	■ Head tone, accurate pitch		
3.1.3 Sing musical phrases.	A. Show the contour of phrases while singing.	■ Singing phrases with sustained breathing		
3.1.4 Sing songs in simple harmony.	A. Differentiate between unison, and harmony. B. Sing simple types of harmony.	■ Vocal ostinatos ■ Ostinato accompaniments ■ Rounds ■ Echo harmony		

Program Goal 3.2: Performing on instruments, alone and with others, a varied repertoire of music.

Outcomes The learner will:	Indicators/Objectives The learner will:	Key Content/Key Ideas	Instructional Strategies	Assessment
3.2.1 Perform short melodies.	A. Play melodic patterns.	■ Play patterns with 3–5 pitches	■ Teacher modeling ■ Body percussion ■ Barred instruments ■ Boomwhackers ■ Small groups rotating	■ Performance assessment ■ Rubric ■ Peer feedback ■ Teacher observation ■ Videotape ■ Written assessment ■ Self-assessment
3.2.2 Perform accompaniments on a variety of instruments.	A. Play an ostinato to accompany a song.	■ Level bordun ■ Simple appegiated bordun		

Program Goal 3.3: Improvising melodies, variations, and accompaniments.

Outcomes The learner will:	Indicators/Objectives The learner will:	Key Content/Key Ideas	Instructional Strategies	Assessment
3.3.1 Echo rhythmic patterns.	A. Echo rhythmic phrases of 8 to 12 beats.	■ Echo: rhythm, style, dynamics, tempo	■ Call & response ■ Question/answer	■ Performance assessment ■ Teacher observation

Program Goal 3.4: Composing and arranging music within specified guidelines.				
Outcomes The learner will:	Indicators/Objectives The learner will:	Key Content/Key Ideas	Instructional Strategies	Assessment
3.4.1 Create a rhythmic composition or accompaniment.	A. Vary the rhythm of a known piece. A. Create a simple rhythmic interlude or ostinato to a known piece. B. Create a simple rhythmic composition or accompaniment.	▪ Rhythms ▪ Note values ▪ Ostinato ▪ Interlude ▪ Accompaniment vs. melody ▪ Composition	▪ Listening examples ▪ Class examples ▪ Small group examples ▪ Composition criteria	▪ Performance assessment ▪ Rubric ▪ Checklist ▪ Videotape ▪ Self-assessment

Program Goal 3.5: Reading and notating music.				
Outcomes The learner will:	Indicators/Objectives The learner will:	Key Content/Key Ideas	Instructional Strategies	Assessment
3.5.1 Demonstrate rhythm reading skills.	A. Read, notate, and perform rhythms.	▪ Quarter note, quarter rest, eighth note pairs, half note, half rest, dotted half note in 2/4, 3/4, and 4/4 meters	▪ Sight-reading examples ▪ Games ▪ Flashcards ▪ Magnet/felt boards ▪ Floor staff ▪ Dry erase boards ▪ Music literature ▪ Student conducting ▪ Daily practice	▪ Listening assessment ▪ Written assessment ▪ Teacher observation ▪ Application through games ▪ Performance assessment
3.5.2 Demonstrate note reading skills on the staff.	A. Identify the musical alphabet. B. Identify treble clef lines and spaces.	▪ Application of musical alphabet to staff—bottom to top, left to right		
3.5.3 Identify symbols and traditional musical terms.	A. Identify music symbols and terms.	▪ Staff, treble clef, f, p, <, >, measure, bar line, double bar line, repeat sign, fermata, slur, staccato, tie, D.S., D.C., legato, allegro, and largo		

Program Goal 3.6: Listening to, analyzing and describing music.

Outcomes The learner will:	Indicators/Objectives The learner will:	Key Content/Key Ideas	Instructional Strategies	Assessment
3.6.1 Identify simple musical forms.	A. Identify ABA form.	■ Same/different ■ Same/similar ■ Phrases/sections	■ Listening examples ■ Movement ■ Manipulating shapes ■ Word wall ■ Sound bank ■ Matching pictures to sounds ■ Games ■ Attend a concert ■ KWL ■ Web mapping ■ Live demonstration	■ Listening assessment ■ Written assessment ■ Journaling
3.6.2 Use appropriate terms when describing music.	A. Use musical terminology discriminately.	■ Piano, forte, melody, unison, ostinato, crescendo, decrescendo, tempo		
3.6.3 Identify a variety of instruments.	A. Identify characteristics of orchestral families and instruments.	■ Woodwind—flute, clarinet, oboe, bassoon; Brass—trumpet, French horn, trombone, tuba; Strings—violin, viola, cello, bass; Percussion—timpani, snare drum, cymbals, bass drum		

Program Goal 3.7: Evaluating music and music performed.

Outcomes The learner will:	Indicators/Objectives The learner will:	Key Content/Key Ideas	Instructional Strategies	Assessment
3.7.1 Evaluate a music performance or product.	A. Evaluate a performance or composition.	■ Use student/teacher-generated criteria	■ T-chart ■ Listening selections ■ Videos ■ Venn diagram ■ Concept web	■ Rubric ■ Journaling ■ Self assessment

Program Goal 3.9: Understanding music in relation to history and culture.

Outcomes The learner will:	Indicators/Objectives The learner will:	Key Content/Key Ideas	Instructional Strategies	Assessment
3.9.1 Identify the role of music in our culture.	A. Identify/describe the genre or style of music in our daily lives (i.e., classical, march, pop, folk).	■ Instrument timbres ■ Musical style ■ Music written for a specific purpose	■ Expository reading ■ Powerpoint – o-drive ■ Videos ■ Icons ■ Venn diagram ■ KWL ■ QAR ■ Web mapping ■ Story maps	■ Journaling ■ Written assessment ■ Listening assessment ■ Writing
3.9.2 Identify music from various genres and historical periods.	A. Listen to and identify examples of music, instruments, and composers of the Baroque era.	■ Bach ■ Handel		

Olathe School District #233
3rd Grade Objectives/Key Content at a Glance

#1—Singing	#2—Playing Instruments	#3—Improvising	#4—Composing
■ use appropriate posture for singing ■ independently sing simple songs with accurate pitch ■ show the contour of phrases while singing ■ differentiate between unison and harmony ■ sing simple types of hamony	■ play melodic patterns of 3 to 5 pitches ■ play a level bordun ostinato or simple arpeggiated bordun ostinato to accompany a song	■ echo rhythmic phrases of 8 to 12 beats	■ vary the rhythm of a known piece ■ create a simple rhythmic interlude or ostinato to a known piece ■ create a simple rhythmic composition or accompaniment

#5—Reading/Notating	#6—Listening/Analyzing	#7—Evaluating	#8—Relating Disciplines	#9—History/Culture
■ read, notate and perform rhythms using: quarter note, quarter rest, eighth note pairs, half note, half rest, dotted half note in 2/4, 3/4, and 4/4 ■ identify the musical alphabet ■ identify treble clef lines and spaces ■ identify music symbols and terms: staff, treble clef, f, p, <, >, measure, bar line, double bar line, repeat sign, fermata, slur, staccato, tie, D.S., D.C., legato, allegro, and largo	■ identify ABA form ■ discriminately use the following musical terminology: piano, forte, melody, unison, ostinato, crescendo, decrescendo, tempo ■ identify characteristics of orchestral families and instruments: woodwind—flute, clarinet, oboe, basoon, brass—trumpet, French horn, trombone, tuba, string—violin, viola, cello, bass, percussion—timpani, snare drum, cymbals, and bass drum	■ evaluate a performance or composition using student/teacher-generated criteria		■ identify/describe the genre or style of music in our daily lives (i.e., classical, march, pop, folk) ■ listen to and identify examples of music, instruments, and composers of the Baroque era (i.e., Bach, Handel)

Resources

Arts and integrating arts in the curriculum

Andrews, Laura J., and Patricia E. Sink. 2002. *Integrating music and reading instruction: Teaching strategies for upper-elementary grades.* Reston, VA: MENC.

Beaty, Janice J. 1977. *Building bridges with multicultural picture books for children 3–5.* Upper Saddle River, NJ: Merrill / Prentice Hall.

Blecher, Sharon, and Kathy Jaffee. 1998. *Weaving in the arts.* Portsmouth, NH: Heinemann.

Boston, Bruce O. 1996. *Connections: The arts and the integration of the high school curriculum.* New York: The College Board Publications Department.

Brewer, Chris, and Don G. Campbell. 1991. *Rhythms of learning: Creative tools for developing lifelong skills.* Tucson, AZ: Zephyr Press.

Burnaford, Gail, Arnold Aprill, and Cynthia Weiss, eds. 2001. *Renaissance in the classroom: Arts integration and meaningful learning.* Mahwah, NJ: Lawrence Erlbaum Associates.

Consortium of National Arts Education Associations. 1994. *National Standards for Arts Education.* Reston, VA: MENC.

Cornett, Claudia E. 2003. *Creating meaning through literature and the arts.* 2nd ed.

Upper Saddle River, New Jersey: Merrill / Prentice-Hall.

Dodge, Diane Trister, Laura J. Colker, and Cate Heroman. 2002. *The creative curriculum: Connecting content, teaching, and learning.* Washington DC: Teaching Strategies.

Donohue, Keith, ed. 1997. *Imagine! Introducing your child to the arts.* Washington DC: National Endowment for the Arts.

Fiske, Edward B., ed. 1999. *Champions of change: The impact of the arts on learning.* Washington DC: Arts Education Partnership and the President's Committee on the Arts and the Humanities.

Flohr, John W. 2004. *Musical lives of young children.* Upper Saddle River, NJ: Prentice-Hall.

Gardner, Howard. 1990. *Art education and human development.* Los Angeles: The Getty Center for Education in the Arts.

Getty Center for Education in the Arts. 1993. *Perspectives on education reform: Arts education as catalyst.* Santa Monica, CA: Getty Center for Education in the Arts.

Goldberg, Merryl. 1997. *Arts and learning: An integrated approach to teaching and learning in multicultural and multilingual settings.* New York: Longman / Addison Wesley.

Harris, Theodore L., and Richard E. Hodges, eds. 1995. *The literacy dictionary: The vocabulary of reading and writing.* Newark, DE: International Reading Association.

Hillman, Grady. 1996. *Artists in the community: Training artists to work in alternative settings.* Washington DC: Americans for the Arts and the Institute for Community Development and the Arts.

Hirsh-Pasek, Kathy, and Roberta Michnick Golinkoff, with Diane Eyer. 2003. *Einstein never used flash cards.* New York: Rodale.

Hyerle, David. 1996. *Visual tools for constructing knowledge.* Alexandria, VA: Association for Supervision and Curriculum Development.

Longley, Laura, ed. 1999. *Gaining the arts advantage: Lessons from school districts that value arts education.* Washington DC: President's Committee on the Arts and Humanities and Arts Education Partnership.

Mantione, Roberta D., and Sabine Snead. 2003. *Weaving through words: Using the arts to teach reading comprehension strategies.* Newark, DE: International Reading Association.

McCarthy, Bernice. 2000. *About learning.* Wauconda, IL: About Learning.

Piazza, Carolyn L. 1999. *Multiple forms of literacy: Teaching literacy and the arts.* Upper Saddle River, NJ: Prentice-Hall.

Prince, Eileen S. 2002. *Art matters: Strategies, ideas, and activities to strengthen learning across the curriculum.* Tucson, AZ: Zephyr Press.

Remer, Jane. 1996. *Beyond enrichment: Building effective arts partnerships with schools and your community.* Washington DC: American Council for the Arts.

Richards, Janet C. 2003. *Integrating multiple literacies in K–8 classrooms: Cases, commentaries, and practical applications.* Mahwah, NJ: Lawrence Erlbaum Associates.

Task Force on Children's Learning and the Arts: Birth to Age Eight. 1998. *Young children and the arts: Making creative connections.* Washington DC: Arts Education Partnership.

Welch, Nancy, ed. 1995. *Schools, communities, and the arts: A research compendium.* Tempe, AZ: Arizona Board of Regents.

Multiple intelligences and brain research

Armstrong, Thomas. 1993. *7 kinds of smart: Identifying and developing your many intelligences.* New York: Plume.

Armstrong, Thomas. 1994. *Multiple intelligences in the classroom.* Alexandria, VA: Association for Supervision and Curriculum Development.

Dennison, Paul E., and Gail E. Dennison. 1989. *Brain gym: Teacher's edition.* Rev. ed. Ventura, CA: Edu-Kinesthetics.

Gardner, Howard. 1993. *Frames of mind: The theory of multiple intelligences.* 2nd ed. New York: HarperCollins.

Gardner, Howard. 1993. *Multiple intelligences: The theory in practice.* New York: Basic Books / HarperCollins.

Hubert, Bill. 2001. *Bal-A-Vis-X: Rhythmic balance/auditory/vision exercises for brain and brain-body integration.* Wichita, KS: Bal-A-Vis-X.

Jensen, Eric. 2001. *Arts with the brain in mind.* Alexandria, VA: Association for Supervision and Curriculum Development.

Lazear, David. 2003. *Eight ways of teaching: The artistry of teaching with multiple intelligences.* Andover, MA: Skylight.

Wolfe, Patricia. 2001. *Brain matters: Translating research into classroom practice.* Alexandria, VA: Association for Supervision and Curriculum Development.

Writing

Bromley, Karen, Linda Irwin DeVitis, and Marcia Modlo. 1999. *50 graphic organizers for reading, writing, and more.* New York: Scholastic.

Kemper, Dave, Patrick Sebranek, and Verne Meyer. 1998. *All write: A student handbook for writing and learning.* Wilmington, MA: Great Source Education Group / Houghton Mifflin.

McCarthy, Tara. 1998. *Descriptive writing.* New York: Scholastic.

McCarthy, Tara. 1998. *Narrative writing.* New York: Scholastic.

McCarthy, Tara. 1998. *Persuasive writing.* New York: Scholastic.

Neuman, Susan B., Carol Copple, and Sue Bredekamp. 2000. *Learning to read and write: Developmentally appropriate practices for young children.* Washington DC: National Association for the Education of Young Children.

Sebranek, Patrick, Dave Kemper, and Verne Meyer. 1999. *Write source 2000: A guide to writing, thinking, and learning.* Wilmington, MA: Great Source Education Group / Houghton Mifflin.

Schickedanz, Judith A. 1986. *More than the ABCs: The early stages of reading and writing.* Washington DC: National Association for the Education of Young Children.

Journals and magazines

Teaching Artist Journal. Mahwah, NJ: Lawrence Erlbaum Associates.

Scripp, Larry, ed. *The New England Conservatory Journal for Learning through Music.* Boston, MA: New England Conservatory.

Videotapes

The arts and children: A success story. 1996. Washington DC: Arts Education Partnership.

Arts for life. 1990. Los Angeles: Getty Center for Education in the Arts.

Teaching in and through the arts. 1995. Los Angeles: Getty Center for Education in the Arts.

Zike, Dinah. n.d. *How to use Dinah Zike's big book of books.* San Antonio, TX: Dinah-Mite Activities.

Children's books

Andrews-Goebel, Nancy. *The pot that Juan built.* New York: Lee and Low Books.

Bahti, Mark. 1996. *Pueblo stories and storytellers.* Tucson, AZ: Treasure Chest Books.

Bang, Molly. 2000. *Picture this: How pictures work.* New York: SeaStar Books.

Banyai, Istvan. 1995. *Zoom.* New York: Puffin Books / Penguin Putnam.

Christelow, Eileen. 1995. *What do authors do?* New York: Clarion Books / Houghton Mifflin.

Christelow, Eileen. 1999. *What do illustrators do?* New York: Clarion Books / Houghton Mifflin.

Cooper, Elisha. 2001. *Dance!* New York: Greenwillow Books / HarperCollins.

Grimes, Nikki. 1999. *My man blue.* New York: Dial Books for Young Readers / Penguin Putnam.

Hoberman, Mary Ann. 2001. *You read to me, I'll read to you.* Boston: Little, Brown and Company.

Janeczko, Paul, ed. 2002. *Seeing the blue between: Advice and inspiration for young poets.* Cambridge, MA: Candlewick Press.

Mariotti, Mario. 1988. *Hanimations.* New York: Kane/Miller.

Medearis, Angela Shelf. 2000. *Seven spools of thread: A Kwanzaa story.* Morton Grove, IL: Albert Whitman and Company.

Jaffe, Nina, and Steve Zeitlin. 1998. *The cow of no color: Riddle stories and justice tales from around the world.* New York: Henry Holt and Company.

Lionni, Leo. 1959. *Little blue and little yellow.* New York: HarperCollins.

Raczka, Bob. 2002. *No one saw: Ordinary things through the eyes of an artist.* Brookfield, CT: The Millbrook Press.

Raczka, Bob. 2003. *Art is ... .* Brookfield, CT: The Millbrook Press.

Schick, Eleanor. 1992. *I have another language: The language is dance.* Orlando, FL: Harcourt Brace and Company.

Tirabosco, Tom. 2001. *At the same time.* New York: Kane/Miller.

Yolen, Jane, and Heidi Elisabet Yolen Stemple. 1999. *The Mary Celeste: An unsolved mystery from history.* New York: Simon and Schuster.

Performing arts

Benzwie, Teresa. 1987. *A moving experience: Dance for lovers of children and the child within.* Tucson, AZ: Zephyr Press.

Birch, Carol L. 2000. *The whole story handbook: Using imagery to complete the story experience.* Little Rock, AR: August House Publishers.

Blevins, Wiley. 1999. *Phonemic awareness songs and rhymes.* New York: Scholastic Books.

Campbell, Don G. 1992. *100 ways to improve teaching using your voice and music.* Tucson, AZ: Zephyr Press.

MENC. 1999. *Music makes the difference: Programs and partnerships.* Reston, VA: MENC.

Fitzpatrick, Jo. 1997. *Phonemic awareness: Playing with sounds to strengthen beginning reading skills.* Cypress, CA: Creative Teaching Press.

Handy, Shirley. *M.O.R.E. of the singing-reading connection, part two.* Hilmar, CA: National Educational Network (workshop).

Igus, Toyomi. 1998. *I see the rhythm.* San Francisco: Children's Book Press.

Joyce, Mary. 1993. *First steps in teaching creative dance to children.* 3rd ed. Mountain View, CA: Mayfield.

Joyce, Morgenroth. 1987. *Dance improvisations.* Pittsburgh: University of Pittsburgh Press.

New York Philharmonic. *New York Philharmonic: An American celebration, special edition for teachers.* Vol. 1. 2001. CD set with teacher's guide.

New York Philharmonic. *New York Philharmonic: Bernstein live, special edition for teachers.* Vol. 2. 2002. CD set with teacher's guide.

Shepard, Aaron. 1993. *Stories on stage: Scripts for reader's theater.* New York: H.W. Wilson.

Spolin, Viola. 1986. *Theater games for the classroom: A teacher's handbook.* Evanston, IL: Northwestern University Press.

Taylor, Bruce D. 1999. *The arts equation: Forging a vital link between performing artists and educators.* New York: Back Stage Books / Watson-Guptill.

Teaching Tolerance. 2003. *I will be your friend: Songs and activities for young peacemakers.* Montgomery, AL: Southern Poverty Law Center (CD and activity book).

Thistle, Louise. 1993. *Dramatizing Aesop's fables: Creative scripts for the elementary classroom.* Parsippany, NJ: Dale Seymour / Pearson Learning.

Wallace, Rosella R. 1998. *Ella Vanilla's multiplication secrets: Building math memory with rhythm and rhyme.* Tucson, AZ: Zephyr Press.

Visual arts

Beyer, Jinny. 1999. *Designing tessalations.* Lincolnwood, IL: Contemporary Books.
Carter, David A., and James Diaz. 1999. *The elements of pop-up: A pop-up book for aspiring paper engineers.* New York: Little Simon / Simon & Schuster.

Diehn, Gwen. 1998. *Making books that fly, fold, wrap, hide, pop up, twist, and turn.* New York: Lark Books / Sterling.

Ernst, Bruno, and M. C. Escher. 2002. *Impossible worlds: 4 in 1: The magic mirror of M. C. Escher; Adventures with impossible objects; Optical illusions; And the graphic work.* Köln, Germany: Evergreen / Taschen.

Gaudelius, Yvonne, and Peg Speirs, eds. *Contemporary issues in art education.* Upper Saddle River, NJ: Prentice Hall.

Golden, Alisa. 1998. *Creating handmade books.* New York: Sterling.

Graves, Ginny. 1997. *Walk around the block.* Prairie Village, KS: Center for Understanding the Built Environment.

Graves, Ginny, and Dean W. Graves. 1999. *Box city: An interdisciplinary experience in community planning.* Prairie Village, KS: Center for Understanding the Built Environment. (Also available in Spanish.)

Jackson, Paul. 1992. *The pop-up book: Step-by-step instructions for creating over 100 original paper projects.* New York: Henry Holt and Company.

Keane, Mark, and Linda Keane. 2000. *Wrightscape: The geometry of Wright.* Milwaukee, WI: Frank Lloyd Wright Inititiative (CD-ROM).

Kitagawa, Yoshiko. 1987. *Creative cards: Wrap a message with a personal touch.* Tokyo: Kodansha International.

LaPlantz, Shereen. 2000. *The art and craft of handmade books.* New York: Lark Books / Sterling.

LaPlantz, Shereen. 2000. *Cover to cover: Creative techniques for making beautiful books, journals, and albums.* New York: Lark Books / Sterling.

London, Peter. 1994. *Step outside: Community-based art education.* Portsmouth, NH: Heinemann.

Seymour, Dale, and Jill Britton. 1989. *Introduction to tessellations.* Parsippany, NJ: Dale Seymour / Pearson Learning.

Stephens, Pamela. 2000. *Bridging the curriculum through art: Interdisciplinary connections.* Glenview, IL: Crystal Productions.

Thompson, Jason. 2000. *Making journals by hand.* Gloucester, MA: Rockport.

Zike, Dinah. 2000. *Big book of books and activities.* San Antonio, TX: Dinah-Mite Activities.

Zike, Dinah. 2000. *Dinah Zike's big book of projects.* San Antonio, TX: Dinah-Mite Activities.

Visual and literary arts

Johnson, Paul. 1997. *Pictures and words together: Children illustrating and writing their own books.* Portsmouth, NH: Heinemann.

Bunchman, Janis, and Stephanie Bissell Briggs. 1994. *Activities for creating pictures and poetry.* Worcester, MA: Davis.

Books to inspire those working in the field

Children's Books

Bucholz, Quint. 1999. *The collector of moments.* New York: Farrar, Straus, and Giroux.

Reynolds, Peter H. 2003. *The dot.* Cambridge, MA: Candlewick Press.

Takao, Yuko. 1995. *A winter concert.* Brookfield, CT: The Millbrook Press.

Adult Books

Adolphe, Bruce. 1996. *What to listen for in the world.* New York: Proscenium.

Babb, Fred. 1998. *Go to your studio and make stuff.* New York: Workman.

Booth, Eric. 1997. *The everyday work of art: How artistic experience can transform your life.* Naperville, IL: Sourcebooks.

Resources compiled by Liz Kennedy, program coordinator, Arts Partners of Wichita, Wichita, Kansas.

Song Reference List

Note: Page numbers in basal series are for teacher's edition.

Songs in *The Music and Literacy Connection*
Brother John, figure 6.2, p. 82
Che Che Koolay, figure 3.3, p. 45
Follow the Drinking Gourd, figure 5.1, p. 68
Skip to My Lou, figure 3.1, p. 41

Exploring Music. Eunice Boardman, Beth Landis, and Barbara Andress. (New York: Holt, Rinehart, and Winston, 1975).
Deaf Woman's Courtship, p. 7
Have You Seen My Honey Bears? pp. 102–103

Exploring Music 2. Eunice Boardman and Beth Landis (New York: Holt, Rinehart, and Winston, 1966).
Honey, You Can't Love One, p. 110

Making Music. Jane Beethoven et al. (Glenview, IL: Scott Foresman, 2002).
Apples and Bananas, grade 1, p. 371
Don Gato, grade 3, p. 344
If You're Happy and You Know It, grade K, p. 94
Love Somebody, grade 3, p. 90

The Musical Classroom: Backgrounds, Models, and Skills for Elementary Teaching. Patricia Hackett and Carolyn A. Lindeman. (Upper Saddle River, NJ: Prentice Hall, 2001).
Don Gato, p. 291
Love Somebody, p. 336
Who's That Yonder, p. 389

Share the Music. René Boyer-Alexander, et al. (New York: McGraw-Hill School Division, 2000).
Apples and Bananas, grade K, p. 86
Love Somebody, grade 2, p. 334

References

American Speech-Language-Hearing Association. 2001. *Roles and responsibilities of speech-language pathologists with respect to reading and writing in children and adolescents.* Rockville, MD: American Speech-Language-Hearing Association.

Andress, Barbara. 1985. The practitioner involves young children in music. In *The young child and music: Contemporary principles in child development and music education. Proceedings of the Music and Early Childhood Conference at Brigham Young University.* Reston, VA: MENC.

Andress, Barbara, ed. 1989. *Promising practices: Prekindergarten music education.* Reston, VA: MENC.

Andress, Barbara. 1998. *Music for young children.* Fort Worth, TX: Harcourt Brace.

Andress, Barbara, and Linda Miller Walker, eds. 1992. *Readings in early childhood music education.* Reston, VA: MENC.

Armbruster, Bonnie B., Fran Lehr, and Jean Osborn. 2003. *Put reading first: The research building blocks for teaching children to read.* Jessup, MD: The Partnership for Reading.

Armstong, Thomas. 2003. *The multiple intelligences of reading and writing: Making the words come alive.* Alexandria, VA: Association for Supervision and Curriculum Development.

Aronson, Elliott, N. Blaney, C. Stephan, J. Sikes, and M. Snapp. 1978. *The jigsaw classroom.* Beverly Hills, CA: Sage.

Barclay, Kathy D., and Lynn Walwer. 1992. Linking lyrics and literacy through song picture books. *Young Children* 47 (4): 76–85.

Bear, Donald R., Marcia Invernizzi, Shane Templeton, and Francine Johnston. 2000. *Words their way: Word study for phonics, vocabulary, and word instruction,* 2nd ed. Old Tappan, NJ: Merrill.

Benjamin, Amy. 1999. *Writing in the content areas.* New York: Eye on Education.

Berends, Polly Berrien. 1997. *Whole child/whole parent.* New York: HarperCollins.

Bergen, Doris. 1998. Stages of play development. In *Play as a medium for learning and development,* ed. Doris Bergen. Olney, MD: Association for Childhood Education International.

Bergen, Doris, and Juliet Coscia. 2001. *Brain research and childhood education: Implications for educators.* Olney, MD: Association for Childhood Education International.

Bernstorf, Elaine. 2003. Music educators: Hidden allies for poor readers. *TMEC Connections* 17 (2): 9–12.

Bloom, Benjamin S., ed. 1984. *Taxonomy of educational objectives. Book 1: Cognitive domain.* New York: Longman. (Orig. pub. 1956.)

Bodrova, Elena, and Deborah J. Leong. 2003a. Chopsticks and counting chips: Do play and foundational skills need to compete for the teacher's attention in an early childhood classroom? *Young Children* 58 (3): 10–17.

Bodrova, Elena, and Deborah J. Leong. 2003b. The importance of being playful. *Educational Leadership* 60 (7): 50–53.

Bredekamp, Sue, and Teresa Rosegrant, eds. 1992. *Reaching potentials: Appropriate curriculum and assessment for young children.* Vol. 1. Washington DC: National Association for the Education of Young Children.

Brophy, Timothy S. 2000. *Assessing the developing child musician.* Chicago: GIA.

Bryant, P. E., M. MacLean, L. L. Bradley, and J. Crossland. 1990. Rhyme and alliteration, phoneme detection, and learning to read. *Developmental Psychology* 26 (3): 429–438.

Burns, Susan M., Peg Griffin, and Catherine E. Snow, eds. (Committee on the Prevention of Reading Difficulties in Young Children, National Research Council.) 1999. *Starting out right: A guide to promoting children's reading success.* Washington DC: National Academy Press.

Campbell, Patricia Shehan, and Carol Scott-Kassner. 2002. *Music in childhood.* 2nd ed. Belmont, CA: Wadsworth-Schirmer.

Catterall, James. 2003. The importance of play in learning. *Journal for Learning through Music.* no. 2 (Summer): 116–118.

Chaille, Christine, and Steven B. Silvern. 1996. Understanding through play. *Childhood Education: Infancy through Early Adolescence.* 72 (5): 274–277.

Clay, Marie. M. 1992. *Becoming literate: The construction of inner control.* Portsmouth, NH: Heinemann.

Consortium of National Arts Education Associations. 1994. *National standards for arts education.* Reston, VA: MENC.

Cooper, David. 1997. *Literacy: Helping children construct meaning.* 3rd ed. New York: Houghton Mifflin.

Copple, Carol, Sue Bredekamp, and Susan Neuman. 2000. *Learning to read and write: Developmentally appropriate practices for young children.* Washington, DC: National Association for the Education of Young Children.

Csikszentmihalyi, Mihalyi. 1978. Intrinsic rewards and emergent motivation. In *The hidden costs of reward: New perspectives on the psychology of human motivation,* eds. Mark Lepper and David Greene. Hillsdale, NJ: Lawrence Erlbaum.

Davies, Mary Ann. 2000. Learning … The beat goes on. *Childhood Education: Infancy through Early Adolescence* 76 (3): 148–153.

Deasy, Richard J. 2002. *Critical links: Learning in the arts and student academic and social development.* Washington DC: Arts Education Partnership.

Diamond, Marian, and Janet Hopson. 1998. *Magic trees of the mind: How to nurture your child's intelligence, creativity, and healthy emotions from birth through adolescence.* New York: Dutton Books / Penguin Group.

Diederich, Paul. 1974. *Measuring growth in English.* Urbana, IL: National Council of Teachers of English.

Eisner, Elliott. 1981. Mind as cultural achievement. *Educational Leadership* 38 (7): 466–471.

Ekwall, Eldon. 1986. *Teacher's handbook on diagnosis and remediation in reading.* 2nd ed. Boston: Allyn and Bacon.

Elkind, David. 2003. Thanks for the memory: The lasting value of true play. *Young Children* 58 (3): 46–50.

Feichtner, Susan Brown, and Elaine Actin Davis. 1991. Why some groups fail: A survey of students' experiences with learning groups. *The Organizational Behavior Teaching Review* 9 (4): 75–88.

Felder, Richard, and Rebecca Brent. 1994. Cooperative learning in technical courses: Procedures, pitfalls, and payoffs. (ERIC Document Reproduction Service No. ED377038.) http://www.ncsu.edu/felder-public/Papers/Coopreport.html (accessed July 1, 2003).

Fields, Marjorie V. 1998. *Your child learns to read and write.* Olney, MD: Association for Childhood Education International.

Fiske, Edward B., ed. 2000. *Champions of change: The impact of the arts on learning.* Washington DC: Arts Education Partnership.

Fogarty, Robin. 1991. *The mindful school: How to integrate the curricula.* Palatine, IL: Skylight.

Foulkes, Mary Ann. 1991. Gifts from childhood's godmother—Patty Smith Hill. In *Readings from childhood education,* vol. 2, eds. James D. Quisenbery, E. Anne Eddowes, and Sandra L. Robinson. Wheaton, MD: Association for Childhood Education International.

Gardner, Howard. 1983. *Frames of mind.* New York: Basic Books.

Gardner, Howard, David H. Feldman, and Mara Krechevsky. 1998. *Project spectrum: Preschool assessment handbook.* Vol. 3 of *Project zero frameworks for early childhood education.* New York: Teachers College Press.

Gerson, Steven M. n.d. *Writing that works: A teacher's guide to technical writing.* Topeka, KS: Kansas Competency-Based Curriculum Center.

Haiman, Peter Ernest. 1991. Developing a sense of wonder in young children:

There is more to early childhood development than cognitive development. *Young Children* 46 (6): 52–53.

Halliday, M. A. K. 1975. *Learning how to mean.* New York: Elsevier North-Holland.

Hansen, Dee, ed. 2002. tARgeTS. Kansas State Department of Education, Topeka.

Hansen, Jane, and David P. Pearson. 1983. An instructional study: Improving the inferential comprehension of good and poor fourth-grade readers. *Journal of Educational Psychology* 75: 821–29.

Harris, Theodore L., and Richard E. Hodges, eds. 1995. *The literacy dictionary: The vocabulary of reading and writing.* Newark, DE: International Reading Association.

Hartenberger, Aurelia. 2003. Levels of conceptual understanding in music. (Electronic communication.)

Harth, Eric. 1993. *The creative loop: How the brain makes a mind.* Reading, MA: Addison-Wesley.

Hirsch-Pasek, Kathy, and Roberta Michnick Golinkoff. 2003. *Einstein never used flash cards: How our children really learn—And why they need to play more and memorize less.* New York: Rodale Press.

Humpal, Marcia Earl, and Jan Wolf. 2003. Music in the inclusive environment. *Young Children* 58 (2): 103–107.

Jablon, Judy, et al. 1994. *Work sampling system: Omnibus guidelines.* Ann Arbor, MI: Rebus, Inc.

Jensen, Eric. 2001. *Arts with the brain in mind.* Alexandria, VA: Association for Supervision and Curriculum Development.

Johnson, David W., Roger T. Johnson, Edythe Johnson Holubee, and Patricia Roy. 1984. *Circles of Learning.* Alexandria, VA: Association for Supervision and Curriculum Development.

Kansas State Department of Education. 2000. LINKS: Literacy instruction now knowledge for teachers implementing state standards. http://www.ksde.org/outcomes/links.pdf.

Kansas State Department of Education. 2000. *Standards for listening, viewing and speaking including information retrieval and media production.* Topeka, KS: Kansas State Department of Education. http://www.ksde.org/outcomes/speaking.pdf.

Kern, Petra, and Mary Wolery. 2003. The sound path: Adding music to a child care playground. *Young Exceptional Children* 5 (3): 12–20.

Lazear, David. 1991. *Seven ways of teaching: The artistry of teaching with multiple intelligences.* Palatine, IL: Skylight.

Lochhead, Jack, and Arthur Whimbey. 1987. Teaching analytical reasoning through thinking aloud pair problem solving. In *Developing critical thinking and problem-solving abilities,* ed. James E. Stice. San Francisco: Jossey-Bass.

Lowery, Larry F. 1998. Asking effective questions. Workshop handout at the Lawrence Hall of Science, Graduate School of Education, University of California, Berkeley.

Maria, Katherine. 1990. *Reading comprehension instruction: Issues and strategies.* Parkton, MD: York Press.

Marzano, Robert. 2003. *What works in schools: Translating research into action.* Alexandria, VA: Association for Supervision and Curriculum Development.

McCarthy, Tara. 1998. *Expository writing.* New York: Scholastic.

Meyen, Edward, Glenn Vergason, and Richard Whelan, eds. 1996. *Strategies for teaching exceptional children in inclusive settings.* Denver: Love Publishing.

Moats, Louisa C. 1999. *Teaching reading IS rocket science: What expert teachers of reading should know and be able to do.* Washington DC: American Federation of Teachers.

Nagy, William E. 1988. *Teaching vocabulary to improve reading comprehension.* Washington DC: International Reading Association. Quoted in Cooper 1997, 236.

National Reading Panel. 2000. *Teaching children to read: An evidence-based assessment of the scientific research literature on reading and its implications for reading instruction.* Washington, DC: National Institute of Child Health and Human Development.

Ogle, Donna M. 1986. Know-Want-Learn, K-W-L. Manual accompanying videotape *Teaching reading as thinking*. Alexandria, VA: Association for Supervision and Curriculum Development.

Owocki, Gretchen. 1999. *Literacy through play*. Portsmouth, NH: Heinemann / Reed Elsevier.

Parten, Mildred. 1930. Social participation among preschool children. *Journal of Abnormal and Social Psychology* 23: 243–269.

Pearson, P. David, and Dale D. Johnson. 1978. *Teaching reading comprehension*. New York: Holt, Rinehart, and Winston.

Perrault, Charles. 1990. *Puss in boots*. Trans. by Malcolm Arthur. New York: Farrar, Straus, and Giroux.

Perrault, Charles. 1991. *El gato con botas*. Trans. by Aida Marcuse. New York: Mirasol / Farrar, Straus, and Giroux.

Piazza, Carolyn L. 1999. *Multiple forms of literacy: Teaching literacy and the arts*. Upper Saddle River, NJ: Prentice Hall.

Purves, Alan. 1992. Reflections on research and assessment in written composition. *Research in the Teaching of English* 26 (Feb. 1992) : 108–22.

Raphael, Taffy E. 1986. Teaching question answer relationship, revised. *The Reading Teacher* 39: 516–522.

Rice, D. 1990. Commentaries. *Journal of Aesthetic Education* 24 (1): 95–99. Quoted in Wright 2003.

Rogers, Cosby S., and Janet K. Sawyers. 1988. *Play in the lives of children*. Washington DC: National Association for the Education of Young Children.

Rumelhart, D. E. 1980. Schemata: The building blocks of cognition. In *Theoretical issues in reading comprehension,* eds. R. J. Spiro et al. Hillsdale, NJ: Lawrence Erlbaum.

Shaywitz, S. E., B. A. Shaywitz, K. R. Pugh, R. K. Fulbright, R. T. Costable, W. E. Menel, et al. 1998. Functional disruption in the organization of the brain for reading in dyslexia. *Proceedings of the National Academy of Sciences, USA* 95 (5): 2636–2641.

Short, Ruth A., Mary Kane, and Tammy Peeling. 2000. Retooling the reading lesson: Matching the right tools to the job. *The Reading Teacher* 54 (3): 284–95.

Shuler, Scott, ed. 2002. *The arts: A guide to K–12 program development.* Connecticut: The Connecticut State Board of Education.

Sims, Wendy. 1993. Guidelines for music activity and instruction. In *Music in prekindergarten: Planning and teaching,* ed. Mary Palmer and Wendy Sims. Reston, VA: MENC.

Sims, Wendy, ed. 1995. *Strategies for teaching prekindergarten music.* Reston, VA: MENC.

Sloutsky, Vladimir. 2003. Is a picture worth a thousand words? Preference for auditory modality in young children. *Child Development* 74 (3): 822–833. Quoted in Preschoolers tune into sounds, *Advance for Speech-Language Pathologists and Audiologists* (June 7, 2003): 5–6.

Soares, Magda Becker. 1992. Literacy assessment and its implication for statistical measurement. Paper prepared for UNESCO, Division of Statistics, Paris.

Spandel, Vicki, and Richard Stiggins. 1997. *Creating writers: Linking writing assessment and instruction.* 2nd ed. New York: Longman.

Spodek, Bernard, and Olivia N. Saracho. 1998. The challenges of educational play. In *Play as a medium for learning and development,* ed. Doris Bergen. Olney, MD: Association for Childhood Education International.

Stevenson, Sara. 2003. Creative experiences in free play. *Music Educators Journal* 89 (5): 44–47.

Stone, Sandra J. 1995–96. Teaching strategies: Integrating play into the curriculum. *Childhood Education: Infancy through Early Adolescence* 72 (2): 104–107.

Strickland, Susan. 2001–02. Music and the brain in childhood development. *Childhood Education: Infancy through Early Adolescence* 78 (2): 100–103.

Talcott, J. B., C. Wilton, M. F. McLean, P. C. Hanson, A. Rees, G. R. Green, et al. 2000. Dynamic sensory sensitivity and children's word decoding skills. *Proceedings of the National Academy of Sciences, USA* 97 (6): 2952–2957.

Teale, William H, and Elizabeth Sulzby. 1986. *Emergent literacy: Writing and reading.* Norwood, NJ: Ablex.

TESOL (Teachers of English Speakers of Other Languages). 1997. *ESL standards for pre-K–12 students.* Alexandria, VA: TESOL.

Thornburg, Kathy, Susie Cable, Jackie Scott, Wayne Mayfield, and Amy Watson. 2003. *Recommendations for effective early childhood programs.* Columbus, MO: University of Missouri.

Thornburg, K., D. Mauzy, L. Espinsosa, and W. Mayfield. 2003. Missouri's early childhood research findings: Workforce development, teacher education, program quality and child achievement. Presented at the first Faculty Institute of the Association for the Education of Young Children of Missouri, November, Lake Ozark, Missouri.

U.S. Department of Education. No Child Left Behind Web site. www.ed.gov/nclb/landing.jhtml.

Villeneuve, Pat. 1992. *Making sense of art: Aesthetic scanning and questioning strategies.* Lawrence, KS: The Spencer Museum of Art.

Vygotsky, Lev Semenovich. 1978. *Mind in society: The development of higher psychological processes.* Eds. Michael Cole, Vera John-Steiner, Sylvia Scribner, and Ellen Souberman. Cambridge, MA: Harvard Univ. Press.

Wassermann, Selma. 1992. Serious play in the classroom: How messing around can win you the Nobel Prize. *Childhood Education: Infancy through Early Adolescence* 68 (3): 104–107.

Weinberger, Norman. 1997. The neurobiology of musical learning and memory. *MuSICA Research Notes* 4: 3–5. (Online at www.musica.uci.edu/mrn/V412F97.html.)

Wiggins, Jackie. 2001. *Teaching for musical understanding.* New York: McGraw-Hill Higher Education.

Wilson, Robert M., and Linda B. Gambrell. 1988. *Reading comprehension in the elementary school: A teacher's practical guide.* Boston: Allyn and Bacon.

Winter, Jeanette. 1988. *Follow the drinking gourd.* New York: Dragonfly / Alfred A. Knopf.

Wolfe, Patricia. 2001. *Brain matters: Translating research into classroom practice.* Alexandria, VA: Association for Supervision and Curriculum Development.

Wright, Susan. 2003. *The arts, young children, and learning.* Boston: Pearson Education.

Yopp, Hallie Kay, and Ruth Helen Yopp. 2000. Supporting phonemic awareness development in the classroom. *The Reading Teacher* 54 (2): 130–43.

Young, Kimberly, ed. 2000. *Literacy instruction now—Knowledge for teachers implementing state standards (LINKS).* Topeka, KS: Kansas State Department of Education.